T0320987

Praise for

DIVESTITURES

Through her rigorous and well-researched analysis, Dr. Feldman provides an invaluable guide for any executive looking to address one of the most crucial, yet sensitive, corporate challenges: knowing why, when, and how to divest and reshuffle a firm's businesses and resources in pursuit of more value-creating opportunities.

—Laurence Capron
Professor of Strategy and The Paul Desmarais Chaired
Professor of Partnership and Active Ownership, INSEAD

Emilie Feldman shows us how thoughtful divestitures create wins for management and shareholders. For many leaders, the inherent bias for acquisitions and against divestitures creates blind spots for value creation. The entire breadth of this book, covering divestiture strategies, structures, and implementation approaches, is brought to life by the memorable case studies and anecdotes. Our team now refers to these cases by name, adding vocabulary that expands our frame of options available to the companies we advise. I am eager to introduce Emilie's work to my clients. Note: I am less eager to have competing advisers read her work.

—Todd Dubner
Principal, Global Strategy Group, KPMG

Emilie Feldman brilliantly shows that pruning underperforming or non-core businesses is essential to corporate success. This most helpful book shows how to strategize, structure, and implement divestitures to lay the foundations for sustainable growth and profitability.

—Mauro F. Guillén
Dean, Cambridge Judge Business School

Rarely does one find a business book that tackles an important and relevant topic such as divestiture in a forthright and thoughtful manner. In my view, Professor Emilie Feldman's book is one that deserves attention. While the topic of M&A garners broad coverage and highlights why large numbers of them do not produce desirable results, very little is documented or written about the topic of divestitures. From my experience as a CEO, board leader, and board member of public and private companies across a broad range of industries, divestitures consistently produce desirable outcomes in terms of value creation, portfolio focus, improved capital allocation, and better talent deployment. I strongly encourage CEOs and board members to read this book and add divestitures as an active part of their agenda.

—Rajiv L. Gupta
Retired Chairman and Chief Executive Officer of Rohm & Haas,
Retired Chairman of Avantor Inc. and Aptiv PLC

Providing a comprehensive and readable guide to the corporate strategy of divestitures, Feldman vividly illustrates the upsides of divestiture strategy done right and the pitfalls of divestiture strategy done wrong. A tour de force, the book is unique in focusing on divestiture as a critical tool in the strategist's toolbox.

—Constance E. Helfat
J. Brian Quinn Professor in Technology and Strategy,
Tuck School of Business at Dartmouth

Huntsman shrank volumes 70% and grew EPS by 70% since going public. Selling an asset and taking after-tax proceeds to buy something of greater value is one of the most challenging decisions to execute. A company is usually selling an underperforming asset and hoping to buy something of far greater value. Professor Feldman thoroughly explores one of the most overlooked actions a board will ever undertake. This is a long overdue analysis and guide.

—Peter R. Huntsman
Chairman, President, and Chief Executive
Officer of Huntsman Corporation

A very well-written book and an invaluable primer to this very important topic. The author's opening "pruning analogy" is spot on . . . and critical for firms to understand. This is an outstanding resource for an ever-faster-moving world.

—Martin Schroeter
Chairman and Chief Executive Officer of Kyndryl Holdings, Inc.

Explaining the drivers of headline-grabbing corporate breakups, split-offs and reconfigurations, Professor Feldman provides an excellent and timely evidence-based explanation of value creation through strategic divestitures. The book provides consistent evidence that strategic divestitures create significantly higher returns than acquisitions, despite CEOs' disproportionate focus on the latter. This book presents a well-researched approach to choices between modes of divestiture—spinoffs, sales to corporate or private equity buyers, and tracking stocks. Pruning corporate portfolios via divestiture unlocks value for the firm by strengthening its focus on core businesses, improving capital allocation, and developing long-term advantage. The arguments are enriched by detailed narratives illuminating best practices in implementing divestitures. Professor Feldman clearly shows how to unlock substantial value through divestiture as part of corporate scope-changing transactions. A must-read!

—Harbir Singh
Mack Professor and Professor of Management,
The Wharton School, University of Pennsylvania

DIVESTITURES

CREATING VALUE THROUGH
STRATEGY, STRUCTURE, AND IMPLEMENTATION

EMILIE R. FELDMAN

New York   Chicago   San Francisco   Athens   London   Madrid
Mexico City   Milan   New Delhi   Singapore   Sydney   Toronto

1 2 3 4 5 6 7 8 9   LCR   27 26 25 24 23 22

ISBN   978-1-264-27756-8
MHID   1-264-27756-3

e-ISBN   978-1-264-27757-5
e-MHID   1-264-27757-1

This publication is designed to provide accurate and authoritative information in regard to the subject matter covered. It is sold with the understanding that neither the author nor the publisher is engaged in rendering legal, accounting, securities trading, or other professional services. If legal advice or other expert assistance is required, the services of a competent professional person should be sought.
> —*From a Declaration of Principles Jointly Adopted by a Committee of the American Bar Association and a Committee of Publishers and Associations*

McGraw Hill books are available at special quantity discounts to use as premiums and sales promotions or for use in corporate training programs. To contact a representative, please visit the Contact Us pages at www.mhprofessional.com.

McGraw Hill is committed to making our products accessible to all learners. To learn more about the available support and accommodations we offer, please contact us at accessibility@mheducation.com. We also participate in the Access Text Network (www .accesstext.org), and ATN members may submit requests through ATN.

In memoriam, Michael L. Tarnopol,

and with gratitude to his family

To my husband and parents

CONTENTS

PART I
DIVESTITURE STRATEGY

PART II
DIVESTITURE STRUCTURE

PART III
DIVESTITURE IMPLEMENTATION

LIST OF EXHIBITS

ACKNOWLEDGMENTS

I am extremely grateful to Raffi Amit, Lori Rosenkopf, and Harbir Singh for their mentorship and support at Wharton. To paraphrase Newton, *I stand on the shoulders of giants.*

I also thank Dan Levinthal and Nancy Rothbard, the most recent chairs of my department, for having created a working environment that should be the envy of all graduate business schools, and the Mack Institute for Innovation Management for its generous research funding.

INTRODUCTION

Maintaining a tree involves regularly pruning its branches. The designated branches might be competitors for such resources as sunlight, water, or nutrients, or they might be inconsistent with one's conception of the tree. Perhaps they interfere with the tree's desired shape, or dangerously unbalance it; perhaps they are old growth, or now-unproductive grafts. Whatever the cause, the branches are pruned.

Pruning a tree is the arboricultural equivalent of corporate divestitures, transactions in which a company sells one of its businesses to another entity, spins it off into an independent company, or removes it from the company's portfolio through some other structure. The analogy exemplifies some of the different reasons why divestitures are as necessary to the corporate household as pruning is to maintaining the tree.

Consider the following:

Pruning a tree eliminates lower-quality branches and allows its remaining limbs to flourish. The tree will no longer waste its energy fueling the growth of marginalia; instead, it will focus that energy on its more productive branches. Divestitures, too, remove underperforming or even unsuccessful businesses, and allow executives to redirect such critical resources as money, time, and attention to the company's remaining operations. Trees often bear more fruit or flowers after they have been pruned, and companies often yield higher profitability and greater shareholder returns after they have shed business units, especially laggards.

A tree left unpruned can turn into a tangle of crisscrossing, splintered, and overgrown branches, leaving an unsightly mess for passersby to behold. Similarly, there have been major companies that became wild collections of businesses that made little sense together in the same corporate household, their management having neglected to make necessary divestitures. Like a grove with bare branches and sparse foliage, the shares of those companies were regarded derisively by knowledgeable observers. Conversely, the arborist has the ability to shape the tree so that it becomes an object of admiration, and the corporate executive can configure the company so that it is both understandable and attractive to the investment community.

Finally, just as gardens are composed of trees and other plants, companies comprise multiple business units and other assets. As organizational forms, each of them requires a shape, a vision. The splendid Jardins de Marqueyssac in the Dordogne were created by visionaries who acquired specimen trees and carefully tended to their growth, while removing trees that ceased to fit their overall vision; the iconic Berkshire Hathaway was assembled with just as much care by its legendary CEO. In addition to having the ability to expand their gardens and companies, gardeners and executives have the tools to shape them. Just as pruning shears and saws enable the gardener to design the garden, so, too, do divestitures enable the executive to configure the corporation.

CREATING VALUE THROUGH DIVESTITURES

To change metaphors from the garden to the lake, divestitures are the ugly ducklings of corporate strategy when compared to the swans of mergers and acquisitions (M&A) and the geese of organic growth. In every year from 2000 to 2019, S&P 500-listed companies divested less than one business per year on average, and about 70% of them never divested at all.[1] When asked to state which strategy they expected to create more value for their companies over the next two years, 74% of CEOs ranked M&A above divestitures, and fully 90% of CEOs ranked organic growth above divestitures.[2] It is no big surprise, then, that companies divest much less frequently than they acquire:* corporate divestitures only account for about 30% of disclosed annual deal volume and value globally, as shown in Exhibits I.1 and I.2.

Yet there is an echo of Hans Christian Andersen's fairy tale when it comes to value creation; divestitures unexpectedly become swans, perhaps even more majestic swans than M&A, in the lake of corporate transactions. Although the underutilization of divestitures relative to acquisitions might seem to suggest otherwise, investors respond much more favorably when companies divest than when they acquire. Exhibits I.3 and I.4 indicate that in the universe of corporate transactions, the excess shareholder returns to divestiture announcements surpass those of acquisition announcements, and the performance differential between companies that divest and companies that acquire persists for up to 36 months after the completion of these transactions.

The juxtaposition of these two sets of findings highlights the questions that are at the heart of this book: since divestitures demonstrably create value for the companies that undertake them, why aren't they perceived that way, and why aren't they used more frequently?† To shed some light on this matter, consider the following example of a company that failed to divest soon enough.

A CAUTIONARY TALE

From time to time, the expression "*Buddenbrooks* Syndrome" has been used to illustrate the multigenerational growth and decay of a family business (*Buddenbrooks* was Thomas Mann's first novel). But for the familial aspect of the book, one could easily apply the expression to one

---

* While it should be acknowledged that virtually every purchase is another company's sale, sales are but one form of divestiture. Other divestiture structures, such as the various types of spinoffs and joint ventures, split-offs, and tracking stocks, are divestitures that are not offset by concomitant acquisitions. Then, there are the financial press and the databases, which conventionally label a transaction as an acquisition rather than a divestiture, unless the divestiture is announced first. Finally, from a methodological perspective, analyzing the post-divestiture performance of a divesting company is unaffected by the fact that it divested a business operation via a sale to a buyer. All this having been said, however, transactional characterization is certainly skewed by the financial press toward acquisitions.

† Indeed, why aren't they taught more comprehensively in our business schools?

EXHIBIT I.1

Disclosed Volume of Acquisitions Versus Divestitures, 1995–2021[3]

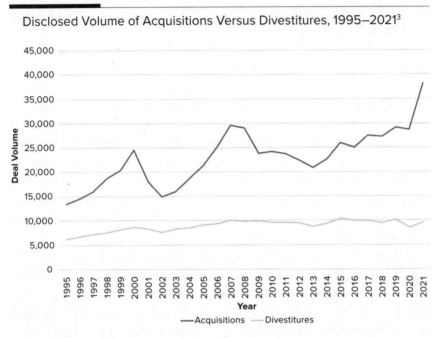

EXHIBIT I.2

Disclosed Value of Acquisitions Versus Divestitures, 1995–2021[4]

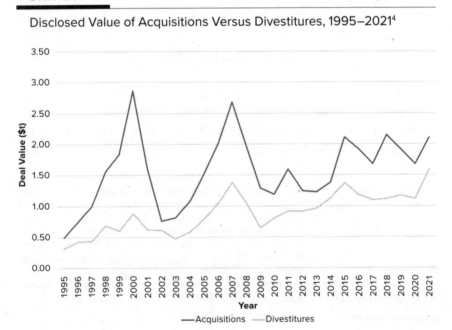

EXHIBIT I.3

Average Cumulative Abnormal Returns upon Disclosed Announcements of Acquisitions Versus Divestitures, 1995–2021[5]

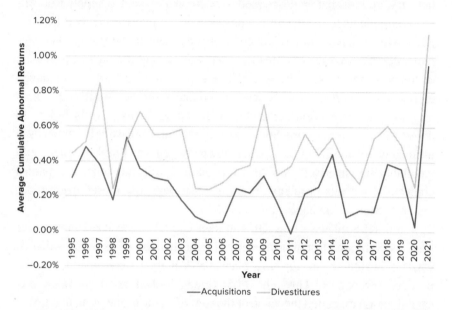

EXHIBIT I.4

Average Compounded Monthly Returns Following Disclosed Completions of Acquisitions Versus Divestitures, 1995–2021[6]

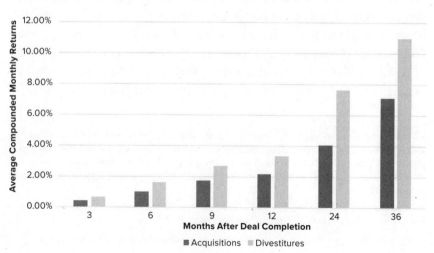

of America's most prominent companies, a company that spans the era from Thomas Edison to Elon Musk, a company that along the way grew organically and through acquisition, reached the pinnacle of American industry, and ultimately descended to become a respected supplier of critical components to the aviation industry. The company is General Electric (GE), which once commercialized electricity, had the largest market capitalization of America's companies, and was among the biggest providers of financial services in the world. The explanation of how GE managed to ride the *Buddenbrooks* "curve" is counterintuitive. While GE's promiscuous diversification certainly set the stage for its fall, its failure to divest those disparate operations in a timely and measured manner was ultimately what sent it careening down the curve. Frankly, one could justifiably be surprised that GE even made it this far; other companies confronted with its problems might have strategically reorganized under the protection of the bankruptcy code.

Exhibit I.5 displays how GE's market capitalization has evolved over time, as compared to the estimated value of the sum of its parts[*]—that is, what its businesses *would have been worth* if they were valued as independent companies. Through 2005, things looked good: GE's market capitalization exceeded the value of the sum of its parts, meaning that investors believed that GE was creating more shareholder value by operating its individual businesses than those businesses would have been worth on a standalone basis.[†] But then the situation flipped in 2006: the value of the sum of GE's parts soared above its actual market capitalization. Although these measures briefly came back nearly into parity between 2008 and 2010 because the global financial crisis caused the value of GE Capital's portfolio to crash, *GE was never again worth more than the sum of its parts.*

What went wrong? By the early 2000s, GE Capital, the company's finance arm, had come to account for an increasingly large share of GE's

---

[*] The empirical methodology developed and employed in Philip Berger and Eli Ofek's canonical 1995 *Journal of Financial Economics* article (which has been cited over 5,000 times as of this book's writing) was used to calculate the estimated value of the sum of GE's parts as of the end of each year. In this exhibit, GE's market capitalization is also depicted as of the end of each year.

Source: Berger, Philip G., and Eli Ofek. 1995. "Diversification's Effect on Firm Value." *Journal of Financial Economics* 37, no. 1 (January 1995): 39–65.

[†] One could say that GE reached the apex of the *Buddenbrooks* curve around this time.

EXHIBIT I.5

GE's End-of-Year Market Capitalization Relative to the Estimated Value of the Sum of Its Parts, 1995–2019[7]

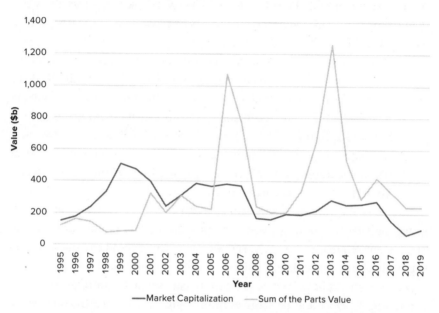

revenues and profits (nearly half, at its peak).[8] Although the cash that GE Capital threw off funded GE's remaining operations, it had become unclear to investors what exactly GE was: Was it a bank, or was it a diversified industrial manufacturer with a core competence in "things that spin" (e.g., jet engines, locomotives, wind turbines, water treatment equipment, and even CT scanners)?[9] Various crises buffeted GE Capital, including insurance losses from the 9/11 terror attacks, the global financial meltdown, and GE Capital's subsequent federal bailout.[10] These challenges made it increasingly more difficult for investors to see the logic behind GE's odd collection of businesses, leading it to become vastly undervalued relative to its fundamentals.

Although the handwriting was on the wall as early as 2006 (see Exhibit I.5), it took GE until 2015 to realize that the time had come for it to divest GE Capital. Various explanations have been offered for this 10-year delay: the magnitude of the tax bill that would result from a sale of GE Capital, the purported need for GE Capital's cash flows to continue funding GE's other businesses, the complexity of the task of divesting, and even the higher priority of empire building, as executives focused on acquiring Alstom to expand GE Power instead.[11] The worst part was that the value of many of GE's core industrial businesses had declined, some irreparably, by the time GE finally did divest GE Capital.

After that, divestitures were a necessity. Over the next several years, GE divested its home appliances business, GE Oil & Gas, GE Rail, its legacy lightbulb business, and GE Capital Aviation Services. Then, in November 2021, GE announced the grand finale, its breakup into three parts: it would spin off its healthcare and power businesses into two new companies and leave its aviation business as a standalone company. After 130 years of operation, one of the most storied companies in the world would cease to exist in its current form.

What is the moral of this story? With only one business left, GE's nearly half-trillion-dollar divestiture program clearly could not have had greater consequences for its corporate mix. But even then, the program was implemented too late. Had GE Capital's divestitures been initiated sooner, GE might have been able to avoid its descent and ultimate breakup, continuing to exist and perhaps even thriving as a smaller version of the diversified industrial manufacturer it had become.

IMPEDIMENTS TO DIVESTITURES

GE's saga raises a threshold question: What causes executives to delay or avoid divestitures, even when it is evident that these transactions will help their companies, and in some cases save them from decline or even extinction? While the answers to this question will be discussed throughout this book, it is worth mentioning some of the major managerial impediments to divestitures up front.

Most fundamentally, divestitures suffer from bad public relations: they tend to be viewed as a last resort to use when something is going wrong, like an acquisition that isn't working out or a business whose performance is deteriorating. Executives often fear that undertaking these transactions would make it *appear* that they were unable to manage the challenges of the underlying problem. Needless to say, the same attitude that impedes problem-solving divestitures also impedes productive divestitures, where maximal value could be obtained if they were executed in a timely manner.

Perceived financial constraints can impede divestitures as well. Generations of executives have been advised to milk, not divest, their cash cows. After all, how does one justify eliminating a predictable source of cash, especially a source of cash for which potential buyers might not pay an acceptable price? Executives equally invoke scale economies and operating synergies as key sources of value that divestitures would disrupt, as well as taxes and transaction costs as major expenses that divestitures would impose. Unfortunately, this attitude comes at a significant opportunity cost: retaining rather than divesting businesses for these kinds of reasons can prevent executives from focusing on the businesses that are more central to their company's strategy. Usually, the costs of this lack of focus far exceed the benefits that cross-subsidization and interdependence used to provide.

Ghosts from the past can also deter divestitures. What does it mean to get rid of the legacy business around which a company was built—especially when that company's name reflects those original operations, or when that divestiture will cost many long-time employees their jobs? What executive wants to be the one to announce that it would be a good idea to sell the founder's original business? These kinds of questions illustrate how historical considerations can hold executives back from divesting as well.

Then, there is a compounding effect. The relative rarity of divestitures means that executives often lack the experience of having observed that divestitures can create value, let alone the experience of having undertaken one of them. So, executives are often unprepared to recognize the need to divest an operation until the problem has become pressing; yet, deferring even a basic discussion about divesting a subsidiary might well preclude the use of certain divestiture structures. Finally, there is another consequence of this lack of divestiture experience: increased effort. In an interview with the author, one executive speculated that the main reason divestitures are underutilized is that most companies don't know how to do them well; for this reason, he estimated that one divestiture is equivalent in workload to *five* acquisitions.[12]

Clearly, the time has come to address the impediments to divestitures and to encourage the development of effective capabilities for these transactions. This book sets out to achieve these objectives.

PURPOSE OF THIS BOOK

There being so much potential value to be realized from divestitures, this book discusses the elements needed to make reasoned divestiture decisions, and to execute and implement them effectively. Hopefully, it also dispels the misconceptions and biases that surround them.

Consistent with the foregoing discussion, this book advances a comprehensive framework for divestitures that addresses three main issues using American tax law and accounting principles:

- Part I analyzes the various *divestiture strategies* that companies can employ and how these transactions create value for them.

- Part II considers the range of possible *divestiture structures* that companies can use, as well as how companies can appropriate value from these transactions.

- Part III explores how companies go about selecting and executing an effective approach to *divestiture implementation.*

The intended audience of this book is threefold: (1) executive management and board members, (2) professional advisors, and (3) members of the academic community. For corporate executives, directors, and their professional advisors, this book presents contemporaneous, actionable, and easy-to-digest insights into divestitures, which are among the most critical and pressing—but also perhaps the least well understood—business decisions that companies face. The concepts and ideas in this book are based upon nearly 20 years of rigorous academic research at two of the world's best universities, and they are illuminated by numerous examples, anecdotes, and interviews. As a result, this book stresses the importance of well-informed divestiture decisions and effective transactional implementation.

As for academics, this book could be used in business school courses and executive education programs involving corporate strategy. Given its underpinnings in research, it can serve as a useful starting point for professors and doctoral candidates seeking to conduct additional research on the phenomenon of divestitures.* Over the last 10 years, the *Strategic*

---

* The endnotes in each chapter provide citations for many of the seminal academic studies on divestitures.

Management Journal (the flagship academic journal in the field of strat-egy) has published 144 articles about acquisitions and alliances, compared to only 20 articles about divestitures.[13] In addition to being underutilized, divestitures also appear to be under-researched, presenting an important gap in the academic literature that scholars should continue to fill.

Finally, it is important to emphasize what this book is *not* intended to be: it is not meant to be a how-to guide for the formulation or imple-mentation of divestiture strategy; instead, it is a starting point. Excellent summaries and professional monographs are available to supplement the matters discussed herein. This book is also not intended to substitute for the advice of counsel. Executives who are considering divestitures should proactively retain seasoned transactional counsel, even before they assem-ble their team of bankers, accountants, and experts.

* * *

The main messages of this book are also threefold. First, beyond the conventional wisdom that divestitures are merely solutions to problems, divestitures are also key strategic tools that executives can use to change corporate scope and advance their companies' overall strategies. Second, the variety of divestiture structures from which executives may choose provides them with the strategic flexibility to match the mode of dives-titure to their companies' objectives and constraints. Third, there is a set of best practices that companies can employ to implement divestitures as effectively as possible. Given that there is little existing guidance on any of these matters, the insights developed in this book are of critical importance for both practitioners and academics seeking to understand and harness the value-creation potential of divestitures.

PART I

DIVESTITURE STRATEGY

CHAPTER 1

Removing Problematic Businesses

INTRODUCTION

Strategy is defined as the actions that executives take to attain one or more of their companies' objectives, which ideally result in greater profitability and higher returns to shareholders. Divestitures are one such action, and they can achieve four primary objectives for the companies that undertake them: divestitures can remove problematic businesses, improve corporate focus, reconfigure the corporate portfolio, and address regulatory requirements. Each of these four strategies is respectively motivated by a distinct factor: underperformance, overdiversification, the need (or desire) to change corporate scope, and government fiat. The differences among these four motivating factors imply substantial variance in the characteristics of companies that divest, from the traits of the businesses that are being divested (e.g., their relative performance or their strategic fit) to the environments in which these companies operate (e.g., their industries or their regulatory contexts). This chapter considers the first of these four divestiture strategies, *the strategy of divesting to remove problematic businesses*.

In stunning reversals for two of the most storied companies in the U.S. economy, in 2021, AT&T announced plans to divest its WarnerMedia division (a product of its 2018 acquisition of Time Warner)* and Verizon

---

* One person who was not at all surprised by the failure of AT&T's acquisition of Time Warner, or by the subsequent WarnerMedia divestiture, was Time Warner's former CEO Jeff Bewkes. The *Wall Street Journal* reported on a book about HBO (*Tinderbox: HBO's Ruthless Pursuit of New Frontiers*) in which Mr. Bewkes is quoted as saying: "The most disappointing thing to me about the AT&T merger [is that I and my board thought AT&T] would basically leave our people alone. . . . We didn't think they would go to such a level of malpractice as to not listen to anybody . . . even though they themselves had no experience in those areas."

Source: Flint, Joe. 2021. "Jeff Bewkes Lashes Out at AT&T in Coming Book." *Wall Street Journal*, November 15, 2021. https://www.wsj.com/articles/jeff-bewkes-lashes-out-at-at-t-in-coming-book-11636974000.

announced its intention to divest Oath (consisting of AOL, Yahoo!, and other media assets it had bought just a few years prior).* The media content and digital advertising industries that AT&T and Verizon had entered via these acquisitions were dominated by a small number of fierce rivals, substitute products abounded, and customers (i.e., eyeballs) could easily defect. As a result, AT&T and Verizon were unable to compete effectively in these industries, leading to underperformance of the acquired businesses: "AT&T was slow to launch a streaming service and struggled to keep up with rivals plowing billions of dollars a year into content,"[1] and Verizon faced a decline in Oath's share of digital advertising spending from 4.1% to 3.3% in 2018 (compared to Google's 37% and Facebook's 20% shares), forcing Verizon to write down Oath's value by $4.5 billion (half of the total price Verizon originally paid to acquire AOL and Yahoo!).[2] In both cases, divestitures were solutions to problems, facilitating exits from unattractive industries and allowing the two companies to recoup at least some of the costs of their failed acquisitions.

As the AT&T and Verizon anecdotes illustrate, the strategy of divesting problematic businesses generally occurs in one or both of two situations:

1. When one of the businesses in a company's portfolio operates in an unattractive industry (or an industry that has become unattractive), making it difficult for that company to compete effectively

2. When a company previously undertook an acquisition that underperformed relative to expectations, or even failed

Consider the following facts and figures about these occurrences:

On the one hand, businesses that operate in weak or declining industries are nearly 25% more likely to be divested than retained by their parent companies,[3] and over two-thirds of the divestitures demanded by activist investors involve businesses operating in poor industries.[4] Between a third and a half of all acquisitions (especially acquisitions of unrelated

---

* One of the author's colleagues was also not surprised by the failure of Verizon's acquisition of Yahoo!, or by its subsequent divestiture of Oath. This person recounted a conversation they had with a group of Verizon executives: "The Yahoo! folks have never been integrated into Verizon. [Verizon employees] even had to use a separate computer, with separate systems, anytime they wanted to email the Yahoo! employees. It was amazing to hear."

Source: Personal communication of the author, May 25, 2021.

businesses) are later divested because they have failed.[5] Consequently, stock market returns usually improve after companies divest businesses that operate in unattractive industries[6] as well as failed acquisitions,[7] especially when these divestitures are impelled by activist investors.[8]

On the other hand, however, a minimum of 18 months usually elapses between the first mention of industry decline in the press and the announcement of a divestiture,[9] and the median time between the purchase and subsequent divestiture of a failed acquisition is about seven years.[10] Survey results indicate that 78% of companies "continue to hold onto assets too long when they should have divested them," and a third of CEOs report that a challenge they face when deciding to divest is the perception that management failure led to divestment.[11] Indeed, nearly 80% of divestitures are preceded by CEO turnover,[12] suggesting that executives prefer to divest when they can plausibly blame the problems that prompted those transactions on their predecessors.

This is the paradox of divesting problematic businesses: although the problems that justify this strategy are usually obvious, executives have a hard time accepting that divestiture is the remedy. And so, a vicious cycle ensues. One of the company's businesses operates in an unattractive industry or one of its acquisitions shows signs of failing, but its executives delay divesting the problematic business in the hope that something positive will occur, such as improved industry conditions or stronger operating results. During the delay occasioned by managerial indecision, the problematic business continues to deteriorate, exerting downward pressure on its intrinsic value, resulting in an otherwise avoidable discounted sale price when the business is ultimately divested.[13] Indeed, *in extremis*, this can lead to a "busted auction," where no buyers materialize or the proposed purchase prices are unacceptable, further reducing the value of a unit that is now viewed as damaged goods.*

This chapter considers industry unattractiveness and acquisition failure as two motivations for divestitures of problematic businesses, as well

---

* This exact situation unfolded when Motorola initially tried to sell its mobile devices unit but the bids were all $1 billion less than Motorola's reservation price. As a result, Motorola was forced to scrap the sale of that unit and spin it off a few years later, as the industry's decline persisted amid fierce competition among mobile devices companies.

Source: Harrigan, Kathryn Rudie. 2012. "Motorola's Spin-Off of Its Cell Phone Business." Columbia CaseWorks ID# CU129.

as the reasons for which (and situations in which) inertia so often plagues these divestitures. The core message is that the value erosion that precedes these transactions might be mitigated or perhaps even avoided if executives were to overcome the financial, behavioral, and historical hurdles that hold them back from divesting problematic businesses in a timely manner.

INDUSTRY UNATTRACTIVENESS

Industry unattractiveness is one motivation for the strategy of divesting to remove problematic businesses, and it raises a recurring question: How can executives determine that one of their company's businesses operates in an industry that is out of favor? Michael Porter's Five Forces[14] framework is a useful tool with which to answer this question. In Porter's framework, industry attractiveness is a function of a company's competitive position in its industry, as reflected by five characteristics:

- The intensity of rivalry between a focal company and its competitors

- The existence of entry barriers that prevent new competitors from entering the industry

- The availability of substitute products to those produced by the focal company

- The power of buyers relative to the focal company

- The power of suppliers relative to the focal company

Industries are attractive when competitive rivalry is low, entry barriers are high, substitute products are scarce, and buyer and supplier power are low. Industries become increasingly unattractive as more of these factors are reversed. Furthermore, industry attractiveness is not necessarily a stable or fixed characteristic, and it can be tempting to conflate industry growth with industry attractiveness. However, fast growth can encourage substitute products and competitive entry, supplier power may be high as scarce inputs (especially human capital) must be divided among numerous profitable opportunities, and buyer power may also be high as consumers face ample choice among products that are competing ever more intensively to attract their attention and their spending.* In other words, industry growth does not guarantee industry attractiveness.

When companies have operations in industries that are (or become) unattractive, it often makes sense for them to exit those industries through divestitures. Consider Loews's decision to divest Lorillard, its cigarette business. Tobacco was once an attractive industry, especially due to low buyer power resulting from the addictive nature of cigarettes and the lack of substitutes for them. Yet litigation against Lorillard and its peers during the 1990s shifted the competitive landscape by highlighting the health risks of cigarettes. This changed consumer preferences for and attitudes toward tobacco. The controlling Tisch family even faced unfair social backlash arising from their company's ownership of Lorillard: an airplane once reportedly trailed a banner over Long Island beaches reading "Larry Tisch sells cancer sticks."[15] In the face of these challenges, Loews wisely began the process of divesting Lorillard,† although Loews's CEO James Tisch emphasized that the divestiture decision was not made because "it is politically correct to get out of the business."[16]

Another useful example of how industry unattractiveness can prompt companies to divest is Alcoa's divestiture of its low-margin, cyclical commodity aluminum business from its more profitable, finished end products business in 2015. The commodity business faced severe pricing pressure from Chinese imports, with prices declining by over 40% since 2011,[17] which destabilized competitive rivalry and lowered entry barriers in the industry. As a result, substitute products became more prominent and buyers gained power because there was nothing to differentiate commodity aluminum other than its price.

It is important to point out that Alcoa's divestiture only occurred in the wake of agitation by activist hedge fund Elliott Management, whose investment thesis was that the company's finished end products business

---

* One need only look to Silicon Valley to observe these tendencies in action: industries such as online messaging or social networking experienced astronomical growth in their early phases, only to have that growth dissipate and key competitors die out as these industries matured.

† In 2002, Loews issued a tracking stock (see Chapter 8) called Carolina Group, which reflected the operations and performance of Lorillard, followed by a split-off (see Chapter 6) of its remaining stake in that business in 2008. As discussed in Part II, this sequence of divestiture structures permitted Loews to monetize its interest in Lorillard (which, despite the social stigma against it, generated a lot of cash), relative to what Loews would have gotten from a single transaction to divest that business.

had far better prospects than the commodity aluminum business.[18] The involvement of an activist investor in this case and other instances (e.g., eBay's divestiture of PayPal following the commoditization of the mobile payments industry[19]) further underscores the point that managerial inertia against divesting problematic businesses is often quite high. This is one of the reasons why it often takes the involvement of activist investors, who have the distance and objectivity to articulate these problems as well as the financial incentives to act on them, to surmount this inertia and get companies to divest.[20]

ACQUISITION FAILURE

Buyer's remorse is the regret that one experiences after making a questionable purchase. However, while individuals may be able to save the receipt and return the item, there are no refunds at the corporate level. There are divestitures, though, which underscores the second motivation for divesting problematic businesses: acquisition failure.

Why do acquisitions fail? This is a critical question that practitioners and scholars regularly debate, and the fact that it has implications for divestitures makes it even more important. The two main sources of acquisition failure are flawed strategic logic and flawed execution, each of which can occur individually or jointly with the other.

Flawed Strategic Logic

Many acquisitions are premised on the notion of some type of complementarity in the operations of the merged companies. As a result, these companies expect to realize revenue synergies from the ability to serve new customer segments, product categories, geographic regions, or sales channels; to access new talent, knowledge, and capabilities; or to improve their pricing power via greater scale. In many acquisitions, however, these strategic benefits never materialize, leading to acquisition failure and ultimately to the divestiture of the previously acquired businesses. In some of these cases, the flaw in strategic logic is that the projected revenue synergies were too optimistic:* accessing new customers and markets is rarely straightforward, pricing and market share assumptions are often not realistic, and translating new knowledge and capabilities into revenue streams is difficult.[21] In other cases, the flaw in strategic logic is more subtle, involving changes in market or industry conditions or in the company's overall strategic direction, altering the value proposition of the acquisition.

Quaker Oats Company's failed 1994 acquisition of Snapple nicely illustrates these issues. The acquisition was premised on a plan to achieve distribution efficiencies by pushing Snapple into the supermarkets that Quaker already served, which made perfect sense when viewed from 30,000 feet. The problem, however, was that the people who bought Snapple were at ground-level, and they bought Snapple with their sandwiches at the corner deli, not at the supermarket. As a result, the marriage collapsed just four years later, and Quaker's $1.7 billion acquisition of Snapple culminated in the latter's divestiture for a $1.4 billion loss to Quaker,[22] leaving investors crying over spilt juice.

A similar example of acquisition failure due to a misunderstanding of customer needs and preferences is eBay's acquisition and subsequent divestiture of Skype. eBay bought Skype in 2005, only to sell it to a private investor group in 2009. Here, the acquisition was predicated on a plan to enable eBay's customers to use Skype's VoIP technology to communicate with sellers about the items they were interested in buying. As one commentator noted, however, "The Skype-eBay acquisition never panned out. The main reason: For most eBay users, email is good enough. Buyers and sellers don't really need a voice call to seal a deal."[23]

Xerox's divestiture of Conduent, formerly Affiliated Computer Services (ACS), also followed an acquisition with flawed strategic logic. Xerox bought ACS in 2010 for $6 billion, seeking to diversify its old-line photocopy and print operations into a more profitable and faster-growing business process outsourcing operation. Under pressure from activist

---

* Consistent with this point, companies in almost 70% of mergers *failed to realize* projected revenue synergies. By comparison, companies in about 60% of mergers do achieve their projected cost synergies (e.g., headcount reductions, the elimination of redundant processes and facilities, the consolidation of shared services and back-office operations, and improvements in purchasing power).

Source: Christofferson, Scott A., Robert S. McNish, and Diane L. Sias. 2004. "Where Mergers Go Wrong." *McKinsey Quarterly*, May 1, 2004. https://www.mckinsey.com/business-functions /strategy-and-corporate-finance/our-insights/where-mergers-go-wrong.

investor Carl Icahn, Xerox announced the spinoff of Conduent in 2016, bumping its share price by 20% on the first day after the separation.[24] In the ACS acquisition, the flaw in strategic logic was the assumption that Xerox's hardware and services businesses could serve the same customers, when in reality few opportunities for synergy really existed between those businesses: "There was some cross-selling, but at the end of the day the two divisions didn't become highly interdependent and offered no strong reasons to stay together."[25]

Flawed Execution

The corporate strategy landscape is littered with tales of acquisitions that dramatically imploded after integration stalled or simply collapsed. The culprit is usually culture clash, in which differences in the leadership styles, approaches to decision-making, compensation structures, and organizational design (among many others) make it difficult, if not impossible, for the merging companies to meld into one. One specific type of deal in which such execution challenges are especially likely to manifest themselves is the so-called merger of equals, where two companies combine in a purportedly equal fashion. These deals are particularly prone to succumb to flawed execution,[26] as resources, processes, and capabilities are adopted from both companies, even though they may be incompatible with one another and those of one company may be superior to those of the other. Similarly, management and directors are typically drawn from both companies, even though this heightens the potential for conflict and for the political accession of undeserving executives. Finally, well-intended endeavors to blend the two companies' cultures and business practices usually fail.[27] As a result, some of the more spectacular divestitures have occurred in response to the flawed execution of acquisitions generally and mergers of equals specifically.

For example, Daimler-Benz and Chrysler's overly optimistic merger of equals in 1998 resulted in the sale of Chrysler to Cerberus Capital Management after 10 years of spousal infighting. Conflicts arose over issues ranging from such trivialities as the size of business cards and the appropriate class of airline service, to such substantive matters as the combined entity's organizational and reporting structure, brand image and identity, and the appropriate processes for financial reporting and investment community liaison.[28] While the merger of Daimler-Benz and Chrysler was initially struck for $37 billion, Chrysler was ultimately sold for $7 billion—an erosion of over $30 billion of value in slightly less than a decade.[29] Put differently, the $37,000 Mercedes bought by your father-in-law would have been more beneficial to the company than its $37 billion merger with Chrysler.

Similarly, the notorious failure of the marriage of AOL and Time Warner culminated in the spinoff of AOL, causing the value of AOL to plummet from $226 billion to $20 billion between the merger in 2000 and the divestiture in 2009.[30] The deal succumbed to the challenges of blending the "old media" and "new media" cultures of the two companies: "The aggressive and, many said, arrogant AOL people 'horrified' the more staid and corporate Time Warner side. Cooperation and promised synergies failed to materialize as mutual disrespect came to color their relationships."[31] These difficulties were exacerbated by the co-leadership structure the two companies adopted; even though Time Warner's CEO Gerald Levin became the CEO of the new company, there was a widespread perception that AOL's Stephen Case, the chairman of the new company, was "calling all the shots."[32]

These colorful episodes highlight an important point: acquisitions that fail due to flawed execution are often preceded by flawed strategic logic. Commentators (and even the protagonists themselves) identify flawed execution as the proximate cause of the failures of and subsequent divestitures in the Daimler–Chrysler and AOL–Time Warner mergers. However, the lack of strategic logic of these deals might well have been obvious from the start. Were the two automobile companies ever really going to benefit from sharing design expertise or leveraging common production facilities? Were the two media companies ever really going to experience convergence between their respective businesses? With the gift of hindsight, it's easy to answer in the negative.

One deal in which flawed strategic logic and flawed execution were clearly both at play was the Morgan Stanley–Dean Witter Discover (DWD) "merger of equals." The strategy behind this transaction was to unite Wall Street and Main Street (DWD was previously owned by Sears, at the time a major retailer to the Main Street crowd), but this logic faced great skepticism from the onset: "The new firm faces the stiff challenge of integrating Morgan Stanley's aristocratic culture . . . with the meat-and-potatoes environment at Dean Witter, whose brokers ply their trade everywhere from suburban office complexes to small-town storefronts. In a way, the merger would be as if Sears and Saks Fifth Avenue decided to join together."[33]

Consistent with these expectations, the execution of the merger quickly unraveled in the face of massive differences in the cultures, attitudes toward risk taking and regulation, and customer management practices of the two companies. The co-leadership structure the two companies adopted added fuel to the fire, in that Philip Purcell (DWD's former CEO) became the CEO of the merged company, but was widely perceived as being unwilling to cede power to John Mack (Morgan Stanley's past, and as it turned out, future CEO) after the five-year term upon which the two executives had agreed.[34] The cultural deterioration and infighting in the combined company grew so toxic that Morgan Stanley employees would reportedly push the "door close" button in the elevator when they saw their DWD colleagues approaching.[35] The relationship culminated in the spinoff of Dean Witter's credit card business (the Discover card) 10 years later.

Before undertaking an expensive acquisition that seemingly makes sense, one should reflect on an epigraph by Yeats: *In dreams begins responsibilities.*[36]

MANAGERIAL INERTIA

Long before Michael Porter introduced his Five Forces, Isaac Newton defined a force of his own: inertia. In corporate strategy, inertia is not a resistance to changes in velocity so much as it is a resistance to changes in strategy. All too often, though, inertia wins against both Porter and practitioners.

While the previous discussion demonstrated that industry unattractiveness and acquisition failure can motivate divestitures, it also highlighted the fact that managerial inertia against this divestiture strategy can be quite high. For example, in all these failed acquisitions, the subsequent divestitures occurred about *10 years* later. Three related factors cause or contribute to inertia: financial considerations that make executives perceive that it is uneconomical to divest, behavioral biases that cause executives to escalate their commitment to certain businesses rather than divest them, and historical connections that hold executives back from divesting businesses with linkages to the past.

Financial Considerations

Executives sometimes perceive the strategy of divesting problematic businesses as uneconomical because it can be costly for companies to divest businesses in which they have made significant prior investments. In these situations, the perception (or reality) is that the proceeds from divestiture will be insufficient to recoup the costs of those prior investments, leading executives to delay or avoid divestitures.* Perhaps unsurprisingly, this mentality is highly likely to manifest itself when it comes to businesses that operate in unattractive industries. Research has documented that so-called exit barriers to divestiture are highest in businesses operating in capital-intensive industries that require highly specialized fixed investments, and when companies have significant fixed obligations (such as debt, pension, or environmental liabilities) in those businesses.[37] These problems tend to occur in old-line, declining businesses that have been operated for a long time—precisely the kind of businesses that operate in unattractive industries. For example, despite diversification moves into faster-growing, more profitable sectors, American Can delayed divesting its eponymous can business for close to two decades because of the significant fixed investments it had made in packaging equipment and technology.[38] Likewise, Esmark was initially unable to divest its meatpacking business (Swift) due to its $135 million of unfunded pension and healthcare liabilities.[39]

A similar mindset arises in the case of failed acquisitions. As mentioned, executives may be reluctant to divest a business at a loss, a situation that is exacerbated when the business was acquired in recent memory. As the vicious cycle described in the introduction to this chapter illustrates, however, divesting a business (particularly one in an unattractive industry) becomes increasingly more difficult with time: employee morale and productivity sag in the face of culture clashes, operational challenges emerge as the reality of flawed strategic decisions sets in or integration plans fail to be executed, and profits are pressured due to an inability to extract the intended revenue and cost synergies. Reputational damage vis-à-vis customers and Wall Street can worsen these problems, leading to declines that persist long past the point when the failed acquisition is ultimately

---

* While executives will frequently allege that such divestitures are uneconomical and that they must be deferred or abandoned, the possibility of taking losses can offer certain tax advantages. See Chapter 5.

divested. And, of course, time works against the divesting company with regard to the likely strategic buyers of its subsidiary.

Behavioral Biases

Compounding the financial considerations that impede divestitures of problematic businesses, executives tend to display (or feign) overconfidence and escalate their commitment to these units, worsening the inertia against divesting them. For businesses operating in unattractive industries, executives' propensity to delay or avoid divestitures derives from the belief, hope, or pretense that the fortunes of those industries will change, that performance will improve, or that the executives themselves can extricate their companies from those problems. However, as Warren Buffett has been known to say, "When an industry with a reputation for difficult economics meets a manager with a reputation for excellence, it is usually the industry that keeps its reputation intact."[40]

Escalation of commitment is even more prevalent in the case of failed acquisitions, as it is difficult for executives to admit that a major decision they made in the past was strategically flawed or an outright mistake, much less that they were unable to implement or execute their own strategy. As a result, not only do executives delay or avoid these divestitures, but to make matters worse, they often continue investing money, time, and other resources in these businesses in the hope that additional investment will improve the situation. Again, when the promised improvement fails to materialize, the financial hurdle for divestiture becomes even higher; the additional investments make it even more difficult to recoup the cost of the failed acquisition.

Avon's ill-fated acquisition of Tiffany & Co. illustrates how escalation of commitment and continued investments compound managerial inertia against divestitures of failed acquisitions. Wall Street reacted with surprise when Avon announced that it was acquiring Tiffany's in 1978: "To some observers, the marriage of Avon and Tiffany seemed improbable. 'The possibility of a merger is so mind-boggling,' said a cosmetics industry consultant. 'Avon is so middle America and Tiffany is so Fifth Avenue. Does this mean we might see Tiffany items sold door to door?' "[41] It took Avon nearly eight years to arrive at the same conclusion. Avon completely failed to integrate Tiffany's operations and customers into its own organization, despite opening branches in new markets, introducing lower-priced items to its line of offerings, and *investing over $50 million* in technology to bring the two companies together.[42]

Even worse, Avon's efforts alienated important Tiffany's constituents. Angela Cummings, one of Tiffany's key designers, left Tiffany's for Bergdorf Goodman, publicly expressing fears that Tiffany's was "becoming more like Kmart than Cartier," and "some of [Avon's] new innovations, such as Tiffany credit cards with payment deadlines, offended longtime Tiffany shoppers who were used to stretching out payments without any penalties."[43] Perhaps as a consequence of these decisions, Tiffany's net income margin more than halved, from 14.4% in 1977 to 5.8% in 1982, despite revenue nearly tripling from $47.8 million to $115 million over the same period.[44] Although Avon knew Tiffany's had been struggling for years, it finally reached an agreement to sell Tiffany's back to its management team in 1985, after the retirement of longtime CEO Walter Hoving (who had in fact orchestrated the acquisition of Tiffany's by Avon in the first place).[45]

Nearly 40 years after its divestiture, Tiffany's again found itself the target of an acquisition, only this time its suitor was more plausible: luxury goods conglomerate LVMH acquired Tiffany's in 2021 with plans "to reboot what it sees as a sleepy brand that hasn't kept pace with Cartier, Chopard, and other luxury jewelers."[46] While LVMH executives have the mistakes of their Avon predecessors to guide them, the integration of Tiffany's is still in its early phases, and the ongoing COVID-19 pandemic continues to complicate the economic recovery that might encourage luxury jewelry purchases. We can only wish them luck.

Historical Connections

Finally, historical connections exacerbate inertia against the strategy of divesting problematic businesses. This is especially likely to occur among businesses that operate in unattractive industries, where historical connections are often the most prominent. For example, research has documented that companies' "legacy businesses"—the original lines of business in which they have participated since the time of their founding—often operate in weak or declining industries, but executives are nevertheless reluctant to divest them due to their professional histories in those organizations.[47] Ray Morris, the CEO of Pet Inc., articulated this mentality perfectly in his description of his company's legacy dairy products business: "It's a declining business, but you don't want to sell your heritage."[48] Inertia against "legacy divestitures" is particularly pronounced among executives with long tenures in their organizations. These individuals may display a disproportionate emotional attachment to their companies' legacy businesses, given their personal histories with those units.[49] Long-tenured executives may also be more beholden to the interests of individuals or coalitions within their companies, making it harder for them to implement major changes like legacy divestitures. This tendency to delay or avoid legacy divestitures is further exacerbated when the company's name is strongly associated with its legacy business.[50] Examples abound, including American Can, as well as many others like IC Industries (i.e., Illinois Central Railroad) and CPC International (i.e., Corn Products Company).*

Historical connections can also result from family relationships, and the presence of one or more members of a founding family in the top management, board of directors, and/or ownership structure of a company can equally contribute to inertia against divestitures. Founding families seek to realize objectives beyond maximizing economic value, such as preserving the founder's legacy and heritage, creating employment opportunities for family members, behaving responsibly toward employees and other stakeholders, and maintaining family harmony and social status. Founding families usually have substantial discretion to pursue these objectives, thanks to their significant ownership stakes and control-enhancing provisions.[51] As a result, founding families often avoid divestitures, even of businesses operating in unattractive industries, since those divestitures might have the potential to disrupt many of their family-specific objectives. Consistent with this point, family-owned and family-managed companies are 16% to 18% less likely to divest than comparable non-family companies.[52]

As an illustration of this tendency, consider the following anecdote. Facing the rapidly declining fortunes of the newspaper industry, the Washington Post Company, owned and controlled by the Graham family, sold *Newsweek* to industrialist Sidney Harman in 2010 for one dollar.† However, "among *Post* and *Newsweek* insiders the consensus is that Graham

---

* As will be discussed in Chapter 11, companies often change their corporate names after divesting legacy businesses to signal that they have exited these units.

† In other words, the value of the tax benefit from giving away *Newsweek* was greater than its intrinsic value, which was zero, or even negative. See Chapter 5.

should have recognized the need to sell years earlier . . . but was blinded by a concern for legacy and sentimentality. That Graham would sell or close the *Post* itself is all but unimaginable. 'The newspaper is the basic foundation not only of the company but of the family . . . The only family that would be less likely to sell its principal asset would be the Sulzbergers at the *New York Times.*'"[53] Contrary to this prediction, however, the Graham family ultimately did end up selling the *Washington Post* to Amazon's Jeff Bezos in 2013.[54]

CHAPTER 2

Improving Corporate Focus

INTRODUCTION

Corporate strategy refers to the process by which companies build and run portfolios of businesses to maximize profitability and shareholder value. Value is created when a company's businesses mutually reinforce each other by drawing on common resources and capabilities, using similar inputs, sharing corporate functions, serving overlapping customers, or otherwise creating synergies by being part of the same corporate household. Divestitures are a tool to remove business units that detract from—or fail to contribute to—these objectives, the expectation being to improve the company's focus on its remaining operations and to enhance its corporate performance. This chapter discusses *the strategy of divesting to improve corporate focus*. Consider the following example:

"Booze, balls, and cabinets":* in 2010, Fortune Brands respectively owned a liquor business, a golf business, and a home and security products business.[1] Only a few months after activist hedge fund Pershing Square announced it had amassed an 11% stake in the company, reportedly with the intention of pushing it to disassemble itself into its constituent pieces,[2] Fortune Brands announced it would do just that (it was a great call on the part of Pershing). The next year, Fortune Brands sold its golf business to an investor group led by Fila Korea for just over $1.2 billion in cash, and then it spun off its home and security business into a new company (Fortune Brands Home and Security), leaving behind its liquor business as a

---

* Wall Street traders love a good line. This one echoes Wall Street's famous characterization of Ling-Temco-Vought's 1967 spinoffs of its Wilson subsidiary's meatpacking, sporting goods, and pharmaceutical operations: "meatball, golf ball, and goofball."

Source: Poole, Claire. 2020. "Merge Ahead." *Texas Monthly*, August 2020. https://www.texasmonthly.com/articles/merge-ahead/.

publicly traded company (renamed Beam Inc.).[3] These focus-improving divestitures paid off handsomely for shareholders: in the 18 months following the spinoff, Beam achieved a total return of 53% and Fortune Brands Home and Security a whopping 229%.[4] While Fortune Brands' strategy was widely praised, one *Wall Street Journal* reporter appropriately wondered why it hadn't been done sooner: "Why does it take four years to realize booze, golf, security equipment, bathroom fixtures and cabinetry do not work together in one company?"[5]

In contrast to the strategy of divesting to remove problematic businesses, where underperformance provides a clear signal that a particular business should be divested, the same is not necessarily true of divesting to improve corporate focus. Many diversified companies are already profitable and create shareholder value—it's just that they could be *more* profitable and create *more* shareholder value if they divested *certain* businesses.

This makes it difficult to know when divesting to improve corporate focus is warranted, since this strategy requires executives to predict the relative future performance of their company in two different states of the world: (1) the one in which the divestiture occurs (i.e., the ill-fitting business is removed from the company), and (2) the other in which the divestiture does not occur (i.e., the ill-fitting business remains part of that company). While forecasting future performance is challenging under the best of circumstances, it is even more so in this situation because of the hypothetical nature of what is known as the "counterfactual case": executives simply cannot know how the company *would* perform once the business is divested.

Fortunately, a tool called the Better Off Test can help companies determine whether a focus-improving divestiture is the appropriate strategy by enabling them to compare the relative value of keeping versus removing certain businesses. When the Better Off Test fails, the value of removing a particular business exceeds the value of keeping it, so the company should divest to improve corporate focus.

THE BETTER OFF TEST: BACKGROUND

The Better Off Test is a strategic tool that can be used to assess whether a company will perform better after divesting one or more of its business units than it would if it retained them in the corporate household.

As originally conceptualized,[6] the Better Off Test was intended to provide executives with the means to assess whether their *diversification* strategies would create value—in other words, generate synergies—for their companies. To proceed with diversification, the Better Off Test challenged executives to affirm that the new business they were contemplating entering would either "gain competitive advantage from its link with the corporation, or vice versa [the corporation would gain competitive advantage from its link with the new business unit]."[7]

The core argument advanced in this chapter is that when the Better Off Test *fails*, a company does not gain (or it no longer gains) competitive advantage from retaining its ill-fitting operation, and thus divestiture is the appropriate strategy. To understand why the failure of the Better Off Test implies that a company should divest to improve corporate focus, it is useful to contrast two examples: (1) one where the Better Off Test passed and the company retained the business unit in question, and (2) another where the Better Off Test failed and the company instead divested that unit.

In a 2019 open letter to shareholders, activist investor Daniel Loeb demanded that Sony consider divesting its imaging sensors business (Imaging and Sensing Solutions [I&SS], later renamed Semiconductors), arguing that it lacked a connection to the rest of Sony's entertainment-based portfolio and made it difficult for investors to understand Sony's overall corporate strategy.[8] Sony CEO Kenichiro Yoshida responded with his own letter to shareholders,[9] in which he cogently described why and how the I&SS business exhibited synergies with the other units in the company—in other words, why the I&SS business passed the Better Off Test and should not be divested. In perhaps the classiest, most measured response ever to an activist investor, Mr. Yoshida explained:

> We have defined Sony's identity as a "creative entertainment company with a solid foundation of technology" and our corporate direction as "getting closer to people." "People" refers to both creators and users. "Technology" refers to the expertise we have in transforming the vision creators have into reality (through image capture and other means), revealing that vision to users (through image rendering and other means) and connecting the two (through digital signal processing). Imaging and sensing technology is integral to this technology. Indeed, it is the most important technology for enhancing Sony's corporate value over the long term.[10]

Consistent with Mr. Yoshida's argument,* Sony did not divest the I&SS business from its portfolio—*it was better off retaining that business.*

In contrast to Sony's experience, consider the second example, United Technologies' decision to divide its company into three parts in 2020: elevators (Otis), air conditioning (Carrier), and aerospace (legacy Pratt & Whitney and operations acquired from Rockwell Collins and Raytheon). This example illustrates how failing the Better Off Test can motivate divestitures to improve corporate focus. CEO Gregory Hayes articulated that the major benefit of the three-way separation was that it would enable United Technologies to focus on its own strategy in the aerospace business, especially the merger with aerospace giant Raytheon: "Executing the separations of Carrier and Otis is also a major milestone to completing the merger of UTC's aerospace businesses with Raytheon to create Raytheon Technologies, the premier aerospace and defense systems and services provider."[11] Analysts added to these points by explaining that under the United Technologies umbrella, Otis had underinvested in services relative to its main competitor (Thyssenkrupp) and that it could profitably boost investments in this area after its spinoff from United Technologies.[12] Similarly, under United Technologies, Carrier was believed to have retained

---

* The CEOs of General Motors and Ford expressed similar logic supporting the Better Off Test in their responses to speculation that their companies might spin off their electric car businesses, as did the CEO of Macy's in response to activist demands that it separate its e-commerce business from its bricks-and-mortar operations. General Motors CEO Mary Barra explained, "I think all the assets we bring to [the EV transition] are stronger and we can go faster because they're together." After reorganizing Ford's traditional and electric car businesses into separate internal divisions to facilitate their independent valuation, CEO Jim Farley explained that "much of Ford's broader operations will be critical to building out its electric car business, including its engineering and manufacturing expertise. . . . The new startups would love to have the industrial know-how of our company. Why spin out [the electric car business] and risk that?" And according to Macy's CEO Jeff Gennette, "We determined that Macy's, Inc. has a stronger future as a fully integrated business, with Macy's and Bloomingdale's together and assessing a broad range of brands, price points and customers across digital and stores."

Sources: Colias, Mike. 2022. "Ford CEO Says No Plans to Spin Off EV Business." *Wall Street Journal*, February 23, 2022. https://www.wsj.com/articles/ford-ceo-says-no-plans-to-spin-off-ev-business-11645645758.

Colias, Mike. 2022. "Ford Creates Separate EV, Gas-Engine Divisions in Major Overhaul." *Wall Street Journal*, March 2, 2022. https://www.wsj.com/articles/ford-creates-electric-vehicle-gas-engine-divisions-in-company-reshape-11646222458.

Motley Fool Transcribing. 2022. "Macy's (M) Q4 2021 Earnings Call Transcript." February 22, 2022. https://www.fool.com/earnings/call-transcripts/2022/02/22/macys-m-q4-2021-earnings-call-transcript/.

certain businesses that would better have been divested, creating opportunities for portfolio review and realignment in Carrier, itself, after its separation.[13] Together, these descriptions illustrate how United Technologies' three businesses were indeed thought to be *better off as independent entities than they were as part of the same corporate household.*

WHEN DO COMPANIES FAIL THE BETTER OFF TEST?

There are three situations in which companies fail the Better Off Test:

1. When certain operations do not fit strategically with the rest of the company

2. When disparities among the company's operations create internal complexity in the organization

3. When diversification makes it difficult for external constituents like investors and securities analysts to understand the company's overall strategy, resulting in undervaluation in the equity market

These three situations are not necessarily mutually exclusive, and companies frequently find themselves facing more than one of them.

Strategic Misfit

The strategic fit, or lack thereof, among the businesses in a corporate portfolio is the first indicator of whether a company passes or fails the Better Off Test, and hence, whether or not that company should divest to improve corporate focus. When there is strategic logic or coherence in a company's portfolio, keeping its units together creates value for the company as a whole,[14] since resources and capabilities can be applied across businesses to generate a sustainable corporate advantage that other companies cannot replicate.[15] This can be true even when a company operates in seemingly disparate industries,[16] in that "core competencies"[17] or common resources[18] can unify production, knowledge, customers, and management practices across business units.

In companies where the strategic fit among businesses is clear, divestitures are not needed because those businesses generate synergies from their continued joint operation, suggesting that the Better Off Test is satisfied. Disney's cross-promotion of its *Star Wars* movies across its disparate operating lines nicely illustrates this point: "*Star Wars* isn't just about the movie, in other words: it's also about the TV shows, toys, video games, books, soundtracks, and theme park rides, all of which bring in revenue and will help fuel interest in this film (and the next one)."[19]

In contrast, when the strategic fit among a company's businesses is low or absent, it may be more valuable for that company to divest one or more of those businesses than to retain them. Businesses that are divested for poor strategic fit are often referred to as "non-core." This reinforces the notion that companies require a unified strategic focus to generate a sustainable corporate advantage. Divestitures of non-core businesses that exhibit a lack of strategic fit are positively associated with stock market performance and operational profitability.[20]

Consider Pearson's 2015 divestitures of the *Financial Times* and Pearson's 50% stake in the Economist Group (owner of *The Economist* magazine), followed by its divestitures of partial stakes in Penguin Random House in 2017 and 2020. For a long time, Pearson had been emphasizing its focus on education, which grew from 63% of its revenues in 2005 to 82% in 2013.[21] As a result, Pearson's newsprint media and book publishing assets became non-core operations that were a poor strategic fit for the company. Following the divestiture of its final 25% stake in Penguin Random House, CEO John Fallon stressed this exact point: "The sale of our remaining stake to our partners . . . enables Pearson now *to be completely focused* on building the world's leading digital learning company, linking education to employability and skills, and reaching more learners around the world to support them through a lifetime of learning."[22]

Internal Complexity

Internal complexity among the businesses in a corporate portfolio is the second indicator of whether a company passes or fails the Better Off Test, and whether that company should divest to improve corporate focus. But what exactly is internal complexity?

When companies are able to coordinate production, operating, and financial decisions across the businesses in their portfolios, it enables them to generate synergies that increase their profitability—in other words, to create economies of scope.[23] However, such synchronization is not cost-free, and the actual task of overseeing and coordinating multiple businesses can be quite complex: the decisions, processes, policies, and outcomes of one business unit are often inconsistent with or even contradictory to those of other operations in the company.[24] Internal complexity is the cost of synchronizing and coordinating the functioning of multiple businesses in the corporate portfolio, relative to the value that is created by the company owning and operating those businesses together.

Companies fail the Better Off Test when internal complexity is high, and one situation in which this occurs is when a company's business units have different compensation practices. Divisional managers in diversified companies are compensated according to market standards for the industries in which their businesses operate and the geographic regions in which they are located.[25] This can result in variance in the compensation practices of the company's different business units, meaning that managers at the same level of the corporate hierarchy may be compensated in different ways. When managers of corporate siblings observe these compensation differences, it can result in perceptions of inequity or unfairness and thus in reduced teamwork,[26] lower productivity and morale,[27] and greater employee turnover.[28]

Focus-improving divestitures are a solution to these challenges,[29] as illustrated by the experience of Janus Capital Corporation in Kansas City Southern (KCS) Industries (a diversified railroad holding company). Compensation differentials between Janus's mutual fund managers and KCS's railroad executives were a major source of friction between the two entities: " 'People in classic industrial backgrounds aren't used to seeing people make $3 million or $4 million in their 30s,' says Michael Herman, a Janus board member. . . . Industry experts estimate that top Janus managers, taking home fat performance bonuses, make even more than that. As for [Janus CEO Thomas] Bailey himself, he took home about $1.8 million in 1998, including bonuses, while [KCS CEO Landon] Rowland's salary and bonus came to less than half that, at about $829,000."[30] KCS later divested Janus and its other financial services operations via its spinoff of Stilwell Financial.

Internal complexity can also be high when a company's capital allocation decisions create conflicts among its businesses, which is especially likely to occur when the profits from one business unit are used to cross-subsidize the needs of other business units. The KCS Industries–Janus example illustrates some of these challenges, too: "Janus executives say the fund firm now accounts for most of KCS's profits. . . . Janus's chief investment officer, Jim Craig, raised a question about KCS's acquisition in 1994 of Berger Associates. . . . When KCS buys other asset managers, Janus's cash flow is 'subsidizing our competitors,' complained Mr. Craig. . . . 'I would like to vanquish our competitors, not subsidize them.' "[31]

Even differences in the regulatory requirements of the various units in a diversified company can create internal complexity. For example, in the aftermath of the global financial crisis, businesses that were previously unregulated found themselves subject to regulation simply by virtue of being in the same corporate household as newly regulated corporate siblings. General Electric's decision to divest GE Capital provides a useful example of a company's response to this problem. The value of the assets that GE Capital controlled made it the equivalent of the seventh-largest bank in the United States, and hence, a "Systematically Important Financial Institution."[32] As a result, General Electric became "subject to tougher regulatory standards because a failure in GE Capital could impact the banking system in the United States," a major motivation for the GE Capital divestiture.[33] This illustrates how regulatory spillovers can lead to the failure of the Better Off Test and to focus-improving divestitures.

In summary, the negative interactions that arise from differences in the operating processes and practices of various units in a diversified company can lead to the failure of the Better Off Test. Rather than there being *economies* of scope that result from keeping those businesses together in the same corporate household, there are in fact *diseconomies* of scope from doing so. When internal complexity results from these kinds of differences, focus-improving divestitures can remove the businesses that contribute to this complexity, making them a valuable strategy.

Undervaluation

Just as internal complexity can lead to focus-improving divestitures, so, too, can the undervaluation that often results from excess diversification—the third indicator of the failure of the Better Off Test.

When a company's external constituents—its investors and the securities analysts that cover it—have difficulty making sense of how the businesses in a corporate portfolio fit together, they may undervalue the company (i.e., the whole) relative to the combined value of its businesses (i.e., the sum of its parts). The undervaluation of diversified companies is commonly known as the "diversification discount" or the "conglomerate discount." Empirical evidence suggests that diversified companies are worth an average of 13% to 15% less than their individual businesses would be worth were they to be broken apart and valued on a standalone basis.[34]* The conglomerate discount experienced by diversified companies grows larger when their businesses exhibit a greater number of disparities in their operating characteristics (capital intensity, growth rates, and profit margins).[35] Importantly, the conglomerate discount can be seen as a direct manifestation of the failure of the Better Off Test: it concretely measures how much shareholder value is destroyed from keeping a group of businesses together in the same corporate household, relative to the projected value of separating those businesses into independent entities.

Undervaluation tends to be high when the units in a diversified company operate in many different industries. A critical factor contributing to the conglomerate discount lies in the nature of Wall Street research: companies are typically covered by securities analysts who specialize by industry,[36] making it difficult for a single individual who is knowledgeable in one area to produce accurate forecasts of the future performance of a company that operates in many other areas. This challenge can be exacerbated when the analyst's specialization is linked to the earliest industry in which one of the company's businesses operated.[37]

Focus-improving divestitures enable companies to reduce the diversification that contributes to undervaluation and, therefore, to attain clearer analyst coverage and improved market valuations.[38] This is reflected in a colorful reaction to the divestiture of the non-media operations of Westinghouse Electric, which had recently acquired CBS, a fabled broadcast conglomerate: "By focusing Westinghouse-CBS on broadcast, [CEO Michael H.] Jordan satisfies Wall Street, which couldn't figure out how to value a $9.5 billion company with one foot in a TV studio and the other in a nuclear-waste dump."[39] Similarly, when Barnes & Noble announced that it would spin off its Nook e-reader and college bookstores businesses in 2014 (although it later spun off only the college bookstores business), "investors applauded the split announcement, pushing up Barnes & Noble stock 5% in midafternoon trading. [One securities analyst commented:] 'It will simplify what has been a very complicated situation. . . . Valuing

---

* This exact analysis was conducted about General Electric in this book's Introduction.

a business that is a physical retailer, a college book retailer, a hardware vendor, and a digital content seller is very difficult.' "[40]

MANAGERIAL INERTIA

Despite the benefits of focus-improving divestitures, managerial inertia against this strategy is not uncommon, for two related reasons:

1. A lack of urgency around focus-improving divestitures, since there is not usually an obvious signal that something is wrong with one of the company's businesses

2. A failure to clearly articulate the company's corporate strategy, limiting management's ability to conduct the Better Off Test and identify businesses that are good candidates for divestiture

Lack of Urgency

As described in Chapter 1, one of the main challenges associated with the strategy of divesting problematic businesses is the tendency of executives to wait too long to divest, hoping that poor industry conditions or failed acquisitions resolve themselves, believing that they have the capabilities to manage their way out of these problems, or simply being unwilling to admit defeat. When it comes to the strategy of divesting to improve corporate focus, the logic that results in managerial inertia is distinct, and perhaps even more problematic: *Why bother divesting a business when nothing is explicitly wrong with it, especially if the company's performance is strong?* In other words, the lack of urgency around focus-improving divestitures can obscure the value of this strategy and prevent executives from undertaking it.

Esmark provides an instructive example of this mentality. Esmark was one of the widely diversified conglomerates of the 1970s and 1980s, consisting of businesses ranging from its legacy meatpacking unit (Swift) to chemicals (Estech), consumer products (International Playtex), automotive speakers and additives (International Jensen and STP), and energy (Vickers Petroleum and TransOcean Oil). The company was deeply undervalued, yet its management delayed divesting its highly profitable energy division for nearly two years, perhaps because the division was so profitable and almost certainly because there was nothing patently wrong with it that would otherwise warrant its divestiture.[41] Ultimately, in the face of analyst reports and financial analyses trumpeting the high standalone value of the energy division (by one estimate, about 40% higher than Esmark's combined market value),[42] Esmark sold the various components of this business for $1.1 billion in October 1980.[43] The investment community applauded this decision: "The reaction to the restructuring plan among financial analysts and management consultants [was] largely favorable. 'I think [CEO Donald P. Kelly] is a hero,' said Oscar S. Schafer, an analyst with Steinhardt Partners of New York."[44]

Several personal considerations amplify inertia against the strategy of divesting to improve corporate focus. For one, corporate size and scope are positively correlated with executive compensation.[45] As a result, executives may be reluctant to divest,[46] given that these transactions directly reduce corporate size and scope and hence, their own personal bottom lines.* Taking these ideas a step further, executives often gain personal utility from expanding corporate scope.[47] From a reputational standpoint, executives that expand corporate scope are perceived as being successful leaders who have achieved growth for their companies. Rather than divest to improve corporate focus, executives may empire build by pursuing acquisitions and other diversification strategies.[48]

These tendencies are exacerbated by the media stigma that often accompanies divestitures. In news articles that are written about acquisitions versus divestitures, the difference in the tone of the words that are used to describe these transaction types is striking: on the acquisition side, words like "opportunity," "growth," "value," and "expansion" stand in stark contrast to words like "lagging," "makeover," "failure," and "retrench" on the divestiture side. Anecdotal evidence confirms this sentiment as well: for example, two high-profile publications respectively entitled articles describing some of General Electric's announcements that it would begin slimming down its portfolio, "Turning GE's Sacred Cows into Hamburger"[49] and "Power Failure."[50] Facing this kind of portrayal in the popular press, it is unsurprising that many CEOs and top executives

---

* The irony of this point is, of course, the fact that stock market performance usually improves after companies divest, suggesting that executives should stand to gain, not lose, from divestitures.

perceive focus-improving divestitures as threatening to their professional reputations.[51]

Unclear Corporate Strategy

One potential solution to the problem of inertia against focus-improving divestitures is for executives to identify their company's corporate strategy, and then to determine whether divestitures might be warranted for certain businesses. However, executives often do not engage in the regular strategic reviews of their portfolios that would enable them to identify and articulate their companies' corporate strategies. This makes it difficult, if not impossible, for them to distinguish the businesses that pass the Better Off Test from those that fail it, and to know which businesses are good candidates for divestiture and which ones are not. Even worse, this can prevent executives from overcoming the inertia that results from the lack of a clear signal that such divestitures may be warranted.

Companies do not engage in strategic reviews of their portfolios on a more frequent basis because there are usually more pressing tasks to attend to, particularly the day-to-day requirements of running the company and the short-term pressures that result from quarterly earnings cycles. As a result, it can be diversionary and difficult for top executives to take the time to analyze whether their company's businesses create more value by being kept together in the same corporate portfolio than they would by being separated into independent entities or sold to different owners.* Indeed, if executives cannot spare the time and devote the effort to do that, then it would be impossible to engage in the process of actually divesting those businesses. This lack of a clear and coherent corporate strategy can impede executives from divesting to improve corporate focus. Consistent with these points, survey results indicate that nearly two-thirds of executives believe it is necessary to initiate or increase the frequency of portfolio reviews, to take a different approach to portfolio reviews, and to provide better guidance on which businesses are core versus non-core

---

* The accepted alternative would be to commission a review by third-party professionals. Apart from the expense of such a review, there are several potential drawbacks that must be recognized. First, the third-party review bears the risk of becoming a "self-fulfilling prophecy," in which the momentum of the review impels the divestiture. Second, one can only imagine the potential consequences if the company ignores the professional advice, and its subsidiary later fails. Third, it is axiomatic that the risk of a potential leak, in this case a leak to the financial community, will increase with the number of persons involved.

as specific actions they could take to identify divestiture candidates more readily.[52]

Activist investors have found it incredibly profitable to swarm into the gap caused by this collective management complacency. Using their own resources, they effectively substitute for executives in conducting the strategic reviews that can result in focus-improving divestitures.* Since 2014, activist investors have launched hundreds of campaigns per year against public corporations, including such household names as Intel, Comcast, GlaxoSmithKline, ExxonMobil, Hasbro, and Unilever.[53] While the changes that activists demand that companies make vary and can include governance, operational, and portfolio actions, divestitures to improve corporate focus are a common demand, appearing in about a quarter of activist campaigns.[54]

Honeywell provides a useful example of how an activist campaign can prompt a company to engage in a strategic review of its portfolio and undertake focus-improving divestitures. In 2017, Third Point disclosed a major ownership stake in Honeywell and demanded that the company divest its aerospace business. In response, Honeywell undertook a comprehensive strategic review of its portfolio and a clear assessment of its corporate strategy, culminating in the divestiture of its transportation

---

* On an investor call in early 2022, for example, activist investor Daniel Loeb of Third Point explained that he saw nearly $1 billion of untapped value in Amazon, which he hinted that the company could realize by separating its disparate e-commerce and cloud operations. Mr. Loeb's fourth quarter investor letter expressed similar sentiments: "After lagging tech peers for most of last year, we significantly increased the size of our investment, reflecting our conviction that Amazon is at an important crossroads as new management considers its long-term strategic plan to move the company forward, which may include several bold initiatives that are the subject of wide market speculation at the proverbial investor water cooler." Mr. Loeb's comments came on the heels of similar remarks by another professional investor that were published in the *Wall Street Journal*.

Sources: Chung, Juliet, Cara Lombardo, and Dana Mattioli. 2022. "Activist Investor Daniel Loeb Sees Roughly $1 Trillion of Untapped Value in Amazon." *Wall Street Journal*, February 17, 2022. https://www.wsj.com/articles/activist-investor-daniel-loeb-sees-roughly-1-trillion-of -untapped-value-in-amazon-11645048496.

Third Point. 2022. "Fourth Quarter 2021 Investor Letter." February 16, 2022. https:// thirdpointlimited.com/wp-content/uploads/2022/02/Third-Point-Q4-2021-Investor-Letter -TPIL.pdf.

Lonsdale, Joe. 2022. "The Case for Splitting Amazon in Two." *Wall Street Journal*, February 7, 2022. https://www.wsj.com/articles/split-amazon-in-two-prime-web-services-aws-logistics -third-party-earnings-report-consumers-antitrust-11644249482.

systems and its homes and global distribution businesses. Honeywell CEO Darius Adamczyk described the portfolio review as follows:

> Today's announcement marks the culmination of a rigorous portfolio review involving a detailed assessment of every Honeywell business. As part of that review, we analyzed numerous criteria, including growth outlook, financial performance, market dynamics, potential for disruption, and, most importantly, assessment of fit as a Honeywell business. . . . These businesses are best positioned to leverage Honeywell synergies from our technologies, financial and business models, and talent.[55]

Although the divestitures that Honeywell ultimately undertook were different from the one that Third Point demanded, the major insight that stands out from Mr. Adamczyk's statements is that Third Point's campaign appears to have prompted Honeywell to assess its corporate strategy—that is, to determine which of its businesses fit well together and generated synergies (i.e., passed the Better Off Test), and which ones did not. This explains why activist campaigns against public corporations are generally greeted favorably by investors, especially when those campaigns demand that companies undertake focus-improving divestitures (a 6% increase in excess shareholder returns upon announcement, by one estimate).[56] Furthermore, the divestitures demanded by activist investors outperform those that executives undertake of their own accord, both in terms of investors' immediate responses to divestiture announcements and in terms of long-run shareholder returns.[57] This discrepancy suggests that companies may be missing opportunities to undertake focus-improving divestitures, perhaps because they are failing to engage in the rigorous portfolio reviews that activists demand and often conduct themselves. These ideas have prompted leading consulting companies to encourage their clients to "think like activists" by more frequently engaging in strategic reviews of their portfolios, more clearly articulating their corporate strategies, and more proactively divesting to improve corporate focus.[58]

CHAPTER 3

Reconfiguring the Corporate Portfolio

INTRODUCTION

On the face of it, divestitures and acquisitions might seem to be at odds with each other: divestitures are used to reduce corporate scope, while acquisitions are used to increase it. But divestitures and acquisitions can be quite complementary, enabling companies to achieve greater efficiency in their existing operations, to explore new opportunities in different strategic domains, or both. In fact, companies regularly use the two types of transactions sequentially to reconfigure their portfolios: 91% of frequent acquirers (defined as companies that made at least ten acquisitions between 2007 and 2017) also divested an average of 11 times during this period, as compared to 67% of infrequent acquirers (which divested only three times).[1]

When companies pursue divestitures *sequentially* with acquisitions—that is, as part of a strategy of portfolio reconfiguration—the potential for value creation is even higher than it is when companies undertake divestitures (or acquisitions) as discrete transactions. To illustrate this point, Exhibit 3.1 presents the average compounded monthly returns of three groups of publicly traded U.S.-based companies that pursued (1) acquisitions, but no divestitures in the following year; (2) divestitures, but no acquisitions in the following year; and (3) divestitures, and at least one acquisition in the year before or after those transactions. Performance is the highest when companies undertake divestitures and acquisitions sequentially (Group 3), followed by divestitures alone (Group 2), and finally by acquisitions alone (Group 1). These results indicate that not only do divestitures create more value for companies than acquisitions, as highlighted in the Introduction to this book, but the winning strategy from a long-term perspective is in fact the combination of divestitures and acquisitions.

EXHIBIT 3.1

Average Compounded Monthly Returns of Companies That Pursue
(1) Acquisitions Without Divestitures the Year After; (2) Divestitures
Without Acquisitions the Year After; and (3) Divestitures with at Least
One Acquisition the Year Before or After[2]

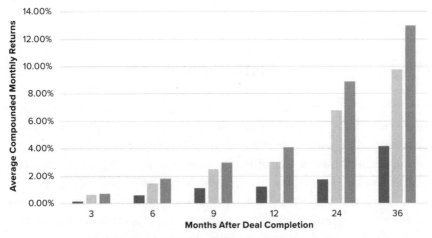

To understand why the potential for value creation is highest when
companies pursue divestitures sequentially with acquisitions, it is instructive to consider the portfolio reconfiguration strategies of two leading
information technology companies: IBM and HP Enterprise (HPE). Each
of them successfully acquired and divested major operations, but in different sequences.

For IBM, acquisition preceded divestiture. IBM bought Red Hat in
2019, solidifying its leading position in the hybrid cloud market. CEO
Arvind Krishna described hybrid cloud as a $1 trillion market opportu-
nity, as more and more customers adopted IBM's platform and leveraged
its artificial intelligence capabilities for managing their data.[3] Only after
this landmark acquisition did IBM divest its managed infrastructure services business, announcing in 2020 that it would spin it off into a new
company,[4] later named Kyndryl. Executive chairman and former CEO
Ginni Rometty highlighted the extent of the portfolio reconfiguration that

this sequence of acquisition and divestiture had achieved: "Our multi-year transformation created the foundation for the open hybrid cloud platform, which we then accelerated with the acquisition of Red Hat. At the same time, our managed infrastructure services business has established itself as the industry leader, with unrivaled expertise in complex and mission-critical infrastructure work. As two independent companies, IBM and [Kyndryl] will capitalize on their respective strengths. IBM will accelerate clients' digital transformation journeys, and [Kyndryl] will accelerate clients' infrastructure modernization efforts."[5] For IBM, the sequence of acquisition followed by divestiture enabled it to rationalize its corporate portfolio around its hybrid cloud strategy.

Conversely, divestiture preceded acquisition for HPE. Shortly after its own separation from HP Inc., HPE continued slimming down, divesting its enterprise services and software businesses. Speaking about the divestiture of the enterprise services business, then CEO Meg Whitman described the transaction as transforming HPE into "a faster-growing company that's intensely focused," with nearly $9 billion of cash on hand, and she also explained that "HPE remains open to new acquisitions, but not large ones."[6] This is exactly what HPE did, buying numerous businesses over the next several years.[7] Many of these acquisitions were of businesses focusing on "secure, next generation, software-defined infrastructure, . . . as well as [HPE's] Helion Cloud platform and software assets."[8] Additionally, several acquisitions were geared at moving "beyond the data center [to redefine] IT at the edge. . . ."[9] Thus, the sequence of divestiture followed by acquisition enabled HPE to free up and reallocate resources into its hybrid information technology and edge-to-cloud strategy.

This chapter analyzes the two distinct pathways through which companies can use divestitures in sequence with acquisitions as part of a strategy of portfolio reconfiguration: companies can divest *after* acquiring to rationalize their portfolios (portfolio rationalization), as IBM did, or they can divest *before* acquiring to redeploy resources (resource redeployment), as HPE did. Portfolio rationalization is valuable in the sense that divestitures facilitate an exit from existing operations once companies have established footholds in new domains through their acquisitions. By the same token, resource redeployment is attractive because divestitures generate a cushion of financial and other resources that can be reallocated into new opportunities through acquisitions, limiting the need to access external markets to fund these initiatives. Importantly, both pathways sidestep some of the managerial inertia that often impedes divestitures, as discussed in Chapters 1 and 2. While the businesses that are divested as part of a strategy of portfolio reconfiguration may indeed be poorly performing, ill fitting, or perhaps even both, the motivation for their divestiture is not necessarily these challenges, but rather the broader strategic shifts of which they are a part. This may make it easier for executives to justify, if only to themselves, the benefits of divesting these businesses.

PORTFOLIO RATIONALIZATION[*]

Portfolio rationalization is defined as the divestiture of unwanted,[†] unneeded, or redundant businesses after companies acquire new businesses. This occurs in the following three situations:

1. Companies "unbundle" and divest incidental businesses they had to buy in the course of other acquisitions.

2. Companies divest some of their own existing businesses after using acquisitions to "trade up" into new and better businesses.

3. Companies divest redundant resources to realize scale efficiencies after acquiring related businesses.

---

[*] Lest there be confusion, portfolio reconfiguration is a distinct concept from portfolio rationalization. Portfolio reconfiguration is a company's use of *any sequence of divestitures and acquisitions* to modify its portfolio and change its strategy. Portfolio rationalization, however, is a company's use of *the specific sequence of acquisitions followed by divestitures*. Portfolio rationalization is therefore a subset of portfolio reconfiguration.

[†] Clearly, it would be counterproductive for a company to portray an unwanted business as such when seeking to divest it, particularly if the divestiture takes the form of a sale. Doing so would negatively impact the value of the divested business in all cases, and it would increase the difficulty of attracting buyers and maximizing the price in a sale. Consistent with this point, investors react negatively to divestitures that are described as removing "undesired units," in contrast to the positive stock market reaction that accompanies divestitures that are described as "strategic."

Source: Montgomery, Cynthia A., Ann R. Thomas, and Rajan Kamath. 1984. "Divestiture, Market Valuation, and Strategy." *Academy of Management Journal* 27, no. 4 (December 1984): 830–840.

Unbundling

Unbundling is premised on the notion that a company divests certain businesses it buys *as part of an acquisition*. For example, InBev did not buy Anheuser-Busch, a diversified beer company, for the killer whales in its theme park. Rather, InBev acquired Anheuser-Busch for the purpose of building scale in the beer industry. Yet as part of the deal, it also got the company's ancillary businesses, the SeaWorld and Busch Gardens theme parks (and other assets, such as Anheuser-Busch's packaging business). InBev clearly did not need or want those non-core businesses.[10] However, they were a necessary part of the acquisition—Anheuser-Busch wouldn't sell its beer business without them. One year later, InBev divested the theme parks, unbundling them from its acquisition of Anheuser-Busch.

This example illustrates that even though the divestiture might occur after a lag, the process of unbundling begins when a focal company concludes a multi-unit acquisition; the buyer must purchase the target in its entirety and then divest (i.e., unbundle) the ancillary businesses. This is depicted in Exhibit 3.2. For example, as part of its transition from chemicals to agricultural and pharmaceutical biotechnology, Monsanto sought to buy G.D. Searle's drug operations due to their strength in biopharmaceuticals. But Searle would not sell that business without its NutraSweet operations.[11] Monsanto eventually bought Searle in its entirety, selling the NutraSweet business after completing the acquisition.[12] Similarly, Disney unbundled TrueX, an advertising technology business, from its acquisition of 21st Century Fox.[13] Since TrueX had little to do with the rest of the entertainment-related assets that Disney acquired in this deal, it was considered a non-core asset from the start. As a result, TrueX was treated as a standalone entity rather than being integrated into Disney's operations, which simplified its subsequent unbundling.[14]

A study using data on manufacturing plants documented that unbundling is a prevalent phenomenon: on average, companies subsequently sell 27% of the plants they obtain in their acquisitions.[15] Additionally, the businesses that are divested in the process of unbundling are usually unrelated to the focal company's remaining operations—the above-mentioned study also found that the manufacturing plants that were sold post-acquisition were disproportionately more likely to be concentrated in the acquiring company's peripheral, rather than core, operations.[16] These findings underscore an important difference between unbundling and divesting in

EXHIBIT 3.2

Depiction of Unbundling

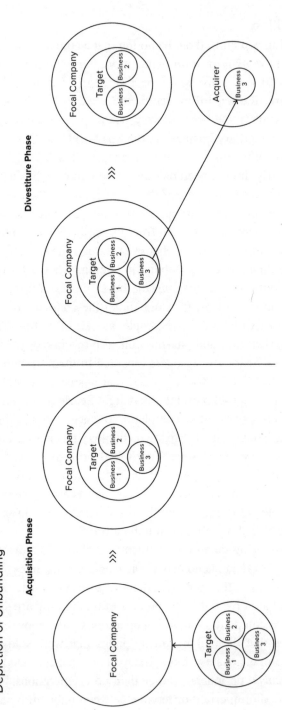

response to acquisition failure. While both types of divestitures involve the removal of previously acquired businesses, the motivation for unbundling is far more benign: exiting an unneeded business, as opposed to removing a problematic business. Because unbundling does not require executives to acknowledge that an acquisition was strategically flawed or incapable of implementation, it is interesting to speculate that there is less inertia against unbundling than there is against divesting failed acquisitions. Consistent with this conjecture, a median of seven years elapses between acquisitions and divestitures when companies divest failed acquisitions,[17] whereas acquisitions and divestitures usually occur contemporaneously when companies unbundle.*

Trading Up

While unbundling is premised on the notion that a company divests certain businesses it buys *as part of an acquisition*, trading up reflects the opposite pattern of activity: a focal company buys a target, but then goes on to divest businesses *from its own organization* rather than from the target after the acquisition. This distinction can be seen by comparing Exhibits 3.2 and 3.3, which illustrate the different origins of the divested business in each of these two situations. Trading up reflects a positive aspect of portfolio rationalization: the focal company refreshes its portfolio by incorporating new businesses via acquisition, and then removing old businesses that no longer advance its strategic objectives via divestiture.[18] Consistent with this point, the businesses that are divested during the process of trading up are usually slower growing and lower margin than the new businesses that are acquired.

The J.M. Smucker Company's divestitures of certain of its slower-growing human foods businesses, following its acquisitions of businesses in the faster-growing pet foods segment, nicely illustrate the process of

---

* At the same time, one challenge that can arise with unbundling is the possibility that the focal company has difficulty finding a buyer for a business it acquired but did not need. In these situations, the divesting company may be forced to hold on to the unneeded business for longer than it intends, starving it of resources and management attention and worsening its quality, much in the same manner as the vicious cycle described in Chapter 1. One way for a company to forestall this downward spiral is to attempt to orchestrate the divestiture of the unneeded business prior to the acquisition that would bring it into its organization. This carries its own challenges, though, in that such planning can lead to leaks or rumors about the acquisition before it even occurs.

EXHIBIT 3.3

Depiction of Trading Up

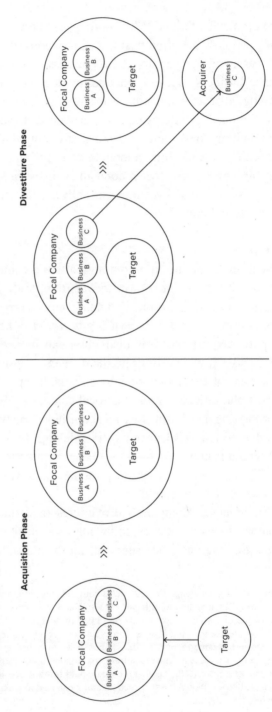

trading up across industry sectors. Smucker's, renowned for its legacy business of jellies and jams, had diversified into several other packaged foods businesses, following which it entered the pet foods segment. Rather than simply continuing to expand, Smucker's traded up, acquiring Big Heart Brands in 2015 and Ainsworth Pet Nutrition in 2018, while subsequently reducing its presence in human foods through the divestitures of its canned milk,[19] shortening,[20] and baking[21] businesses. Indeed, Smucker's even traded up in the pet foods segment by divesting one of its slower-growing brands, Natural Balance, after buying the Nutrish brand in the Ainsworth acquisition.[22] While both brands were marketed as "healthy pet foods," Nutrish generated three times the revenues of Natural Balance,[23] making Nutrish a better opportunity for future growth. CEO Mark Smucker expressed this exact logic in his description of the rationale for the Natural Balance divestiture: "The divestiture reflects our strategy to direct investments and resources toward areas of the business that will generate the greatest growth and profitability."[24]

Treasury Wine Estates (TWE) provides another example of trading up, this time across customer segments. TWE had articulated a "strategic roadmap of transitioning our business from an order-taking agricultural company to a brand-led and capital-light, marketing organization," shifting its portfolio of wines away from commercial and discount brands and into luxury and "masstige" brands ("masstige" being a horrible neologism apparently meaning "premium but attainable").[25] Consistent with this strategy, TWE acquired Diageo's wine business in 2015, which consisted of iconic Napa Valley brands such as Beaulieu Vineyards, Sterling Vineyards, Acacia, Provenance, and Hewitt, as well as Blossom Hill, a U.K. brand.* After this acquisition, TWE sold 12 of its own commercial wine brands at book value to an undisclosed buyer,[26] as well as its Dartmoor, Matheson, and Souverain brands and the Asti Winery (a large-scale production facility in Sonoma Valley).[27] The businesses that TWE divested over the two years after the Diageo acquisition enabled it to rationalize its portfolio of wine brands from 80 to 45, largely focused in the more premium segments of the market.[28]

---

* TWE subsequently unbundled the Blossom Hill winery (i.e., the vineyards and production facilities) that it had bought in the Diageo acquisition, though it kept the actual brand itself.

These two examples reveal some of the similarities and differences between trading up and the divestiture strategies discussed in Chapters 1 and 2. First, trading up is like the strategy of divesting problematic businesses in the sense that both eliminate less-desirable units from a company's portfolio. However, there is an important difference: while the objective of divesting problematic businesses is simply to exit from the less-desirable units, the purpose of trading up is to shift the company's portfolio into better strategic domains, of which the pruning of less-attractive operations is a critical step. Second, trading up is similar to the strategy of divesting to improve corporate focus in that both remove non-core businesses from a company's portfolio. However, the main difference here is that in the case of divesting to improve corporate focus, the divested business is non-core to the company's *existing* portfolio of businesses, whereas in the case of trading up, the divested business is non-core to the *new* portfolio of businesses the company has built via its acquisitions.

Realizing Scale Efficiencies

The strategy of divesting to realize scale efficiencies begins when a company acquires and integrates a target into its own organization, while recognizing that some of the resources of the combined entity are redundant. This prompts the company to divest the redundant resources originating from both companies and potentially to implement other cost-cutting or consolidation measures, thereby achieving economies of scale in production or distribution. This strategy of divesting to realize scale efficiencies (depicted in Exhibit 3.4) occurs most often in industries where (1) cost pressures are significant, (2) companies overlap in the geographic regions or customers they serve, and (3) asset intensity is high (e.g., railroads, airlines, banks, oil).

For instance, Umpqua Bank bought Sterling Financial Corporation in 2013, consolidating capacity in the Pacific Northwest where both regional banks operated. An Umpqua spokeswoman explained that "one of the benefits of the merger is the complementary nature of our footprints."[29] Over the year following the Sterling acquisition, Umpqua proceeded to rationalize its branch footprint, closing 27 branches[30] and selling 6 more to local competitor Banner Bank.[31] Most of the affected branches were within a mile of another Umpqua branch,[32] enabling Umpqua to realize scale efficiencies from headcount reductions and the consolidation of physical facilities.

EXHIBIT 3.4

Depiction of Realizing Scale Efficiencies

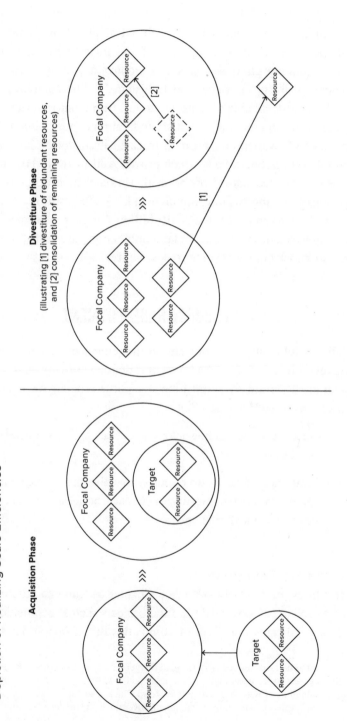

Similarly, the Union Pacific Railroad acquired the Southern Pacific Railroad in 1995, combining two of the major western railroads that ran on "roughly parallel routes and [controlled] most of the huge base of chemical traffic in Texas and Louisiana."[33] The combined operations would therefore be able to consolidate rail traffic onto shorter routes, saving both time and money.* To satisfy federal regulators, Union Pacific sold 335 miles of overlapping railroad track to its historic competitor, Burlington Northern Santa Fe,[34] which proved well worth it. Highlighting the efficiency-oriented nature of the deal, Union Pacific officials noted that "operational savings would amount to at least $500 million a year" relative to operating revenues of about $10 billion the year prior, and an anonymous spokesman explained, "The combinations are just devastating. . . . You can knock hours off some routes. Strategically, it's a superb merger."[35]

RESOURCE REDEPLOYMENT

While portfolio rationalization entails the sequence of acquisition followed by divestiture, resource redeployment is defined as the reverse sequence of divestiture followed by acquisition. Resource redeployment involves two steps, as depicted in Exhibit 3.5:

- Companies divest to free up resources that are tied up in certain of their businesses.

- Companies reallocate the resources that divestitures free up into acquisitions of (and investments into) new businesses, products, technologies, and geographies.

Freeing Up Resources

Divestitures, particularly sales (see Chapter 5), can generate cash, which can be used to pay down debt or fund projects such as acquisitions. Survey evidence indicates that 70% of companies divest operations to generate

---

* This used to happen frequently in railroad mergers. Another example is the 1972 merger of the Illinois Central Railroad and the competing Gulf, Mobile & Ohio Railroad. The merged company found itself with duplicative track from Chicago to New Orleans, which it divested through sales, spinoffs, and even abandonments over the next two decades.

EXHIBIT 3.5

Depiction of Resource Redeployment

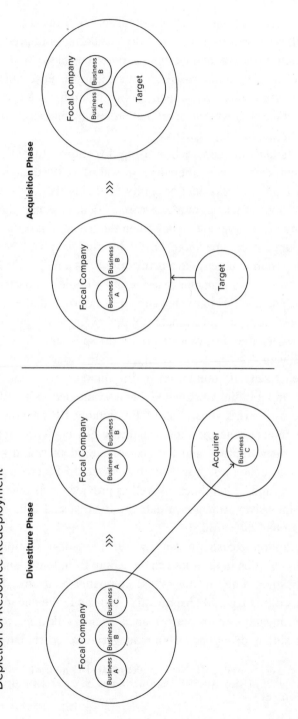

cash proceeds to finance future initiatives.[36] For instance, Cargill divested $2.4 billion worth of assets in 2016, including pork-processing plants, a steelmaking venture, and a crop insurance business,[37] followed by its metals[38] and energy[39] units in 2017. In turn, Cargill subsequently acquired $3 billion worth of businesses, such as Norwegian fish feed producer EWOS[40] and several South American animal protein businesses,[41] and expanded its U.S. meat-processing capacity.[42]

On its face, the approach of using divestitures to generate cash might seem inefficient, since companies in well-developed capital markets can usually readily access debt or equity financing. However, divestitures are often a more efficient source of capital than external financing; when a company is undervalued and/or when the business it is divesting is underperforming, it can be more costly for that company to raise external financing than to undertake a divestiture.[43] As a result, the companies that use divestitures to generate cash are often liquidity constrained, or otherwise face difficulties in raising capital in external markets.

BP provides an unfortunate but apt example of this kind of circumstance. After the Deepwater Horizon oil spill[*] and the ensuing criticism from all walks of American society, from President Obama on down to the average citizen, BP found itself in dire financial straits: its stock price fell by half, and it initially estimated that it would need $20 billion to fund the demand by the U.S. government.[44] Predictably, BP encountered major constraints in accessing the capital markets; any equity it might raise would be extremely dilutive, and the cost of new debt would be prohibitively high because the ratings agencies had lowered BP's credit ratings after the spill.[45] To fund its liabilities, as well as provide for its ongoing (and highly capital-intensive) strategic initiatives, BP divested billions of dollars of assets around the world.

In addition to cash, divestitures free up managerial time and attention. Much as children in families run the gamut from low to high maintenance, some business units in diversified companies consume disproportionate amounts of managerial "bandwidth." This could be due to any number of reasons, including poor performance, industry decline, intense competition, or simply divergence from managerial expertise. Divestitures enable

---

[*] The largest offshore oil spill in history, which released 4.9 million barrels of crude petroleum into the Gulf of Mexico, much of which washed up on the ecologically sensitive Louisiana coastal wetlands.

executives to reallocate their newly liberated time and attention to their companies' other businesses. Indeed, nearly one-third of companies point to the ability to allocate management attention to higher-growth opportunities as a strategic benefit of divestitures.[46]

PepsiCo's experience with its restaurant business provides a useful illustration of how divestitures can free up managerial attention. In the 1990s, PepsiCo owned a portfolio of quick service and casual dining concepts, including Taco Bell, KFC, and Pizza Hut, in addition to its core soda and snacks businesses. The task of growing and expanding these restaurants reportedly caused PepsiCo to take its eye off the ball in connection with its core businesses, thereby creating an opening for archrival Coca-Cola Company to increase its share of certain overseas markets.[47] PepsiCo thereupon spun off Taco Bell, KFC, and Pizza Hut as Tricon Global Restaurants, and sold all its stakes in its remaining restaurant concepts. Free of the distraction of the restaurant business, PepsiCo's top executives were able to restore their focus to the company's core soda and snacks businesses.

Finally, divestitures can free up human and physical capital. When a company divests one of its businesses, employees may become available to work in different parts of the organization, just as physical assets like factories, plants, and machinery may become available to start producing other products. The main factor that shapes the applicability of human and physical capital to other opportunities is the relatedness between the business that is being divested and the company's remaining operations. When businesses are related to one another, the employees and physical plant that divestitures free up may have more crossover opportunities in that company due to their more similar capabilities, knowledge bases, and production processes.

Reallocating Resources

Having used divestitures to free up resources, companies can reallocate these resources to make acquisitions. Consistent with the statistics presented in the introduction to this chapter, over half of companies that undertake spinoffs explicitly state in their filings with the Securities and Exchange Commission that they are doing so "in order to facilitate future M&A activity," and nearly three-quarters of companies pursue acquisitions within one year after a spinoff.[48]

The process of reallocating the resources that are freed up by divestitures into subsequent acquisitions is much like the process of trading up, in the sense that both involve companies shifting their core businesses into new strategic domains. However, whereas trading up implies that companies will acquire new businesses *before* divesting existing units, resource reallocation instead suggests that companies will acquire new businesses *after* divesting existing units. The Treasury Wine Estates example illustrates this distinction, which can also be seen by comparing Exhibits 3.3 and 3.5. As described previously, TWE's acquisition of Diageo's wine business occurred *before* TWE's divestitures of numerous commercial and discount wine brands, reflecting a strategy of trading up into the premium segment of the market. By comparison, Diageo's acquisition of numerous specialty brands of liquor occurred *after* the sale of its wine business to TWE (and others). In contrast to TWE's strategy of trading up, Diageo's strategy was instead one of resource redeployment, since it reallocated the resources freed up by its divestitures (including the $550 million in proceeds it received from the sale of its wine business to TWE) into its remaining core business of premium hard alcohol brands.[49]

The resources that divestitures free up are usually reallocated into acquisitions of businesses that are related to the company's remaining operations.* Research has documented that between 40% and 70% of companies that spin off unrelated businesses subsequently acquire new businesses that are related to their remaining operations.[50] Conagra's multi-year series of divestitures followed by acquisitions reflects this pattern of activity. The strategy began with multiple divestitures of businesses that were unrelated to its core consumer and commercial foods businesses. Conagra spun off its foodservice portfolio of frozen potato products as Lamb Weston Holdings,[51] and it sold its private label brands,[52] its ingredients distributor,[53] and its flavors and seasonings business.[54] In turn, the acquisitions that Conagra pursued after these divestitures deepened

---

* One situation in which resource redeployment typically fails is when companies reallocate the resources that divestitures free up into areas where they lack relevant capabilities and expertise, rather than using those resources to enter domains in which they are equipped to compete effectively. These mistakes can result from various factors, such as an incorrect assessment of the fit between the resources that divestitures free up and the new areas companies choose to enter, empire-building tendencies, and even opportunism or the desire to foreclose competitors.

its presence in its remaining businesses. For example, the acquisition of Angie's Artisan Treats strengthened Conagra's popcorn business; the acquisition of Thanasi Foods bolstered Conagra's meat snacks business; and most significantly, the acquisition of Pinnacle Foods deepened Conagra's presence in frozen foods by adding Birds Eye, Gardein, and other frozen brands to its existing portfolio in this space.[55] Notably, CEO Sean Connolly kicked off this strategic transformation shortly after his appointment as CEO (in line with the point from Chapter 1 that about 80% of divestitures are preceded by CEO turnover), in conjunction with a corporate name change (ConAgra Foods was renamed Conagra Brands after the Lamb Weston spinoff) and a change of corporate headquarters from Omaha to Chicago (see Chapter 11).[56]

Nestlé provides another good example of resource reallocation into acquisitions of related businesses. After contributing its ice cream business into a joint venture (Froneri) with PAI Partners in 2016 (see Chapter 8) and selling its iconic American candy business (including the Butterfinger, Baby Ruth, and Crunch brands) to Ferrero Rocher in 2018, Nestlé acquired a number of health-related businesses: Aimmune Therapeutics, Atrium Innovations, Persona, Vital Proteins, Freshly, and Zenpep.[57] Similarly, almost immediately after it sold its North American water business to private equity firms One Rock Capital Partners and Metropoulos & Co.,[58] Nestlé acquired Essentia[59] and Nuun,[60] expanding its portfolio of premium and functional water brands, which already included San Pellegrino, Acqua Panna, and Perrier. In all, between 2017 and 2021, Nestlé announced or closed "more than 75 transactions, representing about 18% of its portfolio. . . . [I]n just the past three years, Nestlé has made more than $30 billion in deals, and by all accounts the buying and selling frenzy is far from over."[61] In remarks about the company's strategy, Nestlé CFO François Xavier Roger emphasized the importance of reallocating the resources that are freed up by divestitures to acquisitions of related businesses: "It's not just about going shopping because we have a strong balance sheet, a credit card or whatever. We want to be disciplined about what we do as well. So, we want to make sure that when we go for acquisition, they meet our main three criteria and strategic fit with what we want to do, which is essentially around nutrition, health and wellness, or high growth categories."[62]

CHAPTER 4

Addressing Regulatory Requirements

INTRODUCTION

The preceding chapters analyzed three different roles that divestitures play in strategy: they remove problematic businesses resulting from industry unattractiveness or acquisition failure, they improve corporate focus when companies diversify too widely from their core operations, and they facilitate the reconfiguration of the corporate portfolio when used sequentially with acquisitions. Each of these motivations for divestitures underscores the strategic importance of these transactions, which is reflected in the positive shareholder returns that often accompany them.

In contrast, this chapter examines situations in which companies are mandated to divest certain assets or businesses to address regulatory requirements pertaining to competition, national security, and other political considerations.* Although the specific regulatory requirements that impel these divestitures vary, the common feature that unites them is that government fiat, rather than managerial choice, is the impetus to divest. As a result, compared to the strategically motivated divestitures discussed in Chapters 1–3, shareholder returns to the regulatorily mandated divestitures discussed in this chapter are less positive, which makes intuitive sense because "these actions are not freely undertaken by management and therefore are not necessarily in the shareholders' best interests."[1]

---

* While this chapter focuses on divestitures that are mandated by U.S. regulations, regulatorily mandated divestitures in other countries may be motivated by different sets of principles.

COMPETITION

AB InBev's $100 billion-plus acquisition of SABMiller in 2016 (the largest beer merger in history) vastly expanded its presence in faster-growing emerging markets, especially Africa, where beer volumes were expected to grow more than 44% through 2025, three times faster than the rest of the world.[2] As a result, the merger raised significant antitrust concerns about the level of competition in the beer market. In the United States, the combined company would command a 70% market share and control the country's only two beer distribution networks.[3] In China, the merged company would account for nearly 40% of the market, particularly through its stake in the joint venture that sold one of the country's leading beer brands, Snow.[4] In Europe, regulators raised concerns that the merger would promote tacit coordination at higher price levels among rival brewers.[5] For the merger to proceed, AB InBev would therefore have to divest some businesses to alleviate these and potentially other antitrust concerns.

And divest it did, to the tune of $27 billion—more than a quarter of what AB InBev paid to acquire SABMiller in the first place.[6] In the United States, AB InBev sold SABMiller's share of the MillerCoors joint venture to its partner, Molson Coors, giving Molson Coors the global rights to the Miller brand. AB InBev also agreed not to limit the ability or incentive of independent distributors to sell and promote its rivals' products, or to acquire another brewer (especially craft brewers, a fast-growing segment of the U.S. market) without prior Department of Justice approval.[7] In China, AB InBev agreed to sell SABMiller's 49% stake in the CR Snow joint venture to its partner, China Resources Enterprise, and in Europe, AB InBev agreed to sell certain of SABMiller's brands to Japan's Asahi Group.[8] While significant, these divestitures played a major role in enabling AB InBev to advance its emerging market growth strategy, since regulators wouldn't have permitted it to acquire SABMiller without them.

Background

The Department of Justice (DOJ) and the Federal Trade Commission (FTC) are the primary regulatory agencies responsible for enforcing competition in the United States, and the laws on which they rely are commonly known as the "antitrust" laws. U.S. antitrust laws are designed to preserve "free and unfettered competition as the rule of trade."[9] The first law passed in support of this objective was the Sherman Antitrust Act of 1890, which barred unreasonable "contracts, combinations, or conspiracy in restraint of trade" as well as "monopolization, attempted monopolization, or conspiracy or combination to monopolize."[10] In the early days of the Sherman Act, especially during Theodore Roosevelt's administration, antitrust suits were brought against companies and trusts that were deemed to be monopolizing competition. These included canonical cases such as Northern Securities Trust, Standard Oil of New Jersey, American Sugar Refining, Swift Meatpacking, and American Tobacco, in which companies were respectively accused of monopolizing the railroad, oil, sugar, meatpacking, and tobacco industries.[11] The primary remedy for indictments against these entities was to break them apart—that is, "to bust" the trusts. For example, Standard Oil was dissolved into 34 different companies, and American Tobacco broke apart into four separate companies (American Tobacco, R.J. Reynolds, Liggett & Myers, and Lorillard).* Many decades after this era, the DOJ brought a similar suit against AT&T, charging that it was monopolizing telephone communications across the United States. Rather than divest Western Electric, its supplier of telephone equipment (the remedy that the government was demanding), AT&T proposed and reached a consent decree in which it divested the Regional Bell Operating Companies (the RBOCs, or "Baby Bells"), which provided local telephone service to customers across the United States.[12] Interestingly, all but one of the seven Baby Bells eventually re-amalgamated themselves into two of the major telephone companies, Verizon and (new) AT&T, which offer mobile and landline telephony in addition to numerous other services.

The antitrust laws were strengthened by the passage of the Federal Trade Commission (FTC) Act and the Clayton Act in 1914, as well as the establishment of the Antitrust Division within the DOJ in 1919. The FTC Act outlaws "unfair methods of competition" and "unfair or deceptive acts or practices."[13] The Supreme Court has held that any violation of the Sherman Act is also a violation of the FTC Act, meaning that this law has enabled the FTC to bring suits against companies for the same kinds of activities that might violate the Sherman Act (which the FTC does not technically enforce). The Clayton Act expanded the scope of antitrust law

---

* Many of the great companies that traded publicly before the explosion in mergers were these very divestitures (viz., Standard Oil of New Jersey, R.J. Reynolds, American Sugar Refining, Hercules Powder, ADT, etc.).

to address practices that the Sherman Act did not specifically prohibit, especially mergers where the effect "may be substantially to lessen competition, or to tend to create a monopoly."[14] These are the primary laws by which the government can mandate divestitures.*

Assessing the Competitive Implications of Mergers

The assessment of whether a particular merger will lessen competition or create a monopoly hinges, *inter alia*, on the definition of the relevant market. This definition is based on the products or services sold by the merging parties, and on the geographic regions in which they sell them.

When two companies that operate in the same product or geographic market merge (a horizontal merger), the fact that the combined company might hold a greater share of the relevant market could increase market concentration. As a result, the combined company might have a greater ability to coordinate with the remaining companies in that market on prices, output, or capacity, or unilaterally to raise prices, restrict output, or reduce service quality on its own.

In addition to the anticompetitive potential of horizontal mergers, vertical mergers can also raise the possibility of competitive harm. Vertical mergers consist of "strictly vertical mergers (those that combine firms or assets at different stages of the same supply chain), 'diagonal' mergers (those that combine firms or assets at different stages of competing supply chains), and vertical issues that can arise in mergers of complements."[15] In all these cases, the DOJ and FTC seek to regulate mergers that foreclose or raise the costs of other companies accessing key inputs, outputs, or distribution channels, thereby preventing them from competing effectively in relevant markets.[16]

Using Divestitures to Address Competitive Concerns

The consequence of these issues is that the DOJ and the FTC scrutinize mergers that have the potential to limit competition or create monopolies in relevant markets. When these regulatory bodies find that the potential for anticompetitive behavior is significant—as they did in the introductory

---

* Subsequent antitrust laws dealt with ancillary matters. For example, in 1976, the Hart-Scott-Rodino (HSR) Antitrust Improvements Act further updated the Clayton Act, requiring companies that planned to undertake certain large deals to notify and receive advance approval from the government.

anecdote about AB InBev's acquisition of SABMiller—they often require the merging companies to divest certain businesses or assets as a pre-condition to their combination.* Alternately, the merging companies may proactively agree to divest certain businesses before proceeding with their combination. Either way, these divestitures have the effect of reducing the share of the relevant market that is occupied by the combined entity and therefore the concentration in that market, which, in theory, should protect consumers from anticompetitive practices.

The most familiar examples of divestitures following horizontal merg-ers occur in markets where scale-based advantages are important: one company buys another to consolidate its position in a particular product or geographic market, achieving cost savings as a result. However, this consolidation is exactly what creates the potential for market power and anticompetitive behavior, since the merger results in fewer competitors and hence, less consumer choice in those markets. For instance, in the air-line industry, companies often divest landing slots, gates, and other airport facilities in relevant product markets (defined as flights that consumers can take to or from a particular airport) to achieve antitrust approval for their deals. When American Airlines and USAirways merged in 2013, the DOJ and seven state attorneys general brought a complaint alleging that the merger of American Airlines and USAirways would "entrench" the com-bined airline at Reagan National in Washington, D.C., "where it would control 69% of take-off and landing slots, thus effectively foreclosing entry or expansion by competing airlines," and that the deal would more gener-ally lessen system-wide competition and consumer choice in the industry.[17] To gain antitrust approval for their merger, American Airlines and USAir-ways divested various airport facilities in Boston, Chicago, Dallas, Los Angeles, Miami, New York, and Washington, D.C.

---

* In January 2022 remarks to the New York State Bar Association's Antitrust Section, Jon-athan Kanter, the new head of the DOJ's Antitrust Division, opined that regulators should simply block mergers that carry the potential for competitive harm rather than compromise by allowing remedial divestitures. Whether or not his opinion becomes policy, Mr. Kanter's pro-nouncement will have major implications both for the types of mergers that companies pursue, and for the divestitures that might have been mandated to address competitive considerations.

Source: Department of Justice. 2022. "Assistant Attorney General Jonathan Kanter of the Anti-trust Division Delivers Remarks to the New York State Bar Association Antitrust Section." January 24, 2022. https://www.justice.gov/opa/speech/assistant-attorney-general-jonathan -kanter-antitrust-division-delivers-remarks-new-york.

Similarly, to receive antitrust approval for its purchase of 21st Century Fox, Disney divested 22 of Fox's regional sports networks (RSNs), where the DOJ alleged that "without the required divestitures, the proposed acquisition would likely result in higher prices for cable sports programming licensed to multichannel video programming distributors ('MVPDs') in each of the local markets that the RSNs serve."[18] To receive antitrust approval for its purchase of VCA Inc. (which operated a nationwide chain of specialty veterinary clinics), Mars (yes, the candy company, which owns a large pet care business) divested 12 of its own specialty clinics in overlapping geographic markets. The FTC, which brought the complaint, alleged that without these divestitures, Mars's acquisition of VCA would reduce competition for specialty and emergency veterinary services: "Without a remedy, the acquisition would likely lead to higher prices for pet owners and lower quality in the specialty and emergency veterinary services they receive. These effects are unlikely to be mitigated through timely new entry, as opening a specialty or emergency services veterinary clinic presents some unique challenges, including the need to recruit specialist veterinarians with considerably greater training than general practice veterinarians."[19]

In contrast to these examples of divestitures following *horizontal* mergers, the AT&T–Time Warner merger provides a useful example of why regulators might require divestitures before allowing *vertical* mergers to proceed. The DOJ brought an antitrust challenge against the AT&T–Time Warner merger, arguing that "a post-merger AT&T would be both a leading pay-television service provider, including through its DirecTV subsidiary, and an owner of sought-after programming, via Time Warner's portfolio, which included the Turner networks and HBO. AT&T would be able to force rival pay-television systems to pay more for Turner networks such as TNT and CNN after the merger."[20] As a potential remedy to its concerns, the DOJ proposed divestitures of certain assets, such as DirecTV or the Turner channels. "But AT&T fought back in its closing brief, noting the DOJ presented 'no basis to impose any remedies at all, much less divestitures that would destroy the value of the transaction.'"[21] Ultimately, the DOJ's challenge against the AT&T–Time Warner merger failed and the deal proceeded as planned, although the merger's vertical combination of media and content businesses was largely unwound by AT&T's divestitures of DirecTV and Time Warner just a few years later. *Even an antitrust win was apparently no match for a flawed acquisition strategy.*

The major challenge with divestitures that regulators mandate for competitive reasons is that they are often more complex and difficult to execute than divestitures that executives choose to undertake of their own accord. Divestitures that are imposed by regulators as preconditions to resolve competitive challenges are, by definition, intertwined with the mergers that created those challenges in the first place. This means that a company must manage the divestiture process simultaneously with—and often under the time constraints imposed by—the acquisition process. This can limit the company's ability to respond to changing circumstances or the demands of the acquisition, and also requires significant time, attention, and resources. Additionally, the fact that regulatorily mandated divestitures are not optional could compromise the company's negotiating position vis-à-vis potential buyers of the businesses or assets it is being forced to divest. This could compel the company to accept a discounted valuation rather than fair market value for the divested assets, or, if the price for those assets is too low, to abandon an otherwise attractive acquisition. The remedy to these problems is proactive planning, in which companies assess "trade-offs among minimizing the impact on deal value, satisfying regulatory concerns, attracting interested bidders, limiting separation complexity . . . [and] also identifying walkaway conditions—namely, those in which the original deal would no longer make economic sense. . . . Such preparation delivers a huge pay-off by minimizing the drain on leadership, resources, and the costs of getting into protracted regulatory issues."[22] Even proactive planning may not be a silver bullet, though, in that regulators still have the ultimate discretion to mandate divestitures to permit a particular merger to proceed.

NATIONAL SECURITY

Background

The Committee on Foreign Investment in the United States (CFIUS) is an interagency committee of the U.S. government, chaired by the secretary of the treasury, that is charged with assessing the national security implications of foreign acquisitions of or investments in U.S. companies. CFIUS focuses on foreign acquisitions or investments that have the potential to threaten critical U.S. infrastructure, technology, and intellectual property. Formally, the definition of a "covered" transaction that is subject to CFIUS review is " 'any merger, acquisition, or takeover that is proposed or pending after August 23, 1988, by or with any foreign person which could result in foreign control of any person engaged in interstate commerce in the United States.' By having such a broad definition of what transactions may be subject to CFIUS review, the law gives great discretion to the administration in how to exercise its power to block or impede certain foreign transactions in the United States."[23]

CFIUS was established in 1975 to study foreign investment in the United States, seeking "to support unequivocally [international] investment, consistent with the protection of the national security."[24] Precipitated by the proposed acquisition of Fairchild Semiconductor by Fujitsu (which raised jingoistic concerns over the national security implications of a Japanese company acquiring American chip technology),[25] the Exon-Florio Amendment of 1988 expanded the scope of CFIUS to give it the ability to reject (rather than simply evaluate) acquisitions and investments that had the potential to threaten U.S. national security interests.

More than a decade later, the unprecedented 9/11 terror attacks reawakened the debate over balancing national security interests with the economic benefits of foreign investment in the United States. These issues were brought into sharp relief in 2006 by a proposed transaction in which Dubai Ports World would manage the terminal operations of ports in several major U.S. cities.[26] Although the acquisition was supported by President George W. Bush and many others, overwhelming opposition in Congress and by the public ultimately caused the deal to be scuttled.[27] Later, in 2007, the Foreign Investment and National Security Act (FINSA) was passed, strengthening the national security review process.[28]

Concerns over the rise in foreign direct investment from China, as well as increasing numbers of cross-border mergers between China and the United States,[29] prompted the further strengthening and modernization of CFIUS in 2018. The Foreign Investment Risk Review Modernization Act (FIRRMA) "expanded the scope of transactions subject to [CFIUS] review by granting [it] the authority to examine the national security implications of a foreign company's *non-controlling* investments in U.S. businesses that deal with critical infrastructure, critical technology, or the personal data of U.S. citizens . . . [as well as] real estate transactions—including leases, sales, and concessions—involving air or maritime ports or in close proximity to sensitive U.S. government facilities."[30] The expanded definitions of which transactions would be covered by CFIUS, as well as the breadth of reasons for which CFIUS reviews might need to be conducted, have given CFIUS a more prominent role in corporate strategy decision-making.

Assessing the National Security Implications of Mergers

The process of a voluntary CFIUS review begins with the filing of a notice of the transaction. CFIUS has 30 days to review the transaction and ask for additional information, upon which it has one of two options. CFIUS can approve the transaction, "effectively giving [it] the green light . . . and providing a safe harbor for the parties against future actions that might unwind [it]."[31] Alternately, CFIUS can decide that a formal investigation is required, causing the review to proceed into an additional 45-day investigation period. "During this time, CFIUS meets with all member agencies as well as the parties to the transaction to discuss the transaction itself, its implications on national security, and options for modifying the transaction to mitigate national security concerns. CFIUS will then decide whether to recommend to the president that the transaction be blocked."[32] Companies can choose to withdraw their filings at any time throughout the CFIUS review process, or to propose modifications to their transactions that would then be subject to further review. The U.S. president has the final authority to block transactions that are not modified or voluntarily terminated.

Using Divestitures to Address National Security Concerns

Many CFIUS-mandated divestitures were found to have the potential to threaten U.S. national security interests in infrastructure, technology, and intellectual property. For example, the George H. W. Bush administration ordered the China National Aero-Technology Import and Export Corporation (CATIC) to divest MAMCO Manufacturing, a Seattle-based manufacturer of metal parts for aircraft, due to the importance of MAMCO's production and technological capabilities from a national security perspective.[33] The Obama administration prevented Ralls Corporation, a Chinese company, from building four small wind farm projects near the Boardman Naval Weapons Systems Training Facility in Oregon due to concerns about the sites being used "to gather information on U.S. advanced weapons systems."[34] The Trump administration blocked Singapore-based Broadcom from acquiring Qualcomm due to national security concerns over intellectual property resulting from 5G wireless technology research and development.[35]

One compromise that was employed to avoid a CFIUS-mandated divestiture was the use of an independent voting trust to hold nuclear technology that had the potential to threaten national security. This occurred in 1981, when Kuwait Petroleum Corporation (an enterprise owned by the Kingdom of Kuwait) bought Santa Fe International Corporation. U.S. regulators were concerned—rightly, as it later turned out—that the nuclear technology owned by Santa Fe's subsidiary, C.F. Braun International, could potentially fall into the wrong hands. Accordingly, rather than divest that business, the parties agreed to employ a voting trust to hold C.F. Braun, where its sensitive assets would be shielded from potentially hostile foreign interference. Indeed, the trust protected those assets until Kuwait Petroleum divested C.F. Braun in a sale to Halliburton in 1989, *a year before nuclear wannabe Saddam Hussein invaded Kuwait*.[36*]

Yet CFIUS has occasionally been fallible. In a 1995 transaction that was approved by CFIUS, General Motors divested its Magnequench subsidiary in a sale to an investor group led by the son of a prominent American attorney, but controlled by Chinese investors with ties to Beijing. The transaction resulted in the physical transfer to China of America's only rare earths fabrication facility,[37] even though rare earths are critical for its defense. Later, China demonstrated that it was prepared to use rare earths as a geopolitical weapon when it briefly embargoed their export to Japan during a territorial dispute in 2010.[38]

---

* While C.F. Braun involved national security, independent voting trusts have been used in other situations to isolate decision-makers and other affected parties from their assets and investments, including high-level federal officials who might be conflicted because of their businesses or portfolios, and broadcast licensees with licenses that are subject to future divestiture. Interestingly, however, the Surface Transportation Board (STB) unanimously rejected the use of such a trust in the takeover contest for Kansas City Southern Railroad because the trust "[did] not meet the standards under the current merger regulations." Without meaning to second-guess the STB, the use of a trust in this situation might have facilitated an orderly divestiture of the railroad if its acquisition had later been denied.

Source: Surface Transportation Board Decision. 2021. "Decision: Canadian National Railway Company, Grand Trunk Corporation, and CN's Rail Operating Subsidiaries Control Kansas City Southern, the Kansas City Southern Railway Company, Gateway Eastern Railway Company, and the Texas Mexican Railway." August 31, 2021. https://dcms-external.s3.amazonaws.com/DCMS_External_PROD/1630430814437/50915.pdf.

Three examples highlight the increasing importance under FIRRMA of the personal data of U.S. citizens as a source of national security concerns that can lead to CFIUS-mandated divestitures. First, in March 2019, CFIUS ordered Beijing Kunlun Tech Co. Ltd., a Chinese technology firm, to sell Grindr, a popular LGBTQ dating application that it had acquired between 2016 and 2018. Second, also in 2019, CFIUS ordered iCarbonX, a Chinese company that had developed artificial intelligence technology for improving healthcare, to divest its majority stake in PatientsLikeMe, an online platform for patients facing similar health conditions. Commentators noted that these two divestitures "underscore that CFIUS is more focused than ever on how data can pose a security threat."[39]

A third situation in which concerns about data security prompted consideration of a CFIUS-mandated divestiture occurred when the Trump administration sought to order ByteDance, the Chinese company that acquired the video-sharing app TikTok, to divest its U.S.-based assets in 2020. "U.S. officials have expressed concern that China's authoritarian government would have access to the data TikTok collects from users, including Americans. . . . 'This data collection threatens to allow the Chinese Communist Party access to Americans' personal and proprietary information—potentially allowing China to track the locations of federal employees and contractors, build dossiers of personal information for blackmail, and conduct corporate espionage,' the order says."[40] This order was stymied by various legal challenges until the Biden administration reversed course in February 2021, asking the courts to delay appeals of these decisions while it reviewed the implications of the deal and national security policy more broadly.[41] The episode culminated four months later in an executive order launching a broader review of whether apps controlled by foreign adversaries pose a security threat to the United States,[42] though as of September 2022, reports suggest that TikTok may be nearing a deal with a U.S. company to "store its U.S. users' information without its Chinese parent ByteDance having access to it, hoping to address U.S. regulatory concerns."[43]

For divestitures that are mandated by national security considerations, the combination of CFIUS's broad mandate with shifting political exigencies and preferences can subject companies to uncertainty over whether prior acquisitions or investments (especially those that are not submitted voluntarily for CFIUS review) will be allowed to remain in place. For example, commentators noted that "the primary objection to the [proposed acquisition of Fairchild Semiconductor by Fujitsu] centered on national security. But beyond the spoken objections, some Federal officials concede, was the mounting trade friction with Japan."[44] Similarly, the Dubai Ports World controversy that occurred just after 9/11 was framed "against the backdrop of concern about possible terrorist attacks."[45] Even the TikTok controversy came "at a low point in U.S.-China relations, with an economic face-off between the two countries escalating . . . [and] long-held suspicions hardening that the U.S. aims to sabotage [China's] efforts to grow its technology."[46] These problems are compounded by the "lack of transparency" in the CFIUS review process, as well as the fact that companies have "little recourse" if CFIUS blocks or unwinds their transactions.[47] Together, these issues can hinder companies from planning future initiatives, especially mergers.

As with divestitures that are mandated by competitive concerns, one obvious way for foreign companies to mitigate the uncertainty that is created by U.S. national security regulations is proactive planning for the CFIUS review process. For example, various law firms advise foreign companies to "understand CFIUS issues at the earliest stages of a transaction or even during strategic corporate development planning . . . well before any engagement with CFIUS occurs"[48] and "to think about CFIUS mitigation strategies at the outset of any deal, and to reach out to the Committee before filing the notice to begin a dialogue."[49] Even these solutions are imperfect, though, because CFIUS still has the ultimate authority to block transactions that are voluntarily submitted for review.

OTHER POLITICAL CONSIDERATIONS

The boot of the sovereign is a heavy boot, indeed. And when that boot descends on corporate America, a transaction—even a divestiture—may be the result. In response to the failure of Enron, for example, the George W. Bush administration relentlessly pursued Arthur Andersen, Enron's accounting firm, causing its clients to defect and the firm to fold.[50] Years later, in the depths of the global financial crisis, the Obama administration forced Citigroup to sell Phibro, its commodities trading unit, at book value (a "bargain-basement" price[51]), the reason being that Phibro's contractual obligations to pay bonuses exceeded the administration's compensation guidelines* for beneficiaries of federal bailout funds.[52] While the two incidents might appear to be different, they are actually quite similar: in both cases, it was politically expedient for an administration to punish a perceived malefactor despite foreseeably adverse consequences. Accordingly, competition in the accounting industry was reduced by the failure of Arthur Andersen,[53] and the stockholders of Citicorp (which was 34% owned by the federal government) lost the most profitable operation of their investment at a below-market price. Ironically, the descent of the sovereign's boot was absolutely gratuitous in these two instances; Arthur Andersen's conviction was *unanimously* overturned by the Supreme Court,[54] and Phibro's new owners presumably continued to compensate their investment professionals at generous contractual rates.

*   *   *

This chapter concludes Part I, which has investigated the four divestiture strategies that companies can pursue: removing problematic businesses, improving corporate focus, reconfiguring the corporate portfolio, and addressing regulatory requirements. Exhibit 4.1 summarizes their salient features.

---

* Note that "guidelines" lack the force of "regulations," and regulations lack the force of law.

EXHIBIT 4.1

Summary of Divestiture Strategies

Divestiture Strategy	Primary Motivation	Description	Characteristics of Divested Businesses
Removing Problematic Businesses	Underperformance	Company divests to exit an unattractive industry or to recoup the costs of a failed acquisition	• Businesses operating in industries that have high rivalry, low entry barriers, numerous substitutes, high buyer power, and/or high supplier power • Prior acquisitions that have underperformed or failed due to flaws in strategy and/or execution
Improving Corporate Focus	Lack of fit	Company divests non-synergistic businesses to narrow the focus of its remaining operations	• Non-core businesses that do not fit strategically with the company's remaining operations • Businesses that have diseconomies of scope with the company's remaining operations, resulting in internal complexity • Businesses that make it difficult for investors to understand the company's strategy, resulting in undervaluation in the equity market
Reconfiguring the Corporate Portfolio	Scope change	Company divests after acquiring to rationalize its portfolio, or company divests before acquiring to redeploy resources	• Businesses that the company had to buy as part of prior acquisitions • Businesses from the company's existing portfolio after acquisitions of new businesses • Redundant resources following acquisitions of related businesses • Businesses that contain resources that could be reallocated to acquisitions of new businesses
Addressing Regulatory Requirements	Government fiat	Company is required to divest to address competitive, national security, or other political considerations	• Businesses whose acquisition by the company is expected to result in competitive harm in relevant markets • Businesses whose acquisition or ownership by the company could compromise U.S. national security interests • Businesses that conflict with prevailing political sentiments

PART II

DIVESTITURE STRUCTURE

CHAPTER 5

Sales

INTRODUCTION

Divestiture structures can be placed on a continuum with a dominant structure at each end: sales on the left and spinoffs on the right (see Exhibit 5.1). In a sale, a divesting company transfers one of its businesses to a counterparty in return for cash or other consideration, while in a spinoff, a divesting company distributes shares in one of its businesses to its existing shareholders, resulting in the creation of a separate public company. Between the two ends of this continuum are four additional divestiture structures that combine elements of the structures at each end. Moving from left to right, from sales to spinoffs, the four intermediate structures are joint ventures (in actuality, deferred sales), tracking stocks (essentially, the sale of a business unit's future performance through newly issued shares in its parent), equity carveouts (partial equity sales that are usually paired with spinoffs), and Reverse Morris Trusts (combination spinoff-mergers).*

The divestiture structures depicted in Exhibit 5.1 offer numerous and often conflicting alternatives to the divesting company. They offer the divesting company the ability to realize cash and value by selling a business, or the ability to push that value down to shareholders in a spinoff. The divesting company can sell the operation for a gain or a loss, or it can spin off that business and incur neither. There are even divestiture structures in which the company can spread a sale over time, combine a spinoff with a merger, or avoid the disposition altogether and just sell the future

---

* Additionally, there are four divestiture structures that this book will not discuss in detail. Three of them are minor (like-kind exchanges, rights offerings, and exchangeable securities) and are summarized in Appendix A. One of them (exchange offers that are split-offs for tax purposes) is mentioned in Chapter 6.

EXHIBIT 5.1

Continuum of Divestiture Structures

		Divestiture Structures			
Sales	Joint Ventures	Tracking Stocks	Equity Carveouts	Reverse Morris Trusts	Spinoffs
Generally Taxable	Taxable Over Time	Tax Neutral	Generally Tax Neutral	Generally Tax-Free	Generally Tax-Free

Taxation of Disposition

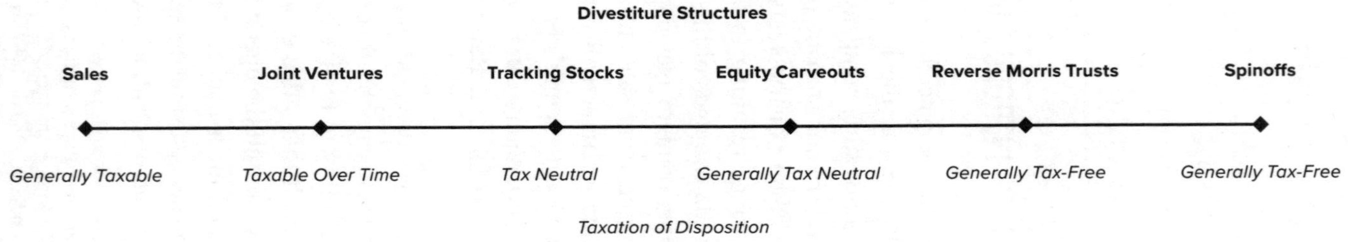

earnings of the subsidiary. Additionally, the characteristics of the divested business (e.g., its tax basis, historical performance, growth prospects, and ability to function as a freestanding entity) can exert a significant influence on the choice of divestiture structure, as can those of potential acquirers (e.g., their willingness to pay and their complementarity with the divested business). It should be obvious that the range of possible divestiture structures provides executives with a reasonably robust "toolbox" from which to select the optimal structure to address these factors.

This chapter focuses on sales, the simple hammer in this toolbox. As illustrated in Exhibit 5.2, sales are a straightforward divestiture structure in which a company transfers one of its businesses to a counterparty in return for cash and possibly other forms of consideration such as debt instruments, equity, assumed liabilities, or some combination thereof. A company identifies the business it wishes to divest and negotiates a mutually acceptable price for it. Upon closing the sale, the divesting company normally severs ties with the former business, freeing its management and board of directors from running that unit. Conversely, the acquirer takes full ownership of the divested business, which the acquirer's management then runs as part of its own organization.

Sales are by far the most common divestiture structure. Exhibit 5.3 depicts the disclosed yearly volume and value of sales undertaken by U.S.-based companies from 1990 to 2021. While the total volume of sales declined after the global financial crisis, the aggregate value of these transactions increased (especially in 2021, due to the post-COVID-19 merger wave), suggesting that companies began undertaking larger deals. This was attributable to several dynamics, chief among them the fact that consolidation and focus came back into favor,[1] fueled by historically low interest rates, massive pools of investment dollars, and the activism of professional investors seeking to maximize the value of their investments. These factors created many opportunities for companies to sell businesses for optimal prices to more focused, better-matched acquirers.[2]

EXHIBIT 5.2

Depiction of Sale

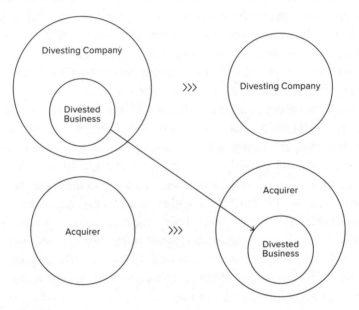

EXHIBIT 5.3

Disclosed Volume and Value of Sales, 1990–2021[3]

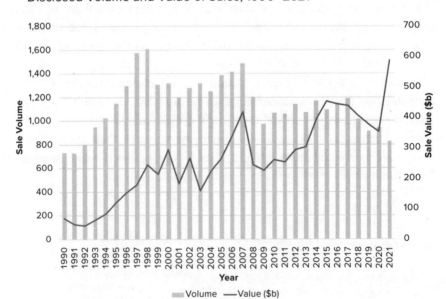

ADVANTAGES

In 2020, Huntsman Corporation sold its chemical intermediates and surfactants businesses (which make ingredients for cleaning supplies and lubricants) to Thailand-based Indorama Ventures. These businesses were among the slowest growing in Huntsman's portfolio, as well as a poor strategic fit with the company's remaining (and faster-growing) downstream and specialty chemicals operations.[4] But these businesses were quite desirable to Indorama, expanding its U.S. presence into higher-margin operating segments and giving it access to valuable facilities on the Gulf Coast and in India and Australia.[5] The sale brought in approximately $2 billion of cash (as well as the transfer of about $76 million of net underfunded pension and other post-employment benefit liabilities), which CEO Peter Huntsman explained would be used "for select strategic and accretive acquisitions, as well as for expansions in our core downstream global footprint, and for continued opportunistic repurchases of our shares."[6]

Sales can be used to achieve all the strategic objectives discussed in Part I: removing problematic businesses, improving corporate focus, reconfiguring the corporate portfolio, and addressing regulatory requirements. As the Huntsman example illustrates, though, sales also offer divesting companies some uniquely valuable financial and tax advantages, three of which make sales an attractive divestiture structure:

1. Sales enable companies to realize value from the businesses they are divesting.

2. Sales generate cash, which can help divesting companies meet their financial needs.

3. In certain cases, sales create tax losses, which can be used to generate refunds of previously paid taxes and/or to reduce current or future tax burdens.

Value Realization

Sales enable companies to realize value from the businesses they are divesting by shifting them into the hands of acquirers where they are likely to be a better fit. Specifically, companies can sell businesses to *strategic acquirers* seeking to generate synergies by combining those businesses with their own operations, or they can sell businesses to *financial acquirers* seeking to turn around and then exit those businesses.

Strategic Acquirers. Companies regularly sell businesses that are unrelated to their remaining operations.[7] As discussed in Chapters 2 and 3, there is often nothing outwardly wrong with businesses that are divested under these circumstances. In fact, many of them are strong performers with sound fundamentals and valuable underlying assets. The motivation for their sale is simply a lack of fit within the divesting companies and the possibility of these companies pursuing better opportunities after the removal of these businesses.

Who buys these types of businesses from divesting companies? Generally, strategic acquirers seeking to generate synergies by combining these businesses with their own operations in related industries.[8] Sales to strategic acquirers are attractive to divesting companies because strategic acquirers usually pay for at least some portion of the synergies they expect to realize from their acquisitions. Indeed, in many cases, strategic acquirers *overpay* for their acquisitions, due to some combination of over-optimistic synergy estimates, "make or buy" decision-making, insufficient scenario planning, managerial hubris, competitive bidding processes, and pressure from investment banks.[9] As evidence of this point, the average premium for acquisitions made by public companies is 63% higher than it is for acquisitions made by private equity firms.[10] Accordingly, selling to strategic acquirers is one way for companies to maximize value from the businesses they divest, since the prices they receive from these sales often far exceed the intrinsic value of these units.

Marathon Petroleum's 2021 sale of Speedway, its chain of gas stations, provides a useful illustration of how sales to strategic acquirers can enable companies to realize value from the businesses they divest. Activist hedge fund Elliott Management had repeatedly called on Marathon to spin off Speedway as part of a three-way separation of its refining, midstream, and retail businesses, which was intended to unlock value for shareholders. Marathon instead sold Speedway to 7-Eleven for $21 billion. While 7-Eleven was caricatured as "paying top price for its shopping trip in the U.S."[11] after initially walking away from the deal at the onset of the COVID-19 pandemic in March 2020,[12] it ultimately justified the Speedway acquisition as "the chance of a lifetime"[13] to expand its existing footprint of convenience stores in the United States and to diversify away from declining prospects in its home market of Japan.[14] 7-Eleven's willingness to pay a premium for Speedway was driven by the $475 to $575 million of synergies it expected to gain each year, as well as $3 billion of tax benefits and $5 billion of net sale leaseback proceeds.[15] On the flipside, one unique advantage of Marathon's decision to sell Speedway to a strategic acquirer may have been its ability to continue supplying gasoline to Speedway through a contractual supply agreement with 7-Eleven. This would allow Marathon to remove its retail business and satisfy Elliott Management's demands, while continuing to extract value from its vertical relationship with its formerly integrated downstream partner.[16]

Financial Acquirers. Companies also sell poorly performing or slow-growing businesses.[17] As discussed in Chapter 1, many such businesses are concentrated in weak or declining industries whose long-term prospects are unlikely to improve. Others are products of failed acquisitions where flawed strategy and/or poor execution have eroded their fundamentals. One benefit of selling such businesses is simply for companies to cut their losses sooner rather than later.

Under these circumstances, the question of who would want to buy such businesses from divesting companies might seem harder to answer. After all, why would any strategic acquirer *voluntarily* choose to buy a declining business in an unattractive industry, much less a business that couldn't be integrated into another organization? Worse, wouldn't the fact that a company was selling that business send a strong signal to strategic acquirers that they should avoid buying it? For these reasons, financial acquirers are often* the natural buyers when companies sell their problematic businesses.

The business model, so to speak, of financial acquirers (especially private equity firms) is to buy underperforming businesses at a discount and turn them around by cutting costs and making strategic investments in them,[18] especially in areas where divesting companies may have failed to do so.[19] Financial acquirers then exit these improved businesses at a profit a few years later. In contrast to strategic acquirers, financial acquirers tend

---

* The opposite certainly does occur, however. For example, the buyers of divested cigarette businesses (a declining industry if there ever was one) have exclusively been other tobacco companies.

not to overpay for their acquisitions, for two main reasons. First, financial acquirers exhibit much more pricing discipline than strategic acquirers. Financial acquirers would sooner abandon a deal than overpay, the reason being that they lack purchase price elasticity: the lower the purchase price, the bigger the future profit upon resale. Second, the main objective of financial acquirers is to rationalize and enhance the performance of businesses they acquire, as opposed to generating operational synergies from them. The fact that financial acquirers usually do not achieve operational synergies—or seek to achieve them—makes them less likely to overpay for their acquisitions than strategic buyers. For both of these reasons, divesting companies that sell businesses to financial acquirers must recognize that their counterpart's motivation is in profound conflict with theirs: the textbook instruction to maximize the sale price must yield to the objectives of expeditiously exiting the divested business and recouping a realistic value for it.

Symantec's $7.4 billion sale of Veritas, its data storage and recovery business, to an investor group led by Carlyle illustrates this point. Although Carlyle's offer was well below the $13.5 billion Symantec originally paid to buy Veritas in 2005, it was still viewed as a fair price for that business. As one commentator put it, "Symantec's sale of Veritas is a positive, in our opinion, in that it lends certainty to a business whose fundamentals have been under pressure for some time and *comes at likely the best valuation Symantec could hope to attain.* . . . The $6.3 billion price net of tax is 2.5 times EV/sales [enterprise value], in line with Symantec's current valuation of 2.2 times."[20]

Tivity Health's 2020 sale of its nutrition business (including the Nutrisystem and South Beach Diet brands) to private equity firm Kainos Capital for $575 million further illustrates these issues. Tivity had originally bought Nutrisystem for $1.3 billion in 2019, seeking to cross-sell diet products with its core wellness programs, like Silver Sneakers. These synergies never materialized, causing Tivity to write down the value of Nutrisystem twice.[21] In a strategic review, Tivity concluded that the declining sales, unprofitability, and write-downs of the nutrition business impaired the value it could expect to recover from selling that business.[22] Given these issues, Kainos was an ideal buyer for the business, thanks to its experience with nutrition brands (it had previously owned SlimFast), its willingness to invest in a turnaround, and its ability to move quickly to complete a deal on Tivity's timeline (thereby avoiding a further erosion of value).[23] The sale enabled Tivity to recoup some value from the nutrition business, which it used to pay down debt and focus on its core healthcare operations.

Cash Generation

Consistent with the final point in the Tivity example, sales generate cash, which companies can use to resolve financial constraints and pay for growth initiatives.[24] Companies are most likely to use sales as the divestiture structure when they need additional funds, which occurs when they are unprofitable, undervalued in the stock market, slower growing, over-levered, or highly capital intensive.[25] In these situations, sales provide companies with a cheaper and/or more easily accessible source of capital than equity, debt, or internal cash flows.[26]

Campbell Soup Company's difficulties illustrate all these points. Campbell overdiversified into the fresh foods and international markets, pursuing ill-fitting and expensive acquisitions of brands like Bolthouse Farms, Snyder's-Lance, and Pacific Foods. As a result, it became significantly overlevered and its stock price plummeted, prompting activist investor Daniel Loeb of Third Point Capital to demand the breakup and sale of the company.[27] Campbell ultimately sold its fresh foods and international businesses piecemeal to various acquirers.[28] The $3 billion of proceeds Campbell brought in from these sales (which it used to pay down debt) likely served as an important and perhaps unique funding source at a time when its internal cash flows and its ability to access external capital markets were constrained by underperformance, excessive borrowing, and declining market value.

Bayer faced a similar situation to that of Campbell in the wake of its troubled acquisition of Monsanto. Bayer took on a large amount of debt to complete the acquisition, but that deal exposed the company to lawsuits claiming that Monsanto's Roundup weed killer had caused cancer. Faced with a plummeting stock price, Bayer announced that it would sell its Coppertone, Dr. Scholl's, and animal health businesses, as well as cut 12,000 jobs.[29] Together, these measures were expected to yield annual savings of nearly $3 billion, "free[ing] up funds for a planned €35 billion to be invested in the company's future through the end of 2022 . . . with R&D accounting for two-thirds of this sum."[30] Even after these initiatives, Bayer continued to divest, agreeing in March 2022 to sell its pest-control unit for $2.6 billion, "a very attractive purchase price" that would enable the company to reduce debt.[31] As with Campbell, it seems unlikely that Bayer would have had the ability to generate this kind of cash flow from either internal or external capital markets, again illustrating how sales can serve as an important funding source for companies facing financial needs.

Tax Considerations

Finally, tax considerations exert a major influence on the decision to employ sales as the divestiture structure. A sale affords the divesting company the benefit of a tax loss when the sale price is less than the tax basis of the divested business—in other words, when the business is sold for a loss. Tax losses can be used to generate refunds of past taxes and/or to offset income and thereby reduce current or future taxes. The ability to generate a tax loss therefore constitutes an important source of value that is not necessarily available in other divestiture structures.[*]

One of the most famous examples of achieving tax advantages through a sale occurred in the Washington Post Company's 2010 sale of *Newsweek* to Sidney Harman (the founder of the audio company Harman International) for *one dollar*, plus the assumption of certain of *Newsweek*'s liabilities.[32] Numerous commentators snarked that the $1 sale price for the entire magazine was less than the $5.95 cover price for a single issue at the time.[33] However, the Washington Post Company's decision made a great deal of sense; *Newsweek* had drastically underperformed in the years leading up to the sale, having lost over $41 million since 2007 and over $2 million in the first quarter of 2010 alone.[34] Selling this business for a minimal price likely achieved the dual purposes of attracting a willing buyer and allowing the Washington Post Company to achieve a favorable tax treatment—a maximal tax loss—while ridding itself of a declining asset.[†]

---

[*] Note, however, that what works for tax purposes usually fails for accounting purposes; companies that focus on maximizing reported income may choose to divest their high-basis subsidiaries using a different divestiture structure, such as a joint venture, which can spread both the tax benefit and the accounting loss over time. See Chapter 8.

[†] Here, Mr. Harman's true investment was the cumulative ongoing funds that he would have had to contribute to run *Newsweek*. Indeed, it was *Newsweek*'s very need for those ongoing infusions that prevented the Washington Post Company from ever spinning it off; *Newsweek*'s operating cash needs were simply too great.

Conversely, a sale becomes less attractive from a tax perspective when it generates a taxable gain—that is, when a business is sold for a price that exceeds its tax basis. For instance, this might occur for a business that (1) has proprietary resources or capabilities, (2) was an early mover in an attractive industry, or (3) was acquired at an advantageous price. In each of these cases, the divesting company's tax basis would likely be lower than the sale prices of these businesses.

In situations where a sale will generate an unacceptable tax bill, companies can employ alternative divestiture structures and techniques. One obvious solution would be to spin off rather than sell the business unit, since spinoffs can be structured as tax-free transactions (see Chapter 6). For instance, many of the large tech companies (e.g., HP, eBay) chose to spin off rather than sell the better-performing, faster-growing businesses in their portfolios (e.g., HP Enterprise, PayPal), presumably in part to avoid the tax hit they might have incurred had they sold those units.

Another solution would be to offset the taxable gains from the sale of one business with the tax losses from the sale of another unit. For instance, returning to the introductory Huntsman–Indorama example, a major downside to that transaction was the tax bill that Huntsman would face from its gain on that sale. In part to mitigate it, Huntsman sold 42.5 million of the shares it owned in Venator Materials PLC *at a loss* to SK Partners LP just a few months later, for approximately $100 million in cash.* The tax strategy behind this deal was brilliant: "by offsetting the capital loss on the sale of Venator shares against the capital gain realized on the sale of [the] chemical intermediates and surfactants businesses," Huntsman reduced its taxes by nearly $150 million.[35] CEO Peter Huntsman even commented that the company was "pleased to have completed [the Venator] transaction before year end enabling us to reduce our current tax obligations by USD 150 million,"[36] emphasizing the tax benefits of the strategy. The tax savings, combined with the $100 million from the sale of the Venator shares, ended up yielding $250 million for Huntsman in 2020.[37]

Finally, a third potential solution would be to use a joint venture to spread the tax bill (and the accounting gain) over an agreed-upon period of time. This will be discussed in Chapter 8.

---

* Venator was a titanium dioxide business that was carved out of Huntsman in 2017 (see Chapter 7). Huntsman retained nearly 80% of Venator's shares at the time of the carveout, some of which it then sold to SK Partners in 2020.

POTENTIAL FOR CONFLICTS

Despite the advantages of sales, the interactions that must occur between divesting companies and acquirers in this divestiture structure create the potential for conflicts. These conflicts can occur during the sale process and/or after the completion of the transaction.

Conflicts During the Sale Process

Conflicts between the divesting company and the acquirer arise during the sale process when adverse and unexpected events occur that impair the value of the divested business. In these cases, the acquirer will usually seek to walk away from the deal. This will leave the divesting company holding the bag, so to speak, with a business that is now perceived as damaged goods (whether or not that assessment is true).

Sometimes, these conflicts can be resolved, with the two parties agreeing to change the terms of the transaction. For instance, in the wake of a massive data breach at Yahoo!, Verizon (perhaps opportunistically) sought to walk away from its deal to buy Yahoo!'s internet business. The transaction was ultimately renegotiated, with Yahoo! accepting a $350 million lower price and agreeing to share the future costs of the data breach with Verizon.[38] In another example, 1-800-Flowers sought to delay its $252 million purchase of PersonalizationMall.com from Bed Bath & Beyond due to the COVID-19 pandemic. Bed Bath & Beyond sued 1-800-Flowers, but the two companies ultimately settled by agreeing to a sale for $245 million, "subject to certain working capital and other adjustments."[39]

At other times, conflicts between the divesting company and the acquirer cannot be resolved and will ultimately result in the termination of the deal. According to one study, about 10% of large M&A transactions are terminated each year,[*] with the most significant reasons being disagreements over valuations, regulatory concerns (e.g., antitrust; see

---

[*] For example, in July 2022, Elon Musk sought to terminate his proposed $44 billion takeover of Twitter "primarily because Twitter hadn't provided the necessary data and information he needs to assess the prevalence of fake or spam accounts." The matter remains unresolved as of this writing.

Source: Needleman, Sarah E., and Cara Lombardo. 2022. "Elon Musk Files Response and Counterclaims to Twitter Lawsuit Over $44 Billion Deal." *Wall Street Journal*, July 29, 2022. https://www.wsj.com/articles/elon-musk-files-response-and-counterclaims-to-twitter-lawsuit-over-44-billion-deal-11659129207.

Chapter 4), and political headwinds (e.g., tax changes, national security issues).[40] For example, even after L Brands reached an agreement to sell a 55% stake in its Victoria's Secret and Pink brands for $525 million to Sycamore Partners in 2020, Sycamore sought to break the deal due to the impact of COVID-19.[41] L Brands had shuttered most of its Victoria's Secret stores at the onset of the pandemic, which Sycamore argued ran afoul of the deal's closing conditions and impaired the brand's valuation.[42] Ultimately, the deal was called off, with L Brands eventually spinning off Victoria's Secret into an independent company instead.[43]

Post-Transaction Conflicts

Even after a sale is complete, post-transaction conflicts between the divesting company and the acquirer can still arise. There are at least three forms these conflicts can take:

- The acquirer claims that the value or performance of the divested business are not what the divesting company portrayed them to be.

- The divesting company and/or the acquirer claim that the other party misconducted itself or mishandled some aspect of the sale process.

- The divesting company and/or the acquirer disagree over the terms of agreements that are put in place to manage the separation and transfer of the divested business.

It is important to recognize that the first two of these post-transaction conflicts are driven by distinct underlying challenges. The first one is a classic lemons problem (as in, "You sold me a lemon"), and it is most likely to occur when the acquirer has difficulty managing or integrating the business into its organization, thereby failing to realize value from the transaction. The second conflict is much more nefarious, resting on claims that the divesting company and/or the acquirer failed to realize the full value of the transaction due to misconduct by the other party.

The long-running saga that unfolded after Albertsons sold 146 of its grocery stores to Haggen in 2014 nicely illustrates both types of conflicts. From the start, Haggen (which was based in the Pacific Northwest) experienced a great deal of difficulty managing this chain of stores (which were mostly located in Southern California), as existing customers left due to a lack of regional name identification and a misaligned pricing strategy.[44]

In turn, Haggen laid off numerous employees, resulting in negative press coverage and grievances from labor unions over the hastily performed layoffs.[45] Shortly after the sale, Albertsons sued Haggen for more than $40 million, accusing it of "fraud for failing to pay millions of dollars for the inventory it acquired in the new stores. In its suit, Albertsons called Haggen's actions 'fraudulent in nature and done with malice.'"[46] In response, Haggen filed a $1 billion lawsuit against Albertsons, claiming that "Albertsons provided inaccurate pricing information during the transition, which resulted in increased prices for customers once Haggen took over . . . deliberately understocked stores ahead of the transition so customers would be dissatisfied and shop at nearby Albertsons and Safeway stores . . . [and] coordinated advertising campaigns to lure customers away from Haggen."[47] Albertsons ultimately settled the lawsuit with Haggen, and, in 2016, actually reacquired some of the stores it had originally sold to Haggen after the latter filed for bankruptcy. This prompted speculation that Albertsons had "shrewdly" reacquired the stores that the FTC had required it to sell to complete its 2015 merger with Safeway. Indeed, in covering the controversy, one grocery industry analyst commented: "You would think somebody would be smart enough to understand what was going on, particularly in the FTC and the federal government. It almost looks like a conspiracy."[48]

In contrast to the first two types of post-transaction conflicts, the third such conflict occurs when there are disagreements over the transition services agreements and contractual arrangements that are put in place to manage the separation and transfer of the divested business. In a transition services agreement, the divesting company and the acquirer usually have opposite interests: the divesting company seeks to shift "all aspects of the divested business over to the acquirer as quickly as possible, with minimal ongoing commitments," while the acquirer often seeks "more robust transition services," with the broadest scope of services and highest service levels at the lowest cost.[49] This discrepancy of interests raises numerous potential areas of conflict, especially over the definitions of each service that will be provided and performance metrics for the extent to which those services will be performed. For example, absent clear definitions, the divesting company and the acquirer may not share a "common understanding of the terms [the transition services agreement] uses (e.g., what each service means)," and "simply stating that transition services should be performed at 'existing service levels' may not be sufficient, especially when the seller does not currently measure such standards."[50] Chapter 9 provides more detail about transition services agreements and the other arrangements that companies put in place to manage ongoing relationships with the businesses they divest.

CHAPTER 6

Spinoffs

INTRODUCTION

Spinoffs[*] are a divestiture structure in which a company distributes shares in a subsidiary to its existing shareholders.[†] This results in the creation of a new, independent, public company, as illustrated in Exhibit 6.1 (two related divestiture structures, split-offs and split-ups, are discussed in a nearby text box). Spinoffs separate the ownership, operations, and valuation of the spinoff company from those of its former parent. Although the divested subsidiary is owned by the parent company until the moment the spinoff is complete, the shareholder bases of the former parent and newly liberated subsidiary will promptly diverge after that, as investors in the two companies independently trade shares, as arbitrageurs close out their positions, and as investment funds adjust their portfolios.[‡] There are other divergences, too: not only will the two companies have their own distinct investor bases, but their corporate identities, boards of directors, and management teams will be different as well.

---

[*] The term "spinoff" is often misused by the press to describe almost any divestiture. Academics also misuse the term to refer to an employee-led startup that separates from another company or from an educational institution (these are more appropriately referred to as "spin-outs"). Similarly, the television industry uses the term "spinoff" to describe a category of TV show that involves popular characters from an earlier TV show (e.g., *Better Call Saul* is a spinoff from *Breaking Bad*).

[†] Indeed, spinoffs are often described as "distributions-in-kind" among legal professionals.

[‡] Technically, shares in the spinoff company begin trading on a "when, as, and if" basis when the date of the transaction is announced, usually a few weeks prior to its closing date. The trades "go regular way" (i.e., they "settle," or they "clear") upon the completion of the spinoff.

EXHIBIT 6.1

Depiction of Spinoff

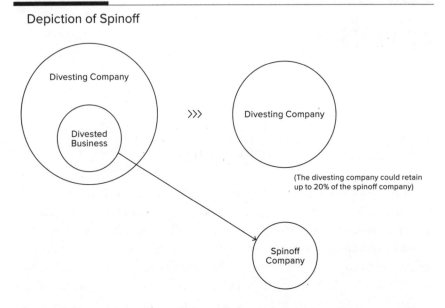

(The divesting company could retain up to 20% of the spinoff company)

Spinoffs are the second most common divestiture structure behind sales. Exhibit 6.2 depicts the disclosed yearly volume and value of spinoffs undertaken by U.S.-based companies from 1990 to 2021.

SPLIT-OFFS AND SPLIT-UPS

Spinoffs are but one of three divestiture structures in which subsidiary shares are distributed to existing shareholders, the others being split-offs and split-ups. In a split-off, the parent company offers its existing shareholders to exchange their shares in the parent company for shares in the subsidiary that is being divested (a few brief words on split-offs appear at the end of this chapter). One can think of it as a share buyback using equity in the spinoff company instead of cash to purchase those shares. In a split-up, the parent company distributes stock in each of its subsidiaries to its shareholders and then dissolves. One can think of it as a liquidation. Spinoffs, split-offs, and split-ups are all tax-free to the extent that no cash or debt instruments are involved in the transaction.

EXHIBIT 6.2

Disclosed Volume and Value of Spinoffs, 1990–2021[1]

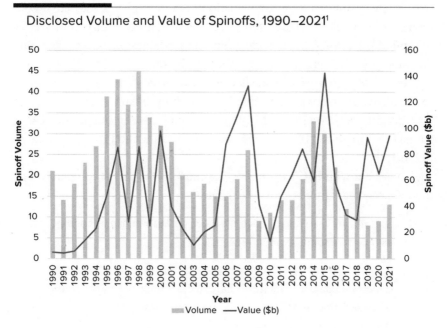

ADVANTAGES

In 2015, the *New York Times*' Andrew Ross Sorkin gave his *DealBook* readers a pop quiz: "Which company has created more value for shareholders over the last two decades: Disney, Microsoft or IAC/InterActiveCorp?"[2] Mr. Sorkin speculated that most people might guess Disney or Microsoft, but the correct answer is in fact IAC, thanks to Barry Diller's strategy of buying nascent digital businesses, growing them to scale, and spinning them off tax-free into independent, public companies when they become strong enough to stand on their own two feet. Although Mr. Diller acknowledged that he did not explicitly intend to create this strategy, "he did recognize that IAC could act as a sort of 'central flywheel' to create, buy and finance companies to later be spun out," describing himself as "an anti-conglomerateur."[3] Indeed, 11 public companies have emerged from IAC between 1995 and 2021, including such well-known companies as Expedia, Ticketmaster, LendingTree, Home Shopping Network, Match Group, and Vimeo, creating $100 billion of shareholder value in the process.[4] As IAC's former CFO, Glenn Schiffman, explained, "The market always places a higher valuation on a pure-play asset than a conglomeration of assets. [IAC itself] trades at a significant discount. We try to remind [investors] that at some point these businesses may be spun out. At some point, it makes sense for them to be on their own. We've found that creativity often gets unleashed when management teams are forced to set a new course with a talented and probing board. A plant needs to be repotted every so often."[5] Mr. Diller echoed this sentiment after IAC's spinoff of Vimeo in 2021: "It appears there is validation in repetition. On to the 12th."[6]

Consistent with IAC's experience, spinoffs offer parent companies and their shareholders three main advantages:

1. Spinoffs are tax-free transactions when parent companies comply with certain statutory requirements.

2. Spinoffs can unlock shareholder value by enabling the parent and spinoff companies, which will have distinct financial and operating characteristics, to be valued on a standalone basis.

3. Spinoffs can improve the operational efficiency of businesses with distinct resource needs and growth prospects by enabling them to function independently of one another.

Tax-Free Transactions

Whereas sales are taxable, spinoffs can be structured as tax-free transactions, making them attractive when the divestiture of a particular business would otherwise generate a taxable gain. Spinoffs are useful in this circumstance because they enable the divesting company to avoid paying the taxes it would otherwise incur if it sold that unit for a profit. By comparison, sales are more attractive than spinoffs when the divestiture of a particular business would generate a taxable loss. There, the divesting company would benefit from the value of the tax deduction, which it could use to (1) offset taxable income in the year incurred, (2) carry back in time to generate a refund, and/or (3) carry forward in time to offset future taxable income. The choice of optimal divestiture structure based on tax considerations is summarized in Exhibit 6.3.

EXHIBIT 6.3

Choice of Optimal Divestiture Structure Based on Tax Considerations

	Tax Effect of Sale	Optimal Divestiture Structure
Value Above Tax Basis	Taxable Gain	Tax-Free Spinoff
Value Below Tax Basis	Tax Benefit From Loss	Taxable Sale

For a spinoff to qualify as tax-free, the parent company must meet four major conditions under Section 355 of the Internal Revenue Code:

- The parent company must distribute "control" of the spinoff company to its shareholders. Control is defined as a distribution of at least 80% of the total combined voting power and at least 80% of any non-voting shares in that entity.[7]*

- There cannot have been a purchase of 50% or more of the stock of the parent company or its former subsidiary in the five years before a spinoff, and no entity can acquire 50% or more of the stock of the parent company or its former subsidiary (the spinoff company) "pursuant to a plan or series of related transactions" within two years before or after a spinoff.[8]†

- The parent company and its former subsidiary must each have engaged in an "active trade or business" for five years before the spinoff. This means that both entities had to have been engaging in "a specific group of activities for the purpose of earning income or profit."[9]

---

* As will be discussed in Chapter 7, this requirement explains why a company that uses an equity carveout to sell a stake in one of its businesses usually retains more than 80% of its shares. In other words, by not compromising its ability to distribute control of the business, the divesting company retains the flexibility to use a tax-free spinoff in combination with an equity carveout of its remaining (less than 20%) stake in that business.

† As will also be discussed in Chapter 7, Reverse Morris Trusts sidestep the latter of these restrictions by enabling a company to spin off and merge one of its businesses with a target company. Reverse Morris Trusts are tax-free transactions so long as the spinoff company is considered the buyer of the target company (i.e., the shareholders of the historic parent company own more than 50% of the merged entity).

- The parent company must be undertaking the spinoff for a legitimate "corporate business purpose" rather than as a "device" for distributing earnings and profits. This means that the spinoff must be motivated "in whole or substantial part . . . [by] a real and substantial non-tax purpose germane to the business of the parent, the spinoff company or both."[10] By contrast, a pure "shareholder purpose," such as increasing shareholder value, will not itself suffice as a reason for undertaking a tax-free spinoff.[11]

While a company can still undertake a spinoff if any of these four conditions are not met, the divestiture would not be accorded tax-free status, meaning that the share distribution would be treated as a dividend to the recipient shareholders.*

Yahoo!'s abortive attempt to spin off its 15% stake in Alibaba provides a useful example of the seriousness of these four tax conditions. While Yahoo! attempted to use a tax-free spinoff to divest a business it called Aabaco, Aabaco was (to be charitable) somewhat unbalanced, consisting of Yahoo!'s $40 billion passive stake in Alibaba together with a minor subsidiary (Yahoo Small Business).[12] While the IRS did not rule specifically on the merits of the spinoff, it *publicly* declined to issue a ruling on the taxability of the proposed transaction while it conducted a broader review of its policies on spinoffs.[13] Various analysts speculated that the IRS's decision not to rule on the taxability of this spinoff was driven by the fact that (1) Aabaco did not conduct an active trade or business (arguing that Yahoo! instead artificially bundled the Small Business unit with its Alibaba stake for appearance's sake), (2) there was no legitimate corporate business purpose to the spinoff, and (3) the transaction was simply intended to confer tax-free status on the distribution of Yahoo!'s substantial and valuable stake in Alibaba.[14]

---

* While *taxable* distributions of subsidiary shares (i.e., taxable spinoffs) are exceedingly rare, circumstances do arise to justify their use. Without intending to be overly technical, distributions are treated as taxable dividends only to the extent of "Earnings and Profits" (the tax analog to retained earnings). Thus, a distribution made by a parent company with no Earnings and Profits would still be a *taxable* distribution, only the taxes would be zero. Entities that could plausibly engage in a taxable spinoff on which the share recipient would not pay taxes include corporations that experienced significant losses and new corporations that were never profitable.

Whatever the reason, the IRS's strategy was brilliant, putting Yahoo! in the preposterous position of distributing shares in Aabaco while simultaneously having to disclose the distribution's foreseeable adverse tax consequences. Unsurprisingly, the deal died; the risk was too great that an overly aggressive tax position would result in a shareholders' lawsuit. One can only feel sorry for poor Yahoo!; while its market value was about $30 billion, its stake in Alibaba was worth nearly $40 billion.[15] Yahoo! continued to pursue its plan to spin off Aabaco for a few months[16] until, faced with pressure from activist investor Starboard Value, it ultimately announced that it would instead sell its core internet business to Verizon.[17] This left behind a stub that was renamed Altaba—presumably, "alternate Alibaba," since it contained Yahoo!'s stake in Alibaba (which was ultimately liquidated, and Altaba shut down).[18] From the perspective of a parent company's board of directors, this example illustrates the importance of complying with the requirements for tax-free spinoffs.

Unlocking Shareholder Value

As highlighted by the IAC example, spinoffs facilitate the separate valuation of businesses that may be hidden in parent companies, thereby "unlocking shareholder value." Per the discussion in Chapter 2, one of the main reasons that diversified companies are often undervalued in the stock market is that they consist of businesses that have different growth prospects and risk profiles, or that simply operate in different industries. These discrepancies can make it difficult for investors to value these companies correctly, since the performance of any one of their businesses may be masked by the performance of the others. Additionally, securities analysts usually lack the expertise to accurately assess business units in different industries, leading the analysts to produce inaccurate forecasts about diversified companies, which could further contribute to their undervaluation.[19]

Spinoffs help resolve these problems by transforming business units into independent public companies, the attributes of which can better and more directly be evaluated by the capital markets. The logic is that these independent companies should be worth more on a standalone basis than they were as part of their former parents, meaning that value will be unlocked for shareholders. Consistent with this logic, parent companies *outperform* their peers by a cumulative excess return of 3.7% over the first

15 months after their spinoffs, and spinoff companies *outperform* their own peers by 17.1% over the 22 months after these transactions.[20] Again, these statistics are driven by the fact that spinoffs often separate business units that have disparate characteristics, facilitating clearer valuations of the independent entities.

In line with these points, Abbott Laboratories chairman Miles White remarked, "Generally speaking, a [spinoff] makes sense when elements of your business have diverging investment identities."[21] This was the case during Abbott's spinoff of AbbVie, which was "among the most successful in history as measured by market value. At the time, pharmaceuticals accounted for more than half of the company's total profit. And the business of drug development is far riskier and more volatile than other key units at Abbott, like its nutrition or medical device businesses."[22] Both Abbott and AbbVie performed remarkably well after the spinoff, with Abbott's share price soaring by 184% and AbbVie's by 158% in the seven years following the divestiture.[23] Similarly, prior to Kraft's separation of its North American grocery business from its global snacks business (Mondelez International), analysts noted that one of the major reasons Kraft was undervalued in the stock market was that the 5% to 7% organic annual revenue growth and double-digit earnings growth of the global snacks business was so different from the more modest, "mid to high" single-digit annual earnings gains of the North American grocery business.[24] As a result, the Mondelez spinoff separated the two disparate parts of Kraft's operations, creating significant growth in the total shareholder returns of both Kraft and Mondelez in the nine months after their separation.[25]

Despite the valuation-related advantages of spinoffs, some small spinoffs may be ill-advised. Regardless of a company's size, there are certain inflexible costs associated with being public.* Accordingly, spinoffs of small subsidiaries may result in a *loss* of market value for the parent and spinoff companies, and criticism for the parent company's executives. Indeed, Warren Buffett is quoted in this book's Conclusion as informing his company's shareholders that he is averse to spinning off subsidiaries *in*

---

* For example, complying with the federal securities laws imposes numerous reporting obligations, which in turn require that the company retain auditors and financial advisors, and that it properly configure its board of directors. This, in turn, requires that the company purchase directors and officers (D&O) liability insurance. And somewhere in that sequence, outside counsel is also retained.

part due to these inflexible costs. *Pace* Mr. Buffett, however, it should be noted that the opposite could also occur: value could be created in a small company spinoff. This would require that the value created by the potential spinoff be great enough to compensate for the "breakage" associated with (1) creating a new public company, and (2) stripping the parent of its crown jewel. Dell's spinoff of VMware, described in Chapter 7, is one such example.*

Improved Operational Efficiency

Spinoffs improve the operational efficiency of the businesses that are separated in these transactions. As described in Chapter 2, diversified companies are highly complex organizations because their subsidiaries often have different resource needs, market opportunities, and growth prospects. This can lead to numerous operational inefficiencies, including in the way that capital and other resources are allocated to different opportunities, whether certain businesses are used to cross-subsidize others, and how compensation is structured to incentivize employee performance.

Spinoffs help resolve these problems by transforming business units that formerly operated in less-efficient corporate households into more-efficient independent companies. Importantly, these new companies have their own strategies, financial statements, leadership teams, and human and physical resources. This enables them to focus directly on their own distinct market and growth opportunities and to function independently, free of any overhang from their former corporate parents and siblings. As a result, businesses that are separated through spinoffs have been shown to enjoy more efficient processes for allocating capital and other resources,[26]

---

* There may also be situations that can justify a defensive spinoff from the parent's perspective, even if the numbers do not support it. For example, the parent company might wish to use a "window of opportunity" to separate itself from a subsidiary. AT&T's divestiture of WarnerMedia (through a Reverse Morris Trust) may be one such example; AT&T shares declined on the day of the announcement. Exelon's spinoff of Constellation (its power generation business) following similar moves by FirstEnergy Corp. and Public Service Enterprise Group Inc. may be another.

Sources: FitzGerald, Drew, Cara Lombardo, and Joe Flint. 2021. "AT&T Agrees to Merge Its WarnerMedia Assets with Discovery." *Wall Street Journal*, May 17, 2021. https://www.wsj .com/articles/at-t-to-combine-warnermedia-division-with-discovery-11621250928.

Blunt, Katherine. 2022. "This New Company Is Betting Big on Nuclear Power in America." *Wall Street Journal*, February 2, 2022. https://www.wsj.com/articles/this-new-company-is -betting-big-on-nuclear-power-in-america-11643820916.

a better ability to pursue independent acquisitions,[27] more powerful financial incentives,[28] and greater focus[29] after these transactions.

eBay's spinoff of PayPal and JDSU's spinoff of Lumentum both provide useful examples of how spinoffs can promote more efficient resource allocation processes. Prior to the eBay–PayPal spinoff, for instance, "the cash-generating eBay enterprise was funding PayPal's growth. Now, however, the roles are reversed: eBay's business has been bolstered heavily by PayPal's strong growth, especially its forays into mobile payment, and PayPal has the necessary cash flows to fund its own future growth."[30] After the spinoff, however, both types of cross-subsidization were eliminated; eBay and PayPal became independent companies, enabling them to focus their own resources on growth in their respective markets. Similarly, JDSU articulated some of the major rationales for its spinoff of Lumentum in the following terms: "to enable a more efficient allocation of capital and resources for both companies; and to enable both companies to benefit from increased operational flexibility, efficiency and support structures tailored to each company's specific needs."[31] Together, these examples and many others illustrate that businesses separated in spinoffs may be better able to direct their investment dollars to the appropriate opportunities as independent entities than they were able to within the confines of their former parents,* where the demands of other businesses, a more limited supply of capital, and perhaps even political dynamics may have impaired the efficiency of their allocation decisions (see Chapter 10).[32]

Finally, as an example of how spinoffs can help resolve inefficiencies in compensation, consider the conglomerate ITT's 2011 spinoffs of its defense business (Exelis) and water technology provider (Xylem). One of the rationales that was provided in the SEC filings for these spinoffs was the following: "In multi-business companies such as ITT, it is difficult

---

* Kellogg's CEO Steven Cahillane articulated this point in the company's 2022 announcement that it would spin off its North American cereals and its plant-based foods businesses, leaving behind its global snacking business as an independent company: "These businesses all have significant standalone potential, and an enhanced focus will enable them to better direct their resources toward their distinct strategic priorities. In turn, each business is expected to create more value for all stakeholders, and each is well positioned to build a new era of innovation and growth."

Source: Wiener-Bronner, Danielle. 2022. "Why Kellogg Is Turning Its Back on Frosted Flakes and Froot Loops." *CNN Business*, June 22, 2022. https://www.cnn.com/2022/06/22/business /kellogg-cereal-snacks/index.html.

to structure incentives that reward managers in a manner directly related to the performance of their respective business units. By granting equity linked to a specific business, equity compensation will be more in line with the financial results of the managers' direct work product."[33] This exact logic—divisional managers are not compensated efficiently in diversified companies, and spinoffs can resolve these inefficiencies—is in fact articulated in the SEC filings of nearly three-quarters of spinoffs,[34] and research has produced empirical evidence documenting this point as well.[35]

POTENTIAL FOR CONFLICTS

As discussed in Chapter 5, sales create the potential for conflicts between divesting companies and acquirers. These conflicts usually revolve around differences between the expected and realized value of the divested business, breaches of representations or warranties, or alleged misconduct by either party. Whereas sales shift the ownership, control, and management of the divested business to an acquirer, spinoffs shift them into a new public company. Thus, spinoffs instead create the potential for conflicts between parent and spinoff companies. These conflicts involve the spinoff company making one (or both) of two types of allegations:

- The parent company opportunistically set the spinoff company up to fail by spinning off a business that would not be viable on a standalone basis and/or by allocating excessive liabilities to it.

- The parent company did not allow the spinoff company to have sufficient input into the spinoff process, enabling the parent company to make decisions that advanced its own interests at the expense of those of the spinoff company.

Allegations of Opportunism
Spinoffs carry a significant potential for opportunism on the part of companies that undertake them. The fact that this divestiture structure enables a company to divest one of its businesses simply by distributing shares in it to existing shareholders (rather than going through the "acid test" of negotiating with buyers and their professional advisors) creates both adverse selection and moral hazard problems. In terms of adverse selection, free

of any pressure from the market mechanism, companies might try to use spinoffs selectively to divest businesses that have no real possibility of functioning as independent companies and therefore, for which they would otherwise be unable to find willing buyers. Indeed, in terms of moral hazard, companies might even attempt to rid themselves of unwanted liabilities by including them in the mix of businesses they are spinning off, while retaining in their own organizations the more valuable businesses.*

Limitations exist to temper both types of opportunism: federal statutes effectively prevent the shedding of pension and environmental liabilities, and laws against fraudulent conveyances are embodied in the statutes and common laws of virtually every state (and in the federal bankruptcy code). These prevent the defrauding of creditors through intentional or constructive transfers of valuable assets to third parties (such as the assets divested in a spinoff) for less than their fair market value. Put succinctly, fraudulent conveyance laws limit companies from spinning off businesses that:

- Are insolvent at the time of the spinoff

- Become insolvent due to that transaction

- Are insufficiently capitalized at the time of the spinoff

- Would incur debts beyond their ability to pay them at maturity[36]

In theory, these limitations against fraudulent conveyances should eliminate both the adverse selection and moral hazard problems by preventing companies from spinning off businesses that would not be able to function independently and/or from loading those businesses with excessive liabilities. Yet, as with most laws, the mere existence of prophylactic statutes doesn't ensure strict compliance with them. Spinoff companies regularly bring fraudulent conveyance litigation against their former parent companies, and these lawsuits have had varying degrees of success.

For instance, following Verizon's spinoff of its print telephone directory business into a new company called Idearc, U.S. Bank, N.A. (Idearc's litigation trustee) sued Verizon, claiming that "the historical print directory business was in decline" and was therefore not viable "due, among

---

* One extreme example of this is the so-called Texas Two-Step, a particularly insidious transaction in which spinoffs are employed to shed mass tort liabilities. See Chapter 9.

other reasons, to the public's declining use of paper telephone directories and increased use of alternative information sources, such as the internet."[37] The litigation also claimed that Verizon had loaded Idearc with so much debt that after the spinoff, "Idearc's balance sheet reflected that its debts exceeded its assets by approximately $9 billion. Not surprisingly, after limping along for some time, Idearc went bankrupt."[38] Verizon ultimately prevailed in this litigation, as a federal district court judge ruled that Idearc had a value of at least $12 billion and was solvent at the time of its spinoff from Verizon.[39]

Conversely, oil and gas company Kerr-McGee spun off its chemicals business into a new company called Tronox in 2006. As part of this transaction, Kerr-McGee allocated to Tronox billions of dollars of environmental, tort, and retiree liabilities.* In addition to these liabilities, Kerr-McGee also caused Tronox to take on significant amounts of debt, the offsetting cash of which Kerr-McGee then upstreamed (see Chapter 7). Unsurprisingly, Tronox filed for bankruptcy and brought fraudulent conveyance litigation against Kerr-McGee and its successor, Anadarko Petroleum,† shortly after the spinoff, claiming that Kerr-McGee had loaded Tronox with excessive debt obligations and liabilities that did not pertain to its operations. Tronox prevailed in this landmark case, with the court finding "clear and convincing evidence" that Kerr-McGee's transfer of liabilities to Tronox was made "with the intent to hinder or delay [Tronox's] creditors . . . [and] for less than reasonably equivalent value" and that they "left [Tronox] insolvent and undercapitalized, [and that Kerr-McGee] reasonably should have believed that [Tronox] would incur debts beyond [its] ability to pay as they became due."[40] The court awarded damages between $5.1 billion and $14.1 billion (the largest amount ever awarded in a bankruptcy proceeding for governmental environmental

---

* Kerr-McGee had initially tried to sell the chemicals business in combination with these liabilities, but their magnitude was so great that reportedly, none of the four bidders that made it to the final round of the auction was willing to proceed with a purchase that included them. For instance, one of the bidders was willing to bid $1.2 billion for the chemicals business without the liabilities, but only $300 million with those liabilities.

Source: Schnapf LLC. 2014. "Bankruptcy Court Finds Kerr-McGee Engaged in Fraudulent Transfer in Tronox Spinoff." April 2014. https://www.environmental-law.net/2013/12/20/bankruptcy-court-finds-kerr-mcgee-engaged-in-fraudulent-transfer-in-tronox-spinoff/.

† Kerr-McGee, free and clear of these liabilities and flush with cash, had become a very attractive company and was subsequently acquired by Anadarko.

claims and liabilities).[41] Kerr-McGee and Anadarko ultimately agreed to pay $5.15 billion to the Tronox Litigation Trust, of which $4.4 billion went toward funding environmental remediation.[42]

Finally, as an example of how fraudulent conveyance litigation can be resolved by settlement, consider Honeywell's 2018 spinoff of Garrett Motion, its transportation systems business. Garrett struggled from the outset as an independent company due to the cyclicality of the auto industry, the company's already high debt burden, and the onset of the COVID-19 pandemic.[43] To make matters worse, as part of the spinoff, Honeywell had allocated a significant portion of its $1 billion asbestos liability stemming from its Bendix brake business to Garrett, requiring it to pay up to $175 million per year on a quarterly basis as part of a 30-year indemnification agreement.[44] Garrett filed suit against Honeywell challenging the validity of the indemnification agreement and claiming that Honeywell had devised the spinoff to offload a liability to Garrett that had nothing to do with its actual operations.[45] Less than a year later, Garrett filed for bankruptcy. During Garrett's bankruptcy proceedings, the two companies negotiated a settlement agreement in which Honeywell released Garrett from the indemnification agreement in return for a payment of $1.21 billion (including an initial cash payment of $375 million, and preferred stock with payments of $35 million in 2022 and $100 million per year from 2023 through 2030) and a seat on Garrett's board until the preferred stock payments fell below a $125 million threshold.[46]

Allegations of Insufficient Input into the Spinoff Process

The second type of conflict that arises in spinoffs occurs when a spinoff company claims that its interests were not adequately represented during the spinoff process, and that in consequence, its former parent company made decisions that enriched its own interests over those of the spinoff company. These types of conflicts can be somewhat intractable. On the one hand, there is a "fundamental premise that the responsibility for [a] spinoff rests with the parent [company's] board and management,"[47] meaning that the parent company affirmatively has the right and responsibility to direct the spinoff process in the manner that it sees fit. On the other hand, however, this "fundamental premise" does put the spinoff company in the tough position of having less involvement in or discretion over the spinoff process than it might like. Of course, when things go wrong, this is exactly the argument that spinoff companies bring against their former parents, usually in court, to try to redress the situation. These types of challenges can manifest themselves in several ways.

For instance, the parent company will decide if and when to undertake a spinoff, as well as which assets to include in the mix. The spinoff company will have no say in these matters; after all, it is simply a controlled subsidiary at the time those decisions are made. The parent company will appoint the spinoff company's future directors and management team and will determine its financial structure. Even more significant, the documents that will govern the administration of the newly independent company (the articles of incorporation and the by-laws) will be drafted by parent company counsel. Unlike a new company that is midwifed with great public fanfare in an IPO, a spinoff company is often abandoned on the church steps with not much more than a blanket and a basket. These imbalances increasingly create incentives for spinoff companies to claim that their former parents embarked on flawed strategies or set them up to fail, as in the fraudulent conveyance examples. To this point, spinoff companies most often make these types of claims when they underperform or fail after they become independent entities.

Relatedly, the parent company's management and board of directors direct the spinoff process. This is totally appropriate; until the moment at which a spinoff is complete, the parent company's management and board of directors will be responsible for overseeing the business that will be spun off.* Importantly, until the moment of partition, the parent company's shareholders will own the company, and the company will own the future spinoff. From the perspective of those shareholders, this configuration means that any shift in value between the parent and its subsidiary will merely be a shift from the one pocket to the other. If the parent company's shareholders are dissatisfied with any aspect of the new spinoff, they have a simple remedy: they can sell the new shares. That the parent company—not the spinoff company—takes the leadership role during the

---

* Indeed, allowing the spinoff company's future management team to be involved in the spinoff process may be inappropriate, in that "these managers may begin to view themselves in a quasi-adversarial position to the parent, as they begin to focus on positioning the business to be spun off in the most advantageous manner."

Source: Wachtell, Lipton, Rosen & Katz. 2020. "Spin-Off Guide." April 2020. https://www.wlrk .com/wp-content/uploads/2020/05/Spin-Off-Guide-2020.pdf.

spinoff process is uncontroversial. Nevertheless, it creates a setting for the spinoff company to claim that it was insufficiently involved in the spinoff process because it was without representation during that period.

Finally, the parent company is responsible for the selection and retention of the legal counsel and investment banks that will manage the spinoff process. Since the parent company is the owner of all the assets—both the assets to be retained and the assets to be divested—it will choose the professional team to manage the spinoff process, and the team will be beholden to the parent company. Again, this arrangement is completely appropriate because the business that is being spun off is still part of the parent company up until the moment at which the spinoff is complete.[*] One analysis indicates that just 2% of spinoff companies had legal counsel that was distinct from that of their parent companies during the spinoff process, and just 1% of spinoff companies had distinct financial representation.[48] Once again, this arrangement provides the background for the spinoff company's claim that its interests were inadequately represented during the spinoff process because it did not have separate legal or financial counsel. For example, in the litigation following the Garrett Motion spinoff, one of the main arguments was that "Garrett did not have independent legal representation during the spinoff process: Honeywell retained the same lawyers to represent both Honeywell and Garrett in connection with the spinoff. The lawyers blindly acceded to Honeywell's wishes, regardless of the best interest of their other client, Garrett."[49] Frankly, the better argument would have been that those lawyers considered the facts and concluded that a conflict did not exist.

All three of these challenges converged and arose during the litigation of the Noble–Paragon spinoff.[†] Following Noble's spinoff of its standard-specification oil rigs into a new company called Paragon Offshore plc, the Paragon Litigation Trust (representing Paragon's creditors) sued Noble,

---

[*] As it is for separate management, "separate legal representation before completion of the spinoff generally is inappropriate as it would unnecessarily exacerbate internal divisions and is inconsistent with the notion that it is the duty of the parent's board to establish the terms of the separation in a manner that serves the best interests of the parent shareholders (who, of course, will also be the initial shareholders of the spinoff company)."

Source: Wachtell, Lipton, Rosen & Katz. 2020. "Spin-Off Guide." April 2020. https://www.wlrk .com/wp-content/uploads/2020/05/Spin-Off-Guide-2020.pdf.

[†] Disclosure: the author represented Noble as an expert witness in this litigation.

claiming, among other matters, that the standard-specification business was unviable as a freestanding entity and that Noble had not provided Paragon with sufficient capital for it to meet its obligations.[50] The Paragon Litigation Trust also claimed that Noble had inappropriately directed the spinoff process by preventing Paragon from having "meaningful input into or control over the terms of the transaction," and from having its own legal or financial representation during the spinoff process.[51] While this litigation was ultimately settled in the wake of Noble's own bankruptcy filing, this example nicely illustrates how conflicts can manifest themselves during the spinoff process.

A FEW BRIEF WORDS ON SPLIT-OFFS

As mentioned at the beginning of this chapter, split-offs are transactions in which the divesting company gives its shareholders the ability to surrender their shares in exchange for shares in the business to be divested. While the tax treatment of split-offs is the same as that of spinoffs, the outcome can be different; unlike spinoffs, split-offs are not *pro rata* distributions. Also, since the proposed exchanges in split-off transactions may not be fully subscribed, split-offs feature the possibility that the divesting parent will distribute its remaining unexchanged subsidiary shares as a spinoff.

General Electric's divestiture of Synchrony took the form of a split-off, as did Eli Lilly's divestiture of Elanco. However, while AT&T ultimately used a Reverse Morris Trust (see Chapter 7) to *spin off* and then merge its WarnerMedia subsidiary with Discovery (creating a new company called Warner Bros. Discovery), it had initially contemplated the alternative of using a Reverse Morris to *split off* and then merge its WarnerMedia subsidiary with Discovery. Opting for the simplicity of the spinoff, which did not involve a formal exchange offer, AT&T's CEO explained his decision:

> John Stankey last week said that the company was debating the best way to separate the two businesses . . . splitting the shareholder base through an exchange offer would help lower the number of AT&T shares circulating—boosting its stock price—though such a complex move would be unprecedented for a company of its size. The company on Tuesday picked the simpler spinoff option—instead of a split—to make the transaction easier for individual investors to digest.[52]

While the formal exchange offer aspect of split-offs will likely limit their popularity, the fact that three iconic companies either employed a split-off or publicly contemplated doing one suggests that more of them may occur in the future.

CHAPTER 7

Appropriating Value from Spinoffs: Equity Carveouts and Reverse Morris Trusts

INTRODUCTION

While the exchange of assets is as old as humanity (an early ironmonger might well have swapped a newly forged hammer for a pair of sandals), and while the sale of assets is as old as civilization (his descendants might have sold it for Sterling), spinoffs are only as old as the modern corporation, a few centuries. The divestiture structures discussed in this chapter, however, are young; there are probably people alive today who can recall their first implementation. This chapter reviews two of them—equity carveouts and Reverse Morris Trusts—as well as a series of techniques that companies can employ to appropriate value from spinoffs, *while still preserving the tax-free nature of the underlying transactions.*

An equity carveout is effectively the sale of an interest in the equity of a corporate subsidiary (also referred to as a "carved-out business"), usually through a public offering. The sale of shares in the carved-out business generates cash proceeds, and the transaction can be structured to be tax-free or taxable, *depending on whether it is the divesting company or the subsidiary that sells the shares* (an important distinction to keep in mind throughout this chapter). Equity carveouts are most often used with tax-free spinoffs as part of two-step transactions. As discussed in Chapter 6, for a spinoff to be tax-free, a parent company must distribute "control" of the spinoff company to its shareholders, defined by law to mean a distribution of at least 80% of the voting (and non-voting) shares in that entity.[1] The sale of up to 20% of the shares of the carved-out business could therefore occur before or after a tax-free spinoff of the company's remaining ownership stake (80% or more of the shares) in that entity.* Thus, equity carveouts generate cash from the sale of carved-out shares without compromising a company's ability to do tax-free spinoffs.

A Reverse Morris Trust is a divestiture structure that combines two tax-free transactions into one: (1) the parent company spins off (or splits off) one of its businesses, which (2) simultaneously merges with another company (referred to as the "target company"). As discussed in Chapter 6, there are limitations on how much of the stock of the parent and spinoff companies can be purchased in the years surrounding a spinoff. Specifically, there cannot have been a purchase of 50% or more of the stock of the parent company or its former subsidiary in the five years before a spinoff, nor can 50% or more of the stock of either entity be acquired as part of a plan or a series of related transactions within two years before or after a spinoff.[2] Reverse Morris Trusts skirt the latter of these limitations and are treated as tax-free transactions *so long as the spinoff company is considered the buyer of the target company* (i.e., so long as the shareholders of the historic parent company own more than 50% of the newly merged entity). Thus, Reverse Morris Trusts enable companies to use mergers in combination with spinoffs without compromising their tax-free status.

Finally, there are various ways that parent companies can structure their future relationships with the businesses they spin off to extract maximal value from them.

EQUITY CARVEOUTS

As defined previously, an equity carveout is the sale of an interest in the equity of a corporate subsidiary. The sale of an equity carveout is typically done through a public offering of less than 20% of the shares of that subsidiary, as depicted in Exhibit 7.1. Exhibit 7.2 presents the disclosed yearly volume and value of equity carveouts from 1990 to 2021.

---

* In practice, companies typically comply with this requirement by distributing slightly more than 80% of the shares to be safe. Accordingly, this chapter tracks the common practice of distributing >80% (rather than ≥80%) of the shares, thereby selling an equity carveout of <20% of those shares.

Equity carveouts are most commonly used in conjunction with spinoffs* in one of the following three ways, all of which ultimately result in the complete divestiture of the subsidiary in question.

Sale of Equity Carveout Before Spinoff

A company could use the public sale of an equity carveout to divest less than 20% of the shares that it owned in a subsidiary in a *taxable* transaction, following which it could do a *tax-free* spinoff of its remaining stake in that entity (see Exhibit 7.3). Publicly traded shares in the equity carveout would create a market for the remaining shares of that subsidiary, thereby setting the value of those shares in anticipation of the future spinoff. Until that spinoff, the divesting company would continue to consolidate the carved-out business for tax and accounting purposes, and the company's share price would presumably reflect the market value of the remaining shares in the carved-out business. There's one problem, though: the sale of the equity carveout is taxable to the divesting company.

Problem Solved:
An Alternate Version of the Previous Transaction

Instead of the *divesting company* selling an equity carveout of its subsidiary's shares, the divesting company could cause its *subsidiary* to sell its own newly issued shares, provided that the number of shares sold does not cause the divesting company's ownership of the subsidiary to fall below 80%. Think of this as a de facto carveout. Here, the sale of newly issued shares is tax-free to the divesting company, since it is the carved-out business that is selling them. However, the divesting company should be able to upstream the proceeds from that sale (e.g., through the repayment of intercompany debt). Exhibit 7.4 illustrates the difference between the two types of pre-spinoff equity carveouts.

---

* Note that equity carveouts can also be used in conjunction with tax-free split-offs, as Eli Lilly did in its divestiture of Elanco (described in more detail later in this chapter).

EXHIBIT 7.1

Depiction of Equity Carveout Without Spinoff

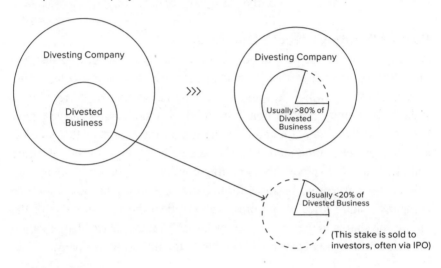

EXHIBIT 7.2

Disclosed Volume and Value of Equity Carveouts, 1990–2021[3]

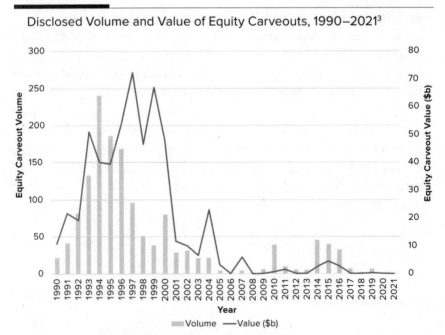

EXHIBIT 7.3

Depiction of Equity Carveout Before Spinoff

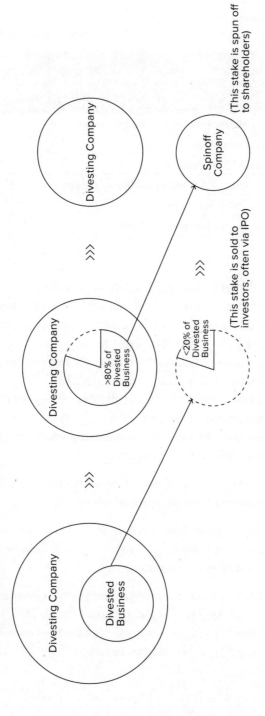

EXHIBIT 7.4

Sample Quantification of Two Alternative Pre-Spinoff Equity Carveouts

	Parent sells subsidiary's shares from its portfolio	Subsidiary sells newly issued shares
Subsidiary shares initially owned by parent	1,000	1,000
Shares sold by parent	195	0
Shares issued by subsidiary	0	242
Subsidiary shares ultimately owned by parent	805	1,000
Total shares after issuance	1,000	1,242
Percent of shares owned by parent	80.5%	80.5%

Spinoff Before Sale of Equity Carveout

Alternatively, a company could first spin off more than 80% of the shares of one of its businesses tax-free, making it an independent, publicly traded spinoff company. Then the divesting company could sell the resulting equity carveout in a taxable transaction, thereby exiting its remaining, less than 20% stake in that entity (see Exhibit 7.5).

The relevant characteristics of all three of these transactional sequences are summarized in Exhibit 7.6.

Equity carveouts have three implications for companies that undertake them, two positive and one negative:

1. Sales of equity carveouts can be structured to be tax-free *and* to generate cash for divesting companies.

2. Publicly traded shares from equity carveouts can facilitate separate valuations of underlying business units whose value may be obscured in larger corporate structures.

3. Equity carveouts have the inherent potential to create conflicts between the controlling and minority shareholders during the period in which divesting companies maintain their controlling stakes in the (now public) carved-out businesses.

EXHIBIT 7.5

Depiction of Spinoff Before Equity Carveout

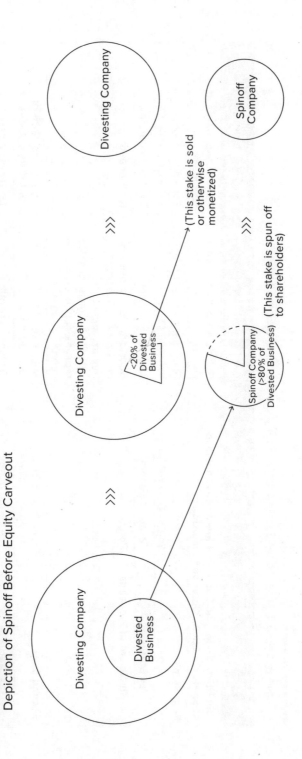

EXHIBIT 7.6

Three Possible Transactional Sequences of Equity Carveouts and Spinoffs

Sequence of Transactions	Equity Carveout Precedes Spinoff		Spinoff Precedes Equity Carveout
	Parent sells shares in subsidiary	Subsidiary sells its own shares	Parent sells shares in subsidiary
Identity of Seller and Source of Shares in Equity Carveout	Parent sells shares in subsidiary	Subsidiary sells its own shares	Parent sells shares in subsidiary
First Step	Parent sells <20% of subsidiary's shares	Subsidiary sells <20% of its own shares	Spinoff of >80% of subsidiary's shares
Tax Status	Taxable to parent	Tax-free to parent	Tax-free to parent
Recipient of Proceeds	Parent	Subsidiary [but subsidiary can upstream cash tax-free to parent under certain circumstances (e.g., repayment of intercompany debt)]	No Proceeds
Second Step	Spinoff of >80% of subsidiary's shares	Spinoff of >80% of subsidiary's shares	Parent sells <20% of subsidiary's shares
Tax Status	Tax-free to parent	Tax-free to parent	Taxable to parent
Recipient of Proceeds	No Proceeds	No Proceeds	Parent

Tax and Cash Implications

While pure spinoffs are tax-free, they generate no cash, and while sales do generate cash, they are not tax-free. In contrast, one of the unique features of equity carveouts is that under certain conditions, they can be tax-free *and* generate cash for the divesting company. As summarized previously, either the divesting company or the carved-out business can issue and sell shares in that business to investors. Each approach has distinct tax and cash flow consequences for the divesting company.

When a company causes its subsidiary to issue and sell newly issued shares, the sale of those shares is not taxable to the divesting company. Some of or all the proceeds from that sale can be upstreamed to the divesting company (e.g., through the repayment of intercompany debt), thereby generating cash. However, if the objective is to set the stage for a future tax-free spinoff by the parent of its remaining investment in its subsidiary, then there is a limit on the number of newly issued shares that the subsidiary can sell, since the parent's post-sale interest must be over 80% to remain tax-free. Executed properly, the divesting company will retain the flexibility to use a tax-free spinoff to divest its remaining stake in the carved-out business at a later date. Given these advantages, most equity carveouts are structured this way (in at least 70% of cases, by one estimate[4]) and many of them are followed by spinoffs.

The tax and cash benefits of this transactional sequence were articulated as two of the main advantages of Eli Lilly's decision to sell an equity carveout of Elanco (its animal health business) in 2018, before divesting its remaining 80.2% stake in that subsidiary through a tax-free split-off (as previously discussed, a type of spinoff for tax purposes) in the form of an exchange offer in 2019. With the proceeds of that public offering, Elanco upstreamed $1.7 billion of net proceeds to Eli Lilly, together with cash from other sources.[5] The decision to structure the divestiture of Elanco as an equity carveout followed by a tax-free exchange, rather than as an outright sale, likely saved Eli Lilly close to $2 billion in taxes, by some estimates: "Lilly received a substantial cash distribution in connection with the IPO and related financings, and could have received even more cash had they just sold Elanco rather than distributed it, but Lilly would likely have had a significant taxable gain. . . . Compared with that option, [the equity carveout] was obviously superior due to the absence of tax leakage."[6]

The beauty of Eli Lilly's equity carveout is that it was Elanco (*the subsidiary*) that sold newly issued shares. However, if *the divesting company* had sold subsidiary shares from its portfolio, then that sale would have been taxable to the divesting company. Baxter Laboratories' 2015 and 2016 transactions to divest Baxalta, its global biopharmaceuticals business, illustrate the reverse of Eli Lilly's transactional sequence. Baxter's tax-free spinoff of an 80.5% stake in Baxalta was followed a year later by a series of taxable transactions in which Baxter sold its remaining 19.5% stake, generating $5.15 billion in gross proceeds that Baxter used to retire debt, contribute to its pension plan, and accumulate treasury stock.[7]

Separate Valuation

The existence of a public market for the shares that are sold in an equity carveout can be beneficial to the divesting company. The sale of those shares results in the separate valuation of the carved-out business (the performance or growth prospects of which might otherwise be obscured), leading to clearer and more accurate valuations of both the divesting company and the carved-out business. This is especially true in situations where an old-line company has a dynamic subsidiary that would trade at a higher earnings multiple as an independent company. The presumably higher multiple accorded to the carved-out business would be reflected in the price of the divesting company's shares, particularly if investors assumed that a subsequent spinoff was imminent. Accordingly, companies regularly carve out businesses that operate in industries with better growth prospects than those of their remaining operations: the average annual revenue growth of carved-out businesses is about 13% over the first two years after these transactions, compared with a growth rate of around 5% for those companies' remaining businesses.[8] Similarly, carved-out businesses have significantly higher operating metrics than their former parents, belong to industries that had positive excess returns during the prior year, and are comprised of assets that are valued highly relative to their book values.[9] The fact that the divesting company continues to own a stake in the carved-out business gives it the opportunity to participate in the upside of its remaining investment.

In 2007, for example, EMC caused VMware (the virtualization software maker it had acquired just a few years prior for $625 million) to sell a 10% equity carveout to public investors for about $1 billion. About half of these proceeds were upstreamed tax-free to EMC as a repayment of intercompany debt and as a payment for VMware's purchase of its headquarters from EMC. More important, trading in the public market unlocked VMware's intrinsic value, which was not previously reflected in EMC's share price. "Calling attention to VMware as a hidden jewel is precisely what EMC was hoping to accomplish. . . . Our contention has been for some time that once people homed in on VMware, they'd see that EMC is undervalued."[10] From a financial standpoint, the carveout "tapped the high market value for virtualization software. . . . VMware's revenue growth topped 90 percent each quarter last year, compared with 20 percent for EMC."[11*] Having separately traded shares gave VMware a stronger currency with which to make acquisitions and to incentivize managers, employees, and especially engineering talent in the hypercompetitive Silicon Valley environment. This also accrued to the benefit of EMC, which was sold to Dell in 2016 (following which Dell succeeded to EMC's ownership of VMware until it finally spun off VMware in 2021).[†]

Fiat Chrysler's equity carveout of Ferrari in 2015 is another example of the valuation-related advantages of this divestiture structure. Ferrari was viewed as "a bit of an odd fit" in the Fiat Chrysler portfolio, given that it targeted a different customer segment than the rest of Fiat Chrysler's brands and there was limited cross-selling between them.[12] As a result, CEO Sergio Marchionne expressed concern that Ferrari's true valuation was hidden in Fiat Chrysler, and that Ferrari itself "was worth 'at least' €10bn—more than half the parent company's market capitalization of $20bn. . . . [He] also said the company should be judged as a maker of luxury goods, which trade on much higher stock market multiples than carmakers."[13] To unlock and monetize some of Ferrari's true value, Fiat

---

* Similarly, seeking to "spark investor enthusiasm in its own shares and capitalize on growing demand for automated driving," Intel announced in March 2022 that it would sell an equity carveout in Mobileye (its self-driving car unit), retaining a majority share in that entity. Intel bought Mobileye in 2017 for about $15 billion, but commentators predicted that "the unit could fetch a valuation of over $50 billion" thanks to its double-digit revenue growth and the strong demand for its technology.

Source: Kellaher, Colin. 2022. "Intel Files to Take Self-Driving Unit Mobileye Public." *Wall Street Journal*, March 7, 2022. https://www.wsj.com/articles/intel-files-to-take-self-driving -unit-mobileye-public-11646669536.

† Dell's acquisition of EMC was interesting in and of itself, in that the parent company of Dell and EMC (Denali) issued a tracking stock in VMware and used it to finance Dell's acquisition of EMC. See Chapter 8 for more detail on tracking stocks.

Chrysler used an equity carveout to sell a 10% stake in Ferrari, part of Mr. Marchionne's plan "to bring down its €8.6bn of net debt while funding an ambitious €48bn investment plan"[14] designed to increase sales and establish global distribution networks for Fiat Chrysler's remaining brands.[15*] Fiat Chrysler divested its remaining stake in Ferrari in a tax-free spinoff just a few months after the equity carveout.

The flipside of these points is that carving out a subsidiary can reveal that the divesting company's remaining operations are *overvalued* in the stock market, the opposite of EMC's (and Dell's) experience with VMware. Supporting this observation, companies that undertake equity carveouts in fact *underperform* comparable companies in their own industries by 9% to 12% over the 36 months after these transactions, while the carved-out businesses *outperform* their peers by up to 29% over the same interval.[16] At times, the underperformance of companies that undertake equity carveouts can be driven by excessive investor sentiment rather than economic fundamentals. In one extreme example, investors imputed a *negative $22 billion* valuation to 3Com after its equity carveout of Palm, even though 3Com's remaining computer network systems and services businesses were still profitable and the company held a large cash position on its balance sheet.[17]

Post-Transaction Conflicts

Equity carveouts carry the very real potential for conflicts to emerge during the period in which the divesting company retains control of the carved-out business. While the carved-out business has its own management team and board of directors that are responsible for running it in such a way as to maximize value for its shareholders, the divesting company will remain its largest shareholder by far. However, decisions that maximize value for the minority shareholders of the carved-out business may or may not maximize value for the divesting company. This can create

---

* Similarly, in September 2022, Volkswagen announced the sale of an equity carveout in luxury carmaker Porsche. The resulting proceeds of this complicated transaction, which was designed in part to preserve control of Porsche by its family heirs, would be used to help Volkswagen "bankroll its transition to electric vehicles and self-driving cars" and to fund a "special dividend."

Source: Boston, William. 2002. "Volkswagen to List Porsche in One of Biggest IPOs in Years." *Wall Street Journal*, September 6, 2022. https://www.wsj.com/articles/volkswagen-to -list-porsche-in-one-of-biggest-ipos-in-years-11662413312.

"friction" and "divided loyalties" between the management and boards of directors of these entities, which can "complicate the [lives] of the parent and the carved-out company."[18]

Because equity carveouts are most often used before or after spinoffs, any conflicts that arise between a divesting company and its carved-out subsidiary are largely transient, manifesting themselves only during the interregnum between the equity carveout and the spinoff. The potential for conflicts during this interim period explains why, when companies use equity carveouts in sequence with spinoffs, the time between these two transactions is usually short.

REVERSE MORRIS TRUSTS

Just as equity carveouts enable companies to generate cash from the sale of carved-out shares without compromising their ability to do tax-free spinoffs, Reverse Morris Trusts allow companies to use mergers in combination with spinoffs without compromising the tax-free nature of those spinoffs. As depicted in Exhibit 7.7, in a Reverse Morris Trust, a parent company spins off one of its businesses. This newly independent spinoff company immediately merges with a target company, which is tax-free under Section 368 of the Internal Revenue Code *if the spinoff company is considered the buyer of the target company*—that is, if the shareholders of the historic parent company own more than 50% of the merged entity. This description makes clear that Reverse Morris Trusts provide a structural means of meeting the requirement that a maximum of just under 50% of the merged spinoff-target company may be transferred without compromising the tax-free nature of that transaction.

EXHIBIT 7.7

Depiction of Reverse Morris Trust

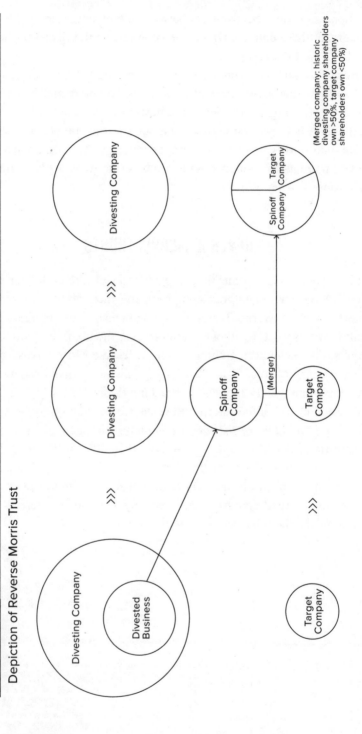

EXHIBIT 7.8

Disclosed Volume and Value of Reverse Morris Trusts, 1998–2021[22]

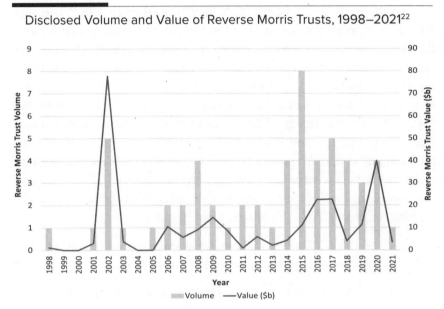

Reverse Morris Trusts first began to be used in 1998, as illustrated in Exhibit 7.8, due to legislative changes that took effect the year before. The name "Reverse Morris Trust" would seem to imply the existence of "regular" or "forward" Morris Trusts. In fact, it does. By way of history, in a Morris Trust, a parent company spins off one of its businesses tax-free to its shareholders. The remainder of the *parent company* then merges with a target company, which is treated as tax-free if parent company shareholders own more than 50% of the merged entity.* However, these transactions came to be perceived as a "device" for a parent company

---

* The name "Morris Trust" originates from a transaction in which American Commercial Bank spun off its insurance business into an independent company and then merged its remaining banking operations with Commercial National Bank of Charlotte. While the shareholders of American Commercial Bank were taxed on the shares of the insurance company they received in the spinoff, the Mary Archer W. Morris Trust resisted the tax bill. The U.S. Court of Appeals for the Fourth Circuit ruled against the IRS in 1966, finding that the Morris Trust and other shareholders had "realized no recognizable taxable gain" in becoming shareholders of the spun off insurance company. This gave rise to "regular" Morris Trusts.

Source: "Commissioner of Internal Revenue, Petitioner, v. Mary Archer W. Morris Trust, North Carolina National Bank, Trustee, Respondent, 367 F.2d 794 (4th Cir. 1966)." https://law .justia.com/cases/federal/appellate-courts/F2/367/794/428100/.

to transfer unwanted businesses to shareholders in a tax-free fashion to facilitate the subsequent merger of its own, wanted businesses.[19] This was viewed as especially problematic when the parent company would cause the unwanted business it was spinning off to take on debt, but retain the proceeds for its own use. As a result, legislation was passed in 1997 treating Morris Trusts for tax purposes as "sales" (which made them taxable), and Morris Trusts ceased to be used that year.[20] After Morris Trusts disappeared, however, Reverse Morris Trusts filled the transactional void.[21] Rather than being regarded as a device to transfer unwanted businesses to shareholders without paying taxes, Reverse Morris Trusts came to be viewed as having a corporate business purpose, since it was the business that was being spun off that subsequently merged with another company.

Reverse Morris Trusts have two unique features:

1. Reverse Morris Trusts permit companies to use tax-free spinoffs in combination with mergers under certain circumstances.

2. Reverse Morris Trusts can create synergies between the spinoff and target companies that merge in these transactions.

Combining Spinoffs and Mergers

Reverse Morris Trusts permit companies to use spinoffs in combination with mergers without compromising the tax-free nature of those spinoffs. Relative to sales and "regular" spinoffs, these benefits are unique to Reverse Morris Trusts: "Outright sales are one option, but the cash received can be subject to heavy taxes. Spinning off a business . . . is another, but IRS regulations can prevent the new company from engaging in M&A transactions for a certain amount of time. . . . Reverse Morris Trusts are an elegant, if complicated, solution. [They combine] the best of both worlds. [They get] the unwanted asset out of the [parent company] tax-free, and shareholders get all the benefit and upside of a prearranged M&A combination."[23]

At the same time, however, because Reverse Morris Trusts require the shareholders of the historic parent company to own more than 50% of the combined entity, the parent company must identify a suitable marriage partner for its child. In that regard, the target company must be less valuable than the spinoff company, and amenable to participate in a complicated transaction. "Finding the right merger partner is tricky: Ideally counterparts are slightly smaller than [the spinoff company] and have to be comfortable giving up control. The stars have to align, but it's very powerful when you can pull it off."[24] Among the Reverse Morris Trusts depicted in Exhibit 7.8, historic parent company shareholders owned a median of 55% of the shares in the merged entities that resulted from these transactions, and the modal value of their ownership was 50.1%.[25]

Reverse Morris Trusts are not devices employed by shady Wall Street operators. Procter & Gamble's (P&G) use of a Reverse Morris Trust* to divest 43 of its beauty brands to Coty nicely illustrates the acceptability of this structure by America's corporate elite.† In that transaction, P&G split off its beauty brands into a new company called Galleria, which simultaneously merged into Coty, with P&G interests accounting for 52% of the merged company relative to Coty's 48%. By one estimate, P&G saved $2 to $4 billion in taxes by using a Reverse Morris Trust, compared to what it would have owed in a sale.[26] Another commentator noted that the $11.4 billion price at which the Coty deal was initially struck fell $1.1 billion short of the $12.5 billion value P&G placed on the 43 beauty brands when the deal was first announced. As one equity analyst pointed out, "If [P&G] were selling [the beauty brands] for cash, it would be another story. They probably saved far more in taxes than the billion-dollar swing amounts to."[27]

The division of ownership between parent and target company shareholders can raise questions over the composition of the management team and board of directors of the combined entity. On the one hand, shareholders of the historic parent company must account for a majority stake

---

* P&G is in fact one of the most active users of Reverse Morris Trusts, having used these transactions to divest its beauty brands to Coty, and both Jif peanut butter and Folgers coffee to The J.M. Smucker Company.

† One novel use of Reverse Morris Trusts is for companies to spin off and merge businesses with special purpose acquisition companies (SPACs). In March 2022, Ligand Pharmaceuticals announced that it would use a Reverse Morris Trust to spin off and merge OmniAb, Inc. (its antibody discovery business) into Avista Public Acquisition Corp. II (a SPAC). According to noted tax expert Robert Willens, "A fertile source for SPAC acquisitions would appear to be unwanted divisions of public corporations. . . . Instead of shedding these divisions via a conventional sale, the public company could engage in a Reverse Morris Trust transaction. . . . We've never had one where the other party to the transaction was a SPAC."

Source: Root, Al, and Luisa Beltran. 2022. "A New SPAC Deal Is a Fresh Idea for the M&A Industry." *Barron's*, March 24, 2022. https://www.barrons.com/articles/spac-acquisitions -stock-51648137117.

in the combined entity for the transaction to be tax-free, which can create an expectation that executives and directors originating from the parent company will account for the majority, if not all, of the combined entity's management team and board of directors.[*] On the other hand, however, the target company is technically the buyer in a Reverse Morris Trust, which can equally create an expectation that its executives and directors will lead the combined entity.[†] More complicated still, in situations where parent and target company shareholders each account for approximately equal shares in the combined entity, the parties may seek to divide their governance structure roughly equally.[‡]

Synergy Potential

Because the participants in the mergers that are part of Reverse Morris Trusts are often synergistic companies, their combination has the potential to be valuable, and the parent company's shareholders could benefit from those synergies. Accordingly, Reverse Morris Trusts should create more value for shareholders than "regular" spinoffs due to the synergistic benefits of combining complementary entities.

---

[*] For instance, H.J. Heinz used a Reverse Morris Trust to combine several of its slower-growing brands with Del Monte Foods. Because Heinz shareholders owned about 75% of the shares in the new Del Monte, it was decided that Heinz would nominate six directors to the new company's board, compared to the old Del Monte's three directors.

Source: Eig, Jonathan, and Robert Frank. 2002. "Heinz to Spin Off Several Units into a Reorganized Del Monte." *Wall Street Journal*, June 14, 2002. https://www.wsj.com/articles /SB1023972164654522120.

[†] For example, when Weyerhaeuser combined its homebuilding business with TRI Pointe Homes using a Reverse Morris Trust, most of the executive team of TRI Pointe Homes continued in their positions, and TRI Pointe Homes nominated five directors to the combined entity's board relative to Weyerhaeuser's four nominees.

Source: Weyerhaeuser Company. 2013. "Weyerhaeuser to Combine Its Homebuilding and Real Estate Development Business, WRECO, With Tri Pointe Homes." November 4, 2013. http:// investor.weyerhaeuser.com/2013-11-04-Weyerhaeuser-To-Combine-Its-Homebuilding-And -Real-Estate-Development-Business-WRECO-With-Tri-Pointe-Homes.

[‡] For example, Hewlett Packard Enterprise (HPE) used a Reverse Morris Trust to combine its enterprise services operations with Computer Sciences Corporation (CSC). Reflecting HPE's and CSC's nearly identical stakes (50.1%–49.9%), the combined entity was renamed DXC Technology, and its board of directors was split 50–50 between directors from HPE and CSC.

Source: Clark, Don, and Tess Stynes. 2016. "HP Enterprise to Spin Off, Merge Services Business." *Wall Street Journal*, May 24, 2016. https://www.wsj.com/articles/hp-enterprise-to-spin -off-merge-services-business-1464121433.

In 2015, for instance, Dow Chemical used a Reverse Morris Trust to merge its chlor-alkali business into Olin Corporation. The two companies projected a minimum of $200 million in annual synergies and cost savings, with revenue synergies from "the combination of complementary businesses, significant scale, integration, cost-advantaged feedstocks, and a broad and diverse end-uses portfolio," as well as cost savings from "network optimization which will facilitate output expansion, significant logistics savings and benefits, and the potential for expansion of existing products produced by Olin and Dow into additional geographies and to additional customers."[28] Both Dow and Olin shareholders were expected to share in the upside of the deal, since Dow's shareholders owned a 50.5% stake and Olin's shareholders a 49.5% stake in the combined entity.[29]

In AT&T's 2021 Reverse Morris Trust of its WarnerMedia assets with Discovery, synergies were projected to result from the union of "complementary and diverse content strengths with broad appeal—WarnerMedia's robust studios and portfolio of iconic scripted entertainment, animation, news, and sports, with Discovery's commanding position in unscripted and international entertainment and sports," as well as the ability to "accelerate both companies' plans for leading direct-to-consumer (DTC) streaming services for global consumers."[30] As in the Dow–Olin example, both AT&T and Discovery shareholders were expected to share in the upside of the merger, since AT&T's shareholders were expected to own 71% of the combined entity and Discovery's shareholders the remaining 29%.[31] This benefit was probably important to AT&T, since it was widely seen as having overpaid for its acquisition of Time Warner in 2018.[32] Accordingly, the ability to participate in the synergistic value created by the Reverse Morris Trust between WarnerMedia and Discovery may have assuaged the pain felt by AT&T's shareholders from its acquisition of Time Warner.

OTHER TECHNIQUES FOR VALUE APPROPRIATION

Equity carveouts and Reverse Morris Trusts enable companies to sidestep the adverse tax consequences that may result from transactions that occur *in sequence with* spinoffs. Additionally, there are several techniques that companies can use *in conjunction with* spinoffs to appropriate additional value from them.

Companies can cause the businesses they plan to spin off to upstream cash or indebtedness to them in the form of intercompany transfers, and companies can even cause these businesses to assume some portion of their preexisting liabilities. These types of intercompany transfers were discussed earlier in the context of equity carveouts, as in the EMC–VMware and Eli Lilly–Elanco examples. One study[33] established that subsidiaries assume debt from their former parents in 60% of spinoffs, pay a dividend to them in 35% of spinoffs, and repay intercompany debt in 21% of spinoffs.* For example, TimkenSteel borrowed $300 million under a credit facility, from which it paid a dividend of $50 million to Timken, its parent company. Prior to its spinoff from Sears Holdings, Lands' End used the proceeds of a $500 million term loan to pay a dividend to its parent company.[34] And in General Mills' spinoff of Darden Restaurants, General Mills transferred $54 million in long-term debt to Darden, and Darden repaid $350 million of intercompany indebtedness to General Mills using a $500 million revolving line of credit it had obtained.[35]

One might wonder how it can be permissible for companies to use intercompany transfers in their spinoffs. In fact, it is perfectly appropriate for companies to do this, because until the moment a spinoff is complete, the business that is being spun off remains part of the parent company's corporate household; value is simply being transferred from one pocket to another, with no net change to the overall value of the corporate parent. Nevertheless, it is unsurprising that *unreasonable* intercompany transfers can and most certainly do result in fraudulent conveyance litigation against the parent company. In these situations, the spinoff company's creditors would claim that intercompany transfers caused it to become insolvent by robbing it of cash or making it unable to pay its debts when due. While the merits of these claims vary from case to case, intercompany transfers (ideally supported by fairness opinions rendered by reputable institutions) are a standard way for companies to monetize their spinoffs.

There are various other ways that companies can appropriate value from their spinoffs. Spinoffs are a unique divestiture structure in the sense

---

* Because companies can do multiple of these in the same transactions, these categories are not mutually exclusive.

that they transform two formerly integrated entities into two separate companies. One consequence of this corporate partition is that the newly independent spinoff company may require the provision of interim services from its former parent. Such services could involve tax matters, cash management, records retention, and facilities leasing, and those services will not come cheap.

Another issue is post-partition control. Chapter 6 explained that there is a 50% limit on the amount of stock that may be acquired in a spinoff company, to preserve the tax-free nature of the spinoff. But once the spinoff is complete, the parent company can no longer dictate the spinoff company's activities. To protect itself from adverse tax consequences, the parent company might implement measures designed to prevent the change of control or the acquisition of the spinoff company. For example, in its spinoff of Resideo, Honeywell's tax matters agreement prohibited Resideo from entering into any "Proposed Acquisition Transaction" involving the acquisition of 40% or more of the equity interests of Resideo.[36] This provision assured that Honeywell (and recipients of the spun off shares) would retain the benefits of the spinoff by preventing Resideo—and predators of Resideo—from engaging in the prohibited accumulation of shares.

Similarly, when a parent company operates in an industry that might make it susceptible to litigation for environmental damages (e.g., chemicals), it might require the spinoff company to help pay for and/or indemnify it against future claims, again preemptively limiting potential value erosion. This situation also occurred in the Resideo spinoff, in which Honeywell caused Resideo to indemnify it from and reimburse it (to the tune of $35 million each quarter through the year 2043) for its liabilities from losses arising from environmental litigation.[37]

Finally, the relationship between the parent and spinoff companies does not necessarily terminate upon the completion of a spinoff, as the two formerly integrated entities might continue transacting with each other at arm's length after they separate. For example, the parent company might continue to supply inputs to the spinoff company, or the spinoff company might continue operating out of the parent company's facilities. Intercompany transfer pricing presents an interesting problem, in that artificially low intercompany pricing will usually switch to contractual pricing after a spinoff. At that point, intercompany transactions would be governed by contracts imposed on the spinoff company prior to its separation.

The spinoff company typically will not have much bargaining power vis-à-vis its former parent, forcing it to accept these prices at least through the life of the contract. This illustrates yet another way that parent companies might be able to appropriate value from their spinoffs, by building such opportunities directly into the agreements that govern them.

CHAPTER 8

Hybrid Divestiture Structures: Joint Ventures and Tracking Stocks

INTRODUCTION

This chapter considers the two final divestiture structures addressed in Part II: joint ventures and tracking stocks. In a joint venture, a divesting company combines one of its businesses with that of a synergistic counterparty. While each of the co-venturers receives an equity stake in the new entity, the divesting company reduces its stake over time, allowing it to exit from its former business. In a tracking stock, a company issues shares that are tied to the performance of one of its subsidiaries, essentially selling interests in that subsidiary's future earnings and liquidation value. This allows investors to trade shares in the tracking stock based on valuations that are separate from those of the company's other business units. However, the parent company continues to own the subsidiary to which the tracking stock is linked.

Joint ventures and tracking stocks are "hybrid" divestiture structures because they enable companies to achieve some of the benefits of divestitures while maintaining an ongoing ownership stake in the underlying business unit. They also share the common characteristic of an average three- to five-year lifespan, in the one case deliberate, and in the other a function of the marketplace.

Both of these hybrid divestiture structures afford companies several benefits. Specifically, joint ventures allow companies to divest businesses that are not amenable to other divestiture structures, especially businesses that are underperforming, large, and often ill fitting. Since joint ventures typically unwind over a few years, they can be more attractive from tax and accounting perspectives than outright sales, in that they spread tax obligations and accounting losses over the life of the venture. Tracking stocks are a useful interim structure by which otherwise uncertain management can raise cash while deciding the ultimate fate of a business unit.

JOINT VENTURES

In its simplest form, a joint venture is a profit-making endeavor between two (or more) parties, to which each venturer contributes consideration such as assets or services. A joint venture could be structured as a corporation or a partnership, in which each venturer holds equity (think: Messrs. Hewlett and Packard). Many of the world's most prominent companies began their lives as joint ventures: Royal Dutch Shell, ARAMCO, Unilever, Eurotunnel, and Zurich Insurance come to mind. As these examples suggest, joint ventures were once common in extractive industries like petroleum and mining, and in binational combinations. In fact, they still are: Google the names of a few major oil companies with the expression "joint venture," and you will get a number of hits. Among the largest publicly traded joint ventures that still exist are Carnival Corporation & plc and Rio Tinto Group. While many of these entities once described themselves as "dual-listed companies" operating under "legal equalization agreements," their underlying operations were conducted through joint ventures. So, feel free to refer to them as dual-listed companies, but as the saying goes: *Call it a goose if you like, but if it looks like a duck and it quacks like a duck, then it's probably a duck.*

Among the many hallmarks of modern finance is its ability to adapt venerable structures to address current needs, and the joint venture was adapted to address the need for a certain kind of divestiture. Picture a company that made the decision to divest a business that could only be sold at a loss. Or picture another company that simply wanted to smooth the accounting or tax effects of a divestiture over time, rather than absorb them all in one reporting period or tax year. In situations such as these, joint ventures provide a structural solution by enabling companies to achieve *phased* exits from certain businesses, thereby spreading the tax and accounting effects of those divestitures over time. Using joint ventures as a divestiture structure may sound obscure, but they are regularly used by some of the biggest corporations in the United States and Europe for precisely this purpose. Appendix B provides a representative list of such transactions.

There are two forms that divesting joint ventures usually take. The first occurs when a divesting company contributes one of its business units to a joint venture with a counterparty that also contributes one of its own business units, as illustrated in Exhibit 8.1. Each party will receive an interest in the joint venture and potentially some other consideration. For example, General Electric (GE) and Vivendi Universal respectively contributed their NBC and Vivendi Universal Entertainment business units into the NBC Universal (NBCU) joint venture in 2004, with GE owning 80% of the joint venture and Vivendi owning the remaining 20%. Six years later, GE bought out Vivendi's stake in NBCU.

The second type of joint venture occurs when the divesting company merges one of its subsidiaries into another company in return for a portion of that company's shares, as depicted in Exhibit 8.2. While this is not technically a joint venture, it has come to be called one, probably because the divesting company will follow the template of selling its shares over time. For example, in 2017, GE merged its oil and gas services business into Baker Hughes, which was renamed "Baker Hughes, a GE Company" (BHGE). GE initially owned a 62.5% stake in BHGE (which, as of March 2022, GE was in the process of winding down), while Baker Hughes's preexisting shareholders owned the remaining 37.5%.* In 2021, GE created yet another joint venture in which it merged its aircraft leasing business, GE Capital Aviation Services (GECAS), into Ireland-based AerCap, following which GE owned a 46% stake in AerCap.

Both types of joint ventures exhibit three main characteristics:

1. Joint ventures spread the tax and accounting effects of sales over time.

2. Joint ventures can create synergies from the combination of complementary businesses.

3. Joint ventures require defined management and governance; think of them as second marriage households where stepsiblings share a room.

---

* This is an abbreviated description of the incredibly complicated joint venture between GE and Baker Hughes; for a fuller description, see: Baker Hughes Incorporated. 2017. "Notice of Special Meeting of Stockholders." May 30, 2017. https://www.sec.gov/Archives/edgar/data/808362/000119312517187240/d535234ddefm14a.htm.

EXHIBIT 8.1

Depiction of Joint Venture

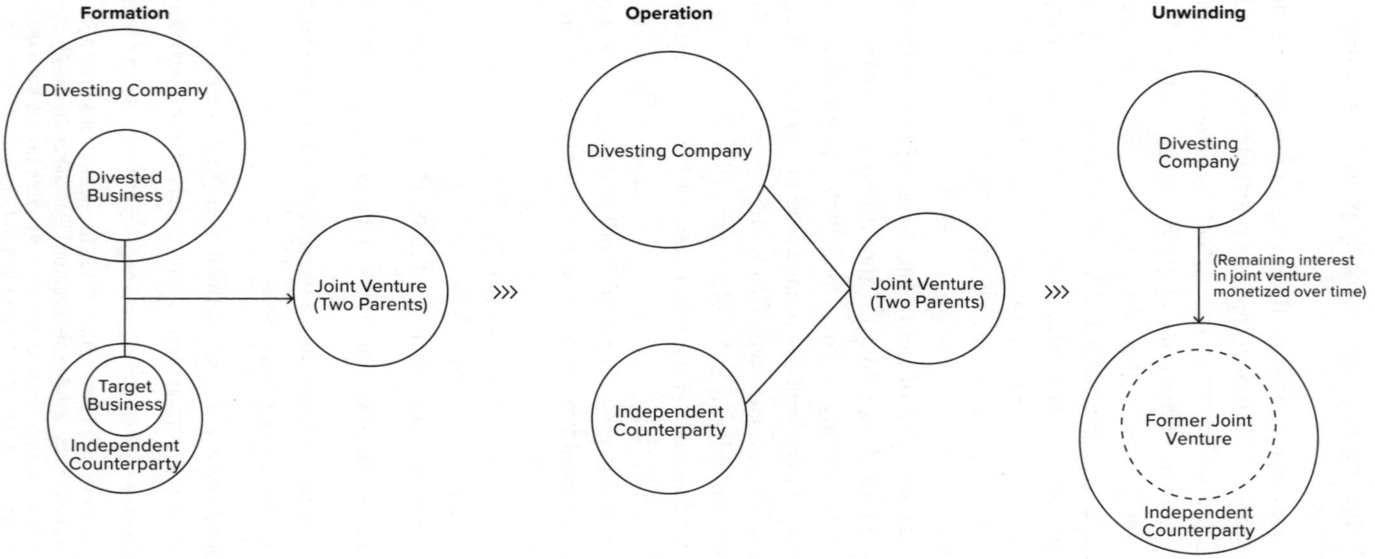

EXHIBIT 8.2

Simplified Depiction of Subsidiary Merger

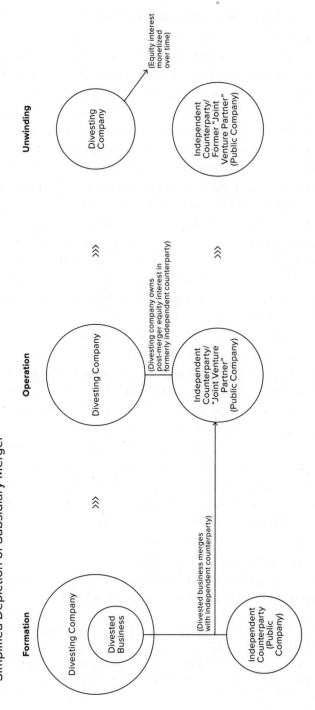

Formation

Divesting Company

Divested Business

Independent Counterparty (Public Company)

(Divested business merges with independent counterparty)

Operation

Divesting Company

Independent Counterparty/ "Joint Venture Partner" (Public Company)

(Divesting company owns post-merger equity interest in formerly independent counterparty)

Unwinding

Divesting Company

Independent Counterparty/ Former "Joint Venture Partner" (Public Company)

(Equity interest monetized over time)

Tax and Accounting Considerations

The attraction of a joint venture is best understood by comparing it to a sale. As described in Chapter 5, sales are taxable transactions in which the divesting company incurs taxes in the tax year in which it sells the business. In contrast, while the formation of a joint venture is usually not a taxable event, the subsequent transactions in which the divesting company reduces its ownership interest in the joint venture are taxable. In other words, the divesting company incurs taxes in each of the tax years in which it reduces its ownership interest in the joint venture.[*]

Consider the situation in which the tax basis of a large, underperforming subsidiary is negligible; perhaps it's an ancient company whose assets were depreciated to zero. For this company, a cash sale of its subsidiary at any price would be taxable. Here, the formation of a joint venture would spread the tax bill over time. Because the divesting company only sells partial stakes in its share of the joint venture at various defined times, it will only have to pay taxes on the gains resulting from each sale in the tax year in which that sale occurred.[†]

The NBCU example usefully illustrates why this is the case. To divest the property, GE first had to acquire 100% control of NBCU from Vivendi. After doing so, GE combined NBCU with $7.25 billion of Comcast's media assets in return for a 49% stake in a new joint venture (renamed NBCUniversal) and $6.5 billion in consideration, while Comcast received ownership of the remaining 51%.[1] The deal included provisions for GE to sell stakes in NBCUniversal to Comcast at "specified times" over a seven-year period, and at a 20% premium to market value.[2] Analysts speculated that an outright sale of its stake in NBCUniversal would have had "huge tax implications for GE, which first bought NBC in 1986 for $6.5 billion."[3] This suggests that GE's low tax basis in NBC carried over to the joint venture with Comcast, and that it was substantially below the $30 to $35 billion value of its share at the time. Assuming a 35% tax rate on the $23.5 to $28.5 billion gain implied by this valuation range suggests that GE would have paid $8 to $10 billion in immediate taxes had it sold its

---

* As to this point, the reader is urged to consult tax counsel when undertaking one of these transactions.

† The converse is true for financial reporting: a combination of a high accounting cost and a low resale value makes a joint venture an ideal way to smooth out the accounting losses on a bad investment over time.

stake in NBCUniversal outright. By comparison, in an earnings confer-ence call, then CEO Jeff Immelt alluded to the tax advantages of using a joint venture rather than a sale to divest GE's stake in NBCUniversal: "We don't anticipate paying any cash taxes at closing. But sometime between closing and the ultimate exit, whether it's at the end of seven years or longer, we'll probably have around $3 billion of cash taxes that we would pay associated with this transaction. It's probably over the next seven to 10 years."[4]

Synergies

In theory, participating in a joint venture allows the divesting company to share in the upside of the combination. However, to be practical, the use of a joint venture as a three-to-five-year divestiture mechanism may not yield much upside over that period. And even then, it will depend on several factors, not the least of which is the quality of the contributed operations. That said, the potential for a joint venture to create value can be significant if it is comprised of two high-quality entities. Synergies may result from complementary capabilities, products, and customers; econo-mies of scale; better bargaining power; and the consolidation of overhead and back-office functions. For example, as part of a broader restructuring, Novartis contributed its over-the-counter (OTC) business to a joint venture with GlaxoSmithKline's (GSK) consumer healthcare business, retaining a 36.5% stake in the combined entity. The two companies shared capabili-ties and expertise in their complementary product and geographic markets over the life of the joint venture, driving a 670-basis-point improve-ment in operating margins and a compound annual sales growth rate of 4%.[5]

Similarly, the joint venture between GE Capital Aviation Services (GECAS) and AerCap offered significant synergistic potential thanks to GECAS and AerCap's "complementary portfolios [of] aircraft, engines, and helicopters" and the combined company's "100 years of experience in the market and a pool of expert talent and leadership . . . broader revenue base, customer diversification, and strong balance sheet."[6] Poor conditions due to the industry cycle and the COVID-19 pandemic would have pre-vented GE from realizing much, if any, of this synergistic value had it tried to sell GECAS. However, the joint venture would enable GE to realize some of that value. As CEO Larry Culp put it, "As the industry recovers, *that equity stake that we have in the combined business undoubtedly will be worth more than it is today.* We would have never sold GECAS for cash at this point in the cycle. Fortunately, that's really not what we're doing today. *We're putting [GECAS] together with an important partner, creating, I think, more value for the GE shareholder over time.*"[7]

Management and Governance

Joint ventures require careful management and governance, requiring the divesting company and its counterparty to define their roles and responsibilities and to articulate a clear timeline over which the divesting company will exit the partnership. Given that the ultimate intention of a joint venture is to enable the counterparty to take over and run the operations of the divested business, albeit in a phased fashion, it most often makes sense for the counterparty's management to lead the joint venture. At the same time, the divesting company often has valuable knowledge of and capabilities in that business to share with the counterparty, so it equally makes sense to create opportunities for the divesting company to do this. Since joint ventures are transitory divestiture structures, it also behooves the divesting company and the counterparty to plan for their termination. While none of these tasks are insurmountable, the failure to define roles clearly or to plan for the end of the joint venture can result in value-destroying conflicts between the divesting company and its counterparty.

GE's ill-fated joint venture between its oil and gas services division and Baker Hughes provides a useful illustration of some of the problems that can result from joint ventures with poorly defined governance structures. As mentioned previously, in this joint venture, GE merged its oil and gas services business into Baker Hughes, resulting in the creation of "Baker Hughes, a GE Company" (BHGE). To avoid tainting its newly liberated subsidiary with the appearance of being damaged goods, GE reassured Wall Street with the announcement that "it is still committed to the oil and gas unit for the long term."[8] Moreover, as part of the deal, GE signed a lock-up provision that prevented it from selling its stake in the joint venture for two years.[9]

What could go wrong? Well, the relationship quickly deteriorated amid "slipping market share, management missteps and culture clashes that have unsettled employees and frustrated suppliers and customers."[10] By way of illustration, "Baker Hughes GE lost market share in 12 of 19 services and equipment sectors between 2016 and 2017. . . . Since the merger, suppliers have chafed under strict cost-cutting demands, and some customers shifted to competitors after abrupt service-fee increases and contract changes. . . . The choppy transition also has driven out veteran Baker Hughes managers in key departments and rattled staff. . . . More than 50 resumes from Baker Hughes employees have landed with one professional recruiter since last summer, according to a headhunter there."[11]

Less than a year after the formation of the joint venture, GE announced its intention to exit the BHGE joint venture over the next few years,[12] initially reducing its ownership stake to 50.2% and giving up four of its five seats on the BHGE board.[13] As part of this transition, Baker Hughes and GE agreed to release GE from the lock-up provision that prevented it from selling its stake in BHGE until July 2019.[14] BHGE also undertook a significant rebranding initiative, in which it changed the company's official name from "Baker Hughes, a GE Company" to "Baker Hughes Co.," switched its ticker symbol from "BHGE" to "BKR," and changed its corporate logo by dropping the GE icon and switching the color scheme from GE's blue to dark green.[15]

TRACKING STOCKS

A tracking stock is a security created by a company that is linked to the performance of one of its businesses (the tracked business). As an issuance of securities, the sale of tracking shares is a tax-free transaction that produces upfront cash for the divesting (parent) company. The parent company still owns the underlying tracked business, and there is not necessarily a change in the structure or operations of the parent company itself (see Exhibit 8.3).

A century ago, the instruments that we now know as tracking stocks were called "participating preferred stocks." However, they gradually fell into disuse until General Motors (GM) revived them under their present name in 1984–1985, when it sold two series of shares that respectively tracked the performance of the recently acquired Electronic Data Systems (EDS) and Hughes Aerospace. GM was motivated to raise money both to conduct its underlying operations and to fund its massive legacy

EXHIBIT 8.3

Depiction of Tracking Stock

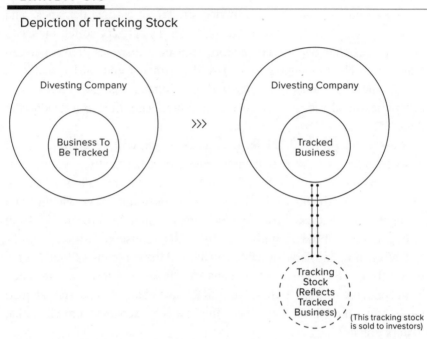

liabilities.* Since the mid-1980s, tracking stocks have occasionally been employed as instruments designed to sell specified future earnings and liquidation value to investors. As depicted in Exhibit 8.4, which shows the disclosed yearly number of tracking stocks issued from 1984 to 2021, the issuance of tracking stocks has tailed off since its peak during the dot-com bubble in the late 1990s.

Why is this the case? Because its income, dividends, and liquidating value are linked to a defined pool of operations, the tracked business can be valued differently from the rest of the parent company's operations. At the same time, the parent company's management and board of directors are still responsible for operating the tracked business, and the parent company's shareholders still have an interest in the tracked business, albeit an indirect interest. This sets up the potential for conflicts when

---

* In those days, Wall Street types referred to GM as an HMO with automobile showrooms.

Source: Sit, Harry. 2008. "Book Review: While America Aged." *The Finance Buff*, June 16, 2008. https://thefinancebuff.com/book-review-while-america-aged.html.

EXHIBIT 8.4

Disclosed Volume of Tracking Stock Issuances, 1984–2021[16]

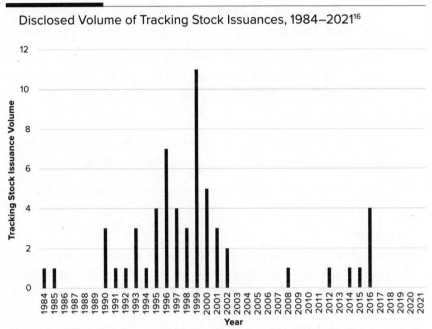

the interests of the shareholders of the tracked business diverge from the interests of the shareholders of the parent company. Together, these considerations put an important question into sharp relief: When it comes to tracking stocks, is the juice worth the squeeze? In other words, given that tracking stocks do not actually separate the tracked business from the parent company's remaining operations, are the potential inefficiencies and conflicts of this divestiture structure worth it? Many investors, analysts, and media commentators think not, and many companies that initially used tracking stocks later retired them or transitioned to other divestiture structures instead.* This explains why tracking stocks have dwindled away as a divestiture structure.

Consistent with this discussion, there are two major trade-offs as well as two significant disadvantages associated with tracking stocks:

---

* For example, GM retired its tracking stocks for EDS and Hughes Aerospace; USX eventually split Marathon Oil from U.S. Steel; and Dell retired its tracking stock for VMware (which had primarily been created as a vehicle to finance Dell's takeover of EMC) during its transition into a public company in 2018.

1. Although tracking stocks facilitate the separate valuation of tracked businesses, companies that issue tracking stocks are often discounted in the stock market.

2. While tracking stocks allow companies to maintain synergies between their tracked businesses and their remaining operations, this can promote inefficient resource allocation and cross-subsidization decisions.

3. Tracking stocks carry a significant potential for conflicts between the shareholders of parent companies and tracked businesses.

4. Problems at parent companies could affect the business units that form the basis of tracking stocks.

Valuation

The main reason why a company might choose to issue a tracking stock is to facilitate the separate valuation of one of its businesses whose value might otherwise be obscured in a larger corporate structure. For example, AT&T explained that its decision to issue a tracking stock in its wireless business in early 2000 was driven by the need to "increase market awareness of the performance and value of our wireless businesses by creating a direct investment vehicle. We expect this will provide greater market recognition and realization of the value individually and collectively, of AT&T and its distinct lines of business represented by each of the AT&T Wireless Group and the AT&T Common Stock Group. . . ."[17] Shortly after AT&T issued the tracking stock for AT&T Wireless, John Malone (the former CEO of Tele-Communications Inc., which AT&T had recently purchased), encouraged AT&T to create additional tracking stocks to facilitate separate valuations of its cable and internet businesses: "You can't sell apples, peaches and bananas together. And right now, AT&T is fruit salad."[18]

This example illustrates that tracking stocks are generally used by companies that are undervalued in the stock market and/or that have businesses whose performance and growth prospects differ substantially from those of the rest of their operations. Tracking stocks can resolve these matters by allowing investors to trade in separate shares representing the tracked business, particularly if those shares attain a separate analyst following. For example, within a few weeks of USX issuing tracking stocks for its U.S. Steel and Marathon Oil businesses, "Marathon had attracted an additional 29 equity analysts to follow it, most of them in the oil sector. Since issuing the separate tracking stocks, both the steel and oil and gas businesses have traded in line with their peers."[19]

Assuming the parent company approves, the tracked business could even use its tracking stock to provide market-based incentives to its managers. For example, Loews pointed to the ability of its tracking stock, Carolina Group (which contained Loews's interest in its tobacco business, Lorillard), to help with the hiring and retention of employees in the stigmatized tobacco industry: "Loews revealed a key reason why it wants to set up the tracking stock: as a recruitment tool . . . Lorillard is currently experiencing difficulty in identifying and hiring qualified personnel in some areas of its business. This difficulty is primarily attributable to the health and social issues associated with the tobacco industry."[20]

Although a main intention of tracking stocks is to improve market valuations, they unfortunately often have the opposite effect: companies that issue tracking stocks frequently trade at a discount in the stock market. There are various reasons why this occurs. One is that tracking stocks can emphasize the weakness of a parent company's untracked businesses by specifically highlighting the strength of the tracked business.* For instance, while tracking stocks representing telecommunications companies' wireless businesses rose 300% to 400% between 1999 and 2002, AT&T's stock price, which reflected the performance and growth prospects of its traditional wireline business, only rose 5% over the same period.[21]

Another reason why companies that issue tracking stocks trade at a discount is that investors may fear that the tracking stock structure will enable executives to cross-subsidize poorly performing businesses, especially when liabilities burden one of those businesses. For example, Pittston created tracking stocks to assign separate valuations to its three businesses: its faster-growing home security and armored car (Brink's) and transportation and freight (BAX Global) businesses, and its coal and minerals (Pittston Minerals) business, which was impaired by the decline of the coal industry and owed significant medical liabilities to retirees. Under the tracking stock structure, Pittston's overall market capitalization was deeply undervalued, which CEO Michael Dan attributed to the

---

* It should be obvious that the alternative of a sale or a spinoff of a valuable subsidiary would make this problem even worse by leaving the weakness of the divesting company's remaining operations exposed for the world to see.

fact that "the coal business and its liabilities have 'cast a shadow' on the other two businesses . . . as investors worry about the cash flow of Brink's and BAX being used to pay the coal liability."[22] In response to this stock market discount, Pittston eliminated its tracking stock structure and sold Pittston Minerals, freeing Brink's and BAX Global from the overhang of the coal business.[23]

Yet a third reason why companies that use tracking stocks often trade at a discount is that tracking stocks are not recognized for inclusion in the major stock market indices, leading to investor turnover when companies issue them. For instance, after Fidelity National Financial (FNF) issued its Fidelity National Financial Ventures (FNFV) tracking stock, FNF was removed from the S&P MidCap index. This forced index funds that replicated the performance of the S&P MidCap index to sell their shares in FNF, resulting in a dramatic decline in FNF's market value.[24] Two years later, FNF announced that it would exchange all FNFV tracking shares for FNFV common shares, separating FNFV into an independent public company. Explained FNF chairman William P. Foley II, "It has become clear that the complexity of our existing corporate structure is holding back FNF's share price in general, and the value of our industry-leading title business in particular . . . the distribution of FNFV to FNFV shareholders enables FNF to revert back to a pure-play, title-only common stock, making FNF index-eligible again and potentially significantly widening the demand for FNF common stock."[25]

Finally, a subsidiary that presents itself to the financial community may appear to be qualitatively different than its peers. One of the criticisms of the USX tracking stock for its oil and gas subsidiary was that it was unlike its competitors, since it could not use the tracking stock as a currency with which to make acquisitions.[26]

Synergies

Although a tracking stock trades and is valued separately from the rest of the parent company, that company still owns and manages the tracked business. This allows the parent company to benefit from financial and operating synergies between its tracked and untracked businesses.

From a financial standpoint, cash proceeds from the issuance of a tracking stock can be used to cross-subsidize other businesses in the parent company.* When Loews issued its Carolina Group tracking stock early in 2002, for example, "Loews' largest holding, its CNA Financial Corp. insurance unit, likely turned in its third consecutive quarterly loss in the final three months of 2001. CNA, which absorbed more than $300 million in claims from the Sept. 11 terrorist attacks, is also facing lawsuits over asbestos claims. . . . Selling Carolina tracking stock [gave] Loews needed cash."[27] Similarly, Liberty Media's tracking stocks permitted it to transfer cash between its subsidiaries when circumstances demanded it. When the COVID-19 pandemic shut down auto racing, Liberty Media transferred a 33% stake in Live Nation from Formula One to Liberty SiriusXM, in order "to give Formula One more financial breathing room . . . while shoring up its balance sheet with more than $1 billion in cash."[28]

Relatedly, tracked businesses can benefit from the stronger credit ratings of their parent companies. For instance, USX explained that its decision to issue tracking stocks for U.S. Steel and Marathon Oil enabled each of those privately owned subsidiary companies to trade publicly "on the basis of the performance of its respective business but [to retain] the overall benefits of a consolidated corporation from a credit standpoint."[29] Indeed, one of the main reasons why USX initially chose to create tracking stocks for rather than spin off U.S. Steel and Marathon Oil is that the USX board believed that spinoffs would weaken the credit ratings of the companies: "It was questionable whether or not steel could have been structured as a stand-alone, viable business with investment-grade credit—given the capital challenges facing it."[30]

From an operational perspective, moreover, tracking stocks permit parent companies to continue to share overhead expenses and potentially even operating synergies among its businesses. For instance, in 1999, Applera issued tracking stocks in its two subsidiaries, Applied Biosystems and Celera Genomics. While the tracking stocks of each of these subsidiaries traded separately on stock exchanges,[31] the two entities shared corporate functions and intellectual property, and products were shifted between them as their strategies evolved. In 2002, for example, the human genome database that Celera had developed was transferred to Applied

---

* Moreover, the issuance of that tracking stock, unlike the issuance of the parent company's common stock, is not dilutive.

Biosystems, which had a more appropriate sales force for it.[32] Similarly, EDS and Hughes helped GM integrate their respective cutting-edge technologies into its automobiles,[33] even though their earnings and cash flows were contractually directed toward their tracking stocks.

This discussion illustrates how the existence of a subsidiary with a tracking stock does not disrupt the historical synergies between it and the untracked businesses, since the tracked business remains part of the corporate household. However, the "elasticity"[34] of tracking stocks can permit the parent corporation to use the resources of the tracked business to artificially boost the performance of its untracked businesses, often by forcing these entities to transact with one another.

The canonical example of this kind of behavior is Sprint, which issued a tracking stock to track the performance of its wireless division (PCS) separately from that of its traditional wireline business (FON) in the early 2000s. Although Sprint had incurred over $16 billion of debt for the PCS division, "that debt actually boosts FON's results, because [Sprint] allocates an interest rate to PCS based on the rate it says PCS would obtain without Sprint's guarantees. The company then counts the difference between the rate charged to PCS and Sprint's actual interest rate as nonoperating income for FON."[35] In terms of business relationships between the two divisions, PCS was "one of FON's biggest long-distance customers. Indeed, PCS is required to purchase its long-distance service from FON. In contrast to the rest of FON, where revenue has been declining, FON revenue from PCS has more than doubled since 1999."[36]

Potential for Conflicts

As Sprint's approach makes evident, a significant disadvantage associated with tracking stocks is the potential for conflicts they create between the parent company and the tracked business. Tracking stocks do not operationally separate the tracked business, meaning that the parent company's management and board of directors are still charged with overseeing it. Thus, in situations where the parent company's interests diverge from those of the tracked business, the management and board may be faced with the potentially intractable challenge of conflicting fiduciary duties: "The fiduciary responsibilities in a tracking stock structure loom large for corporate officers and directors. It is crucial for the board to make sure that one group is not advantaged to the detriment of the other."[37]

For example, Sprint acknowledged in its SEC filings that the "heavier economic interest" that its directors had in FON (its untracked, wireline business) than in PCS (its tracked, wireless business) "could give rise to claims of conflicts of interest when our board of directors makes decisions on matters where the interests of the FON Group and the PCS Group diverge."[38] Although Sprint highlighted the existence of a special board committee to "monitor and resolve" conflicts between FON and PCS shareholders, "corporate governance specialists question how it is possible to simultaneously satisfy two sets of shareholders: 'you can't maximize one without the other suffering to some degree.' "[39] Similarly, when John Malone encouraged AT&T to use tracking stocks to separate its cable and wireless businesses, one of the main reasons why AT&T chose not to pursue this course of action was the potential for fiduciary conflicts it would create. An AT&T representative explained, "The fiduciary responsibilities for the board and management—to make sure we had a good segregation of economics cut out for each class of shareholders—ultimately gave us pause."[40]

Shareholder voting rights are usually the culprit behind conflicts of interest in tracking stocks. Tracking stocks typically carry less voting power than the common stock of parent companies. In the Carolina Group tracking stock, for instance, "[s]hareholders were technically common stockholders of Loews, and so got to vote at Loews annual meetings. But each Carolina share carried one-tenth of a common-share vote. Current Loews common stockholders controlled 98.4% of the combined voting power of Loews, while Carolina shareholders controlled 1.6% of the voting power."[41] These disparities in shareholder voting rights afford companies the discretion to make major corporate decisions that prioritize the interests of their untracked businesses over those of their tracked businesses. For example, if a third party were to make an above-market offer to buy a tracked business that was unacceptable to the parent company's board, the board could block that transaction. Ultimately, because tracking stock investors do not have an actual ownership claim on the underlying tracked business, their interests are subordinate to those of the parent company's shareholders. This makes it imperative for tracking stock investors to consult the corporate documents to determine their rights in connection with such events as dividends, voting, and liquidation, to mention three situations in which conflicts of interest often manifest themselves.

Parent Company Issues

Like it or not, the buyers of a tracking stock must accept the reality that they own an interest in its parent company, albeit an interest that computes its dividends and liquidation value from the results of a defined business unit. What this means is that certain parent company problems will become investors' problems. Take the parent company's credit, for example; since the parent company's loan agreements may regulate the payment of dividends, dividends on the tracking shares could be at risk. But it can get worse than that: a parent company's bankruptcy could affect both the payment of dividends as well as the underlying value of the tracking shares. Finally, there are types of insidious liabilities that are characterized as *joint and several.** What that means is that every corporate entity in the parent's tax control group is equally responsible to pay those liabilities, and as a matter of law those liabilities must be repaid in full before equity can recover.

Picture the "parade of horribles," as it is called in law school. First, the parent company defaults on a bond and the rating agencies downgrade its credit ratings; this affects the prices of all the company's securities, including that of the tracking stock. Then, the company files for bankruptcy and the federal government asserts tax and pension claims against *every* corporation in the control group, including the corporation whose results support the tracking shares. Finally, the parent company emerges from bankruptcy with a reorganization plan that provides little or no recovery for equity. Tracking shares are equity.

This was an illustration of a situation in which a healthy subsidiary (so healthy that its performance once supported a tracking stock) got unexpectedly tagged with liabilities that were incurred elsewhere in the corporate household. To the author's knowledge, no tracking stocks have gone through a bankruptcy. However, GM did issue tracking stocks (which were redeemed) before it went bankrupt, and USX (the leader of an industry that is famous for its unfunded pension liabilities) issued tracking stocks as well. So, to the buyer of tracking shares: *caveat emptor.*

* * *

---

* Examples of joint and several liabilities are federal tax and pension liabilities.

This chapter concludes Part II, which has analyzed the various divestiture structures that companies can use to divest businesses: sales, spinoffs, equity carveouts, Reverse Morris Trusts, joint ventures, and tracking stocks. Exhibit 8.5 summarizes their key features.

EXHIBIT 8.5

Summary of Divestiture Structures

Divestiture Structure	Sale	Spinoff	Equity Carveout	Reverse Morris Trust	Joint Venture	Tracking Stock
Description	Divesting company sells the divested business to a strategic or financial acquirer	Parent company distributes shares in a subsidiary to its existing shareholders, resulting in the creation of a separate, publicly traded spinoff company	Parent company establishes the carved-out business as a separate entity; shares are issued in the carved-out business and (usually) up to 20% are sold to the public	Parent company spins off and merges a subsidiary with a target company; historic parent company shareholders must own the majority of the merged company	Divesting company contributes the divested business to a joint venture in return for a stake in the joint venture and potentially some consideration	Parent company issues stock that tracks the performance of a subsidiary (the tracked business) separately from that of its remaining businesses

(continued)

EXHIBIT 8.5 *(continued)*

Divestiture Structure	Sale	Spinoff	Equity Carveout	Reverse Morris Trust	Joint Venture	Tracking Stock
Key Characteristics	• Value realization from shifting the divested business into the hands of a more appropriate acquirer • Cash generation • Potential tax advantage when the divested business is sold at a loss • Potential for conflicts between the divesting company and the acquirer	• Tax-free when certain statutory requirements are met • Potential to unlock shareholder value by enabling the parent and spinoff companies to be valued separately • Improved operational efficiency by enabling the parent and spinoff companies to function independently • Potential for conflicts between the parent and spinoff companies	• Ability to generate cash from the sale of shares in the carved-out business, without compromising the ability to do a tax-free spinoff before or after the equity carveout • Separate valuation of the carved-out business • Potential for conflicts while the parent company maintains a controlling stake in the carved-out business	• Ability to use mergers in combination with tax-free spinoffs when certain structural requirements are met • Potential synergies from the combination of the spinoff and target companies, which are usually related to each other	• Spread the tax and accounting effects of sales over time • Potential synergies from the combination of complementary businesses • Require careful management and governance to minimize conflicts	• Separate valuation of the tracked business, but potential discount of the parent company • Synergies between the tracked and untracked businesses, but potential for inefficient management decisions • Potential for conflicts between shareholders of the parent company and the tracked business • Potential spillovers of parent company issues

PART III

DIVESTITURE IMPLEMENTATION

CHAPTER 9

Separating the Divested Business

INTRODUCTION

While much ink has been spilled over the years in writing about the implementation of mergers and acquisitions (M&A), divestiture implementation has largely been ignored, or at best, conceptualized as the opposite of M&A implementation. Needless to say, this is simply not the case, which underscores the need for a distinct framework. Divestiture implementation consists of the following three steps, which this chapter and the next two will consider in turn:

1. The divesting company must separate the divested business from its remaining operations.

2. The divesting company must reconfigure internal processes in its remaining businesses, especially corporate overhead expenditures and resource allocation processes.

3. The divesting company must reshape the perceptions of external stakeholders that the divestiture may have impacted.

SEPARATING THE DIVESTED BUSINESS

In 2018, Honeywell International completed the spinoff of Resideo Technologies, its homes and global distribution business. The magnitude of the task of separating Resideo from the rest of Honeywell's sprawling industrial portfolio was enormous: founded in 1906, Honeywell had spent over a century accumulating the processes and systems it would now need to design, implement, and stabilize in Resideo in just two short years. In terms of information technology alone, Resideo's chief information officer, Bruce Mathews, explained, "The scope and scale of this project cannot be overstated. What we're talking about here is nothing less than standing up IT for a whole new company of 13,000 people in just 24 months—*but only after extracting it from a situation where it was very commingled with an even bigger company.*"[1] Additionally, even though the divestiture formally separated Resideo from Honeywell, the transaction did not terminate all relationships between the two companies. For instance, Resideo would continue selling certain products that were branded as "Honeywell Home." To do so, Resideo entered into a trademark licensing agreement with Honeywell, granting it an exclusive license to use the Honeywell Home name for a 40-year term in return for royalties of 1.5% of net sales of those products.[2]

A key source of value in diversified companies is the ability to share physical, intangible, and human assets, corporate functions and services, and even ongoing liabilities among their businesses. When a company undertakes a divestiture, it must determine which of these resources, expenses, and liabilities will follow the divested business versus which ones will remain part of its non-divested operations. As highlighted by the Resideo example, greater interdependence and history between a company's divested and non-divested businesses amplify the complexity of this task. A consultant with whom the author collaborates has a lighthearted but unfortunately true way of noting that divestitures often start out looking like amicable divorces, until the separating parties get down to the brass tacks of who gets the dog and who gets the imported espresso machine. Every divestiture has assets with shared operational and emotional attachments that require objective and effective techniques to separate in a manner that maximizes value.

Furthermore, although divestitures represent the formal separation of the divested business from the rest of the divesting company, the reality is not that straightforward, in that these entities may have continuing interactions (like the Resideo trademark licensing agreement) that persist long past the official closing dates of these transactions (40 years, in that case). Just as divorces can require ongoing alimony payments and shared custody arrangements, the same is true for divestitures: mechanisms must be put in place to govern continuing relationships between the divesting company and the divested business.

The separation of a divested business from the divesting company's remaining operations involves three steps, each of which will be addressed in this chapter:

1. The divesting company must define the scope of the divested business.

2. The divesting company must divide and allocate the resources, expenses, and liabilities the divested business shared with the company's remaining operations.

3. The divesting company must put mechanisms in place to govern any ongoing interactions it will have with the divested business after the divestiture.

DEFINING THE SCOPE OF THE DIVESTED BUSINESS

The first step a company must take in separating a divested business is to define the scope of that business. This means that the divesting company must identify both the specific resources and people that will follow the divested business, and the ones that will remain with the non-divested units. As a McKinsey guide to the successful execution of divestitures explains, "The divestiture team must set a perimeter around the deal—drawing clear lines around the operations (manufacturing sites or equipment, for instance) products (SKU lists), intellectual property (patent rights), and commercial capabilities (sales force) associated with the asset in question. The team should explore critical questions such as which products, geographies, and groups of personnel are in scope for the deal; which contracts will be reassigned; how shared intellectual property will be managed (transferred entirely or licensed); and which systems will remain with the divested asset."[3] These delineations are important because they enable the divesting company to develop a standalone valuation and financial statements for the divested business, smoothing the process of negotiating the terms of the divestiture.[4]

In situations where certain resources clearly belong with the divested business, defining its scope is straightforward. Tangible assets (e.g., facilities, plants, machinery) and intangible assets (e.g., patents, copyrights, trademarks, and other intellectual property) that are directly relevant to the divested business follow it after the divestiture. For example, Nestlé's sale of its U.S. candy business to Ferrero Rocher included Nestlé's confectionery-related manufacturing facilities, administrative offices, and employees.[5] When Pfizer split off Zoetis (its animal health business), the manufacturing sites and equipment that produced animal health products were transferred to Zoetis, while those that produced human health products remained with Pfizer.[6]

Similar patterns of resource allocation occur for employees and managers of the divested business. For instance, when Trinity Industries separated its railcar and infrastructure businesses, "among the first tasks to complete the transition was to help assign operational people for each entity. This was straightforward: railcar personnel would stay with Trinity, and infrastructure specialists would go to Arcosa."[7] When Armstrong World Industries divested its flooring business from its ceiling business, the divisional managers who had previously overseen each of these businesses simply followed them and led the separated companies after the divestiture.[8]

Even suppliers and customers may choose to follow the divested business and cease to transact with the divesting company's remaining businesses. These considerations must be accounted for when defining the scope of the divested business. When Gap proposed to spin off Old Navy, commentators highlighted the magnitude of changes that would likely occur in terms of supplier relationships: "As the company splits, there will likely be a lot of changing relationships at both of the new organizations. Some suppliers that may have had an interest in dealing with only one part of the business may not want a relationship with the other once the split goes into effect. There are going to be cancellation clauses, relationships that are broken because of the change."[9] Similarly, customers who purchased products solely from a business that is being divested might continue transacting with that business after its separation but cease transacting with the divesting company. When L'Oréal sold The Body Shop to Brazilian cosmetics company Natura, for example, many of The Body Shop's eco-conscious and ethics-friendly customers followed it to Natura. Commentators emphasized that this would be a better fit from a customer perspective given the better alignment of their "brand DNA around naturality and ethics."[10] Indeed, many of those customers resented L'Oréal's former ownership of the brand.[11]

DIVIDING SHARED RESOURCES, EXPENSES, AND LIABILITIES

The task of defining the scope of the divested business is more complex when it comes to resources, expenses, and liabilities that the divested business shared with other units in the divesting company. The second step a company must take in separating a divested business is to divide and allocate these shared items between its divested and non-divested operations.

Shared Resources

In general, diversified companies share numerous resources among their businesses. Companies economize on overhead costs by centralizing the provision of common functions and services. Business units share plants, warehouses, and other facilities to achieve production synergies, and patents often apply to the products of multiple subsidiaries. Data and other informational resources are frequently shared across the entire portfolio, as are logos, brands, and corporate names. Certain employees, especially those who manage corporate functions and services, may support several business units. The ability to cross-sell products to the same customers results in scale-based advantages, pricing power, and economies of scope, and the ability to source inputs from the same suppliers leads to greater purchasing power and lower costs.

Accordingly, when a company divests one of its units, it must identify, divide, and allocate the resources that the divested business previously shared with the company's remaining operations. This is not always straightforward. For example, what happens when certain products that will follow the divested business are manufactured in the same facilities as products that the divesting company will continue to produce? Johnson & Johnson CFO Joseph Wolk highlighted this challenge in J&J's divestiture of its consumer health business: that business and the prescription drugs business "are in many cases intertwined. For example, the company generally manufactures pills for over-the-counter medicines and prescription drugs in a similar process in the same type of facility. Over decades of being a combined business, things have become very entangled. Some of that was for efficiency reasons, others because it just made logical sense."[12]

Three specific areas that can cause significant headaches are the division of sales forces, supply chains, and information technology resources that serve both the divested and non-divested businesses. For example, in Symantec's divestiture of Veritas, that unit shared "sales teams and programs" with Symantec's remaining operations.[13] Similarly, one of the reasons Gap reportedly called off its planned divestiture of Old Navy in 2020 was the difficulty of reconfiguring its existing supplier relationships: "Gap Inc. had said that there would be 'dis-synergies' from the split, given how many resources Old Navy and the rest of the company share in terms of buying fabrics, manufacturing facilities, and clout with landlords in negotiating rent."[14] In terms of the division and allocation of shared information technology resources, major systems such as enterprise resource planning and accounting need to be separated. Returning to Honeywell's spinoff of Resideo, for example, the chief information officer described the magnitude of the task of dividing up and allocating the relevant portions of Honeywell's information technology systems to the new company: "It was a question of identifying who was using data and services across 600 different applications and 275 sites globally, and then figuring out how we could separate assets and bring to Resideo what was needed, without causing disruption to [Honeywell's] business."[15]

Human resources issues can also be thorny. In Trinity's spinoff of Arcosa, for instance, vice president and secretary Jared Richardson expressed some of the challenges: "Beyond divvying up personnel and assets, there were seemingly innumerable details that had to be addressed in the primary transaction documents. For example, the employee-matters agreement had to assign responsibility for benefits programs, determine employee seniority levels, and account for collective-bargaining agreements that were in place in certain facilities. There were also issues related to performance-based awards and employee-stock awards that had not yet vested that had to be resolved."[16]

Decisions on how to allocate shared resources can be made based on relevance, need, or other criteria. Motorola's separation of its cell phone business (Motorola Mobility) from its enterprise solutions business (Motorola Solutions) provides a useful example of this point. The two businesses shared at least three sets of resources that were valuable to each entity: the patents for the technology that each business produced, the well-known "batwing" logo (which enjoyed significant brand recognition among customers in both businesses), and fungible resources such as cash. Because Motorola's cell phone business was struggling in the face of intense industry competition, whereas its enterprise solutions business was known for its innovative capacity, all these shared resources were allocated to Motorola Mobility at the time of the separation.[17*]

So far, this discussion has focused on the division and allocation of shared resources that contribute to the day-to-day operations of the divesting company, the divested business, or both. However, it is important to recognize that these allocation questions can even extend to resources that have no operational value. The consultant who compared divestitures to amicable divorces went on to describe a curious example of this point, in which two companies that were being separated in a divestiture each claimed a row of oil paintings of former CEOs that lined a wall of the executive floor. Consider that the separating management teams had already successfully negotiated the allocation of significant resources ranging from R&D laboratories to data centers in the partition of an industrial manufacturer that was over 100 years old, yet it proved difficult for them to agree on how to divide these assets with shared emotional significance. This was the equivalent of who got the dog and who got the espresso machine. Emotional attachment is real, and it matters.

Shared Expenses and Liabilities

In addition to common resources, companies must also divide and allocate the appropriate shares of corporate expenses and liabilities among their divested and non-divested businesses. Well-managed diversified companies typically incur the expenses of centrally providing common functions and services (such as treasury services, finance, information technology, and legal services) to their business units. As the provider of treasury services, these parents may also manage the liabilities associated with those business units. Liabilities can arise from many sources, including normal operations, corporate conduct, internal processes, transactions, litigation, and indebtedness. Accordingly, some proportion of the expense of these

---

* Nonetheless, as will be discussed later in this chapter, in situations where the divesting company and the divested business both need to continue using certain resources after the divestiture, arrangements may need to be made to facilitate ongoing resource sharing. In the Motorola case, for example, even though the technology patents and batwing logo were allocated to Motorola Mobility, the rights to continue using those assets post-divestiture were licensed back to Motorola Solutions.

corporate functions and services and of these liabilities is, at least concep-
tually, attributable to each of a company's businesses.

When a company undertakes a divestiture, the conceptual becomes
real and some "fair share" of these expenses and liabilities must be allocated to the divested business. But what is that fair share? The answer to
that question requires an examination of the nature of the divestiture. In
a divestiture in which the divesting company has a counterparty—a sale,
perhaps—the allocation of expenses and liabilities is negotiated. Fair or
unfair, skewed or not skewed, the counterparties will negotiate this allocation or there will not be a deal.

However, when the divestiture has no counterparty—a 100% spinoff,
for example—the divesting company will often seek to transfer a disproportionate share of its liabilities to the divested business (as described in
Chapter 6, and see the upcoming discussion of the Texas Two-Step, regarding a recent trend in the disposal of mass tort liabilities via spinoffs), and
also to impose a disproportionate share of the corporate expenses through
contractual agreements that survive the spinoff (as discussed in Chapter
7). These practices serve to reduce the divesting company's corporate
overhead and enable it to avoid being saddled with "stranded costs."* However, allocating a larger proportion of corporate expenses to the spinoff
company would lower its profitability and even raise questions about its
viability. As to allocating shared liabilities, relevant laws (e.g., pension,
antitrust, tax, environmental) and contract terms (e.g., terms-of-purchase,
debt instrument) may limit what the divesting company can and cannot
allocate to the divested business.†

A recent trend in disposing of mass tort liabilities via spinoffs is the
so-called Texas Two-Step. In a Texas Two-Step, a company that is the
defendant in mass tort litigation reincorporates itself into a Texas corporation, and then undertakes a "divisive merger" to divide itself into two

---

* As will be discussed in Chapter 10, stranded costs are the costs of any shared services,
assets, or personnel that remain with the divesting company but become underutilized due to
that company's smaller size after a divestiture.

† Note that there are certain types of liabilities that cannot be assigned without creditor assent.
In situations such as these, typical solutions involve the use of indemnification by one of the
parties. There are also certain liabilities that are joint and several among all the corporations
in the group. Apportioning these liabilities, which include tax and pension liabilities involving
the federal government, generally requires government approval.

separate companies, allocating its mass tort liabilities into the one company ("BadCo"), and its viable businesses into the other ("GoodCo"). BadCo is later spun off, and it typically files for bankruptcy in a different state. Instead of recovering from the company's original assets, the mass tort creditors must now recover from a smaller asset base in a very expensive bankruptcy proceeding. In all fairness, a defined amount of financial support is often provided to the mass tort creditors by GoodCo, which has been otherwise released from all claims.

Normally, such behavior would result in fraudulent conveyance litigation against the parent company for having defrauded creditors by transferring excessive liabilities in the divisive merger. However, Texas law provides that mergers operate without any transfer or assignment having occurred, even divisive mergers. Arguably, this rules out the possibility of a fraudulent conveyance, because legally, there has been no transfer (i.e., no conveyance).

To date, only a few companies facing mass tort litigation have used the Texas Two-Step to rid themselves of liabilities (many of those transactions are the subject of ongoing litigation), and Johnson & Johnson is presently involved in the bankruptcy of its consumer health business, which used the Texas Two-Step to shed talc and asbestos liabilities associated with its once-common Baby Powder. This is a developing area of bankruptcy law (which relies on the various state laws to define mergers), going so far as to attract the attention of a U.S. Senate Subcommittee.* Excellent commentary was proffered as testimony in the Subcommittee's hearing[18] and by the legal community.[19]

In an ideal world, allocation decisions would be made on the basis of how intensively the divested business used the various corporate functions and services in its day-to-day operations, and how much of a given liability was attributable to that business. However, it is usually difficult to make this granular of an assessment, and historical cost allocations are rarely a reasonable reflection of what the divested business would really use on an independent basis. As a result, a broad brush may be the best way to allocate corporate expenses between the divested business and the divesting company. Factors like the expected future profitability, growth potential, and competitive prospects of both the divested and non-divested

---

* The U.S. Senate Subcommittee on Federal Courts, Oversight, Agency Action, and Federal Rights heard testimony on February 8, 2022.

businesses can also influence these decisions, since they affect the relative abilities of each of these entities to support a larger or a smaller share of corporate expenses and liabilities.

As described in a Harvard Business School case study, in Humana's separation of its hospital and health plan businesses, $156 million (22% of combined pre-tax operating income) of corporate functions and services and $792 million of long-term debt needed to be allocated between the two businesses.[20] In recognition of the fact that the health plan business had smaller cash flows than the hospital business, Humana allocated almost all of the company's long-term debt ($690 million) to the hospital business, gave the health plan business $135 million in cash, and obligated the hospital business to take out notes paying the health plan business $250 million (plus interest) over five years after the divestiture. However, because the health plan business had stronger growth prospects than the hospital business, Humana allocated more than 50% of the company's overhead expenses to the health plan business, even though it only accounted for about 25% of the company's combined revenues and 10% of its EBITDA prior to the divestiture. In contrast, Motorola Solutions kept all of Motorola's debt and pension obligations post-divestiture, leaving Motorola Mobility free of these burdens.[21] This allocation of corporate expenses reflected the fact that Motorola Mobility was struggling financially and had a more limited growth potential than Motorola Solutions. Together, these two examples illustrate the subjectivity that is inherent in decisions of how to allocate corporate expenses and liabilities.

The subjectivity of these allocation decisions can, in certain situations, come back to haunt the divesting company. In spinoffs where the divested business fails as an independent company, it may have the incentive to claim that its former parent company allocated too great a share of corporate expenses and liabilities to it. For example, the Tronox,[22] Solutia,[23] Paragon Offshore,[24] and Garrett Motion[25] spinoffs resulted in lawsuits against their respective parent companies (or their successors): Kerr-McGee (Anadarko), Monsanto, Noble, and Honeywell. In all these cases, the litigants claimed that these companies had allocated inappropriate shares of debt, environmental liabilities, pension obligations, litigation costs, or some combination thereof to the divested businesses. Without addressing the legal merits of these cases, it's safe to say that they warn the reader that the allocation of corporate expenses and liabilities is far from straightforward and can have ongoing negative repercussions for a divesting company.*

GOVERNING ONGOING INTERACTIONS

Just as children maintain relationships with their parents after they leave the nest, there are many circumstances in which divested businesses might continue to interact with their former parent companies. For example, a divesting company might agree to continue providing certain of the corporate functions and services it once provided to its former subsidiary; the divesting company might agree to the continued sharing of resources with the divested business; or supply relationships might continue between the two entities, albeit at arm's length. Former Zoetis CEO Juan Ramón Alaix nicely summarized some of these possibilities in his description of his company's ongoing relationship with Pfizer: "It can be challenging to manage the evolving relationship with the company from which you're separating. In most cases the former parent company will continue to be a supplier, a shareholder, or a customer, or you'll have service agreements with it—and even though you've been doing business together for a long time, the relationship and priorities change."[26]

These points highlight the fact that mechanisms often need to be put in place to manage ongoing interactions between the divesting company and the divested business *after* a divestiture. These generally fall into two categories: transition services agreements to support the divested business as it leaves the divesting company, and contracts to govern ongoing commercial arrangements between the divesting company and the divested business.

---

* Regulators are also focused on driving equity in the allocation of assets and liabilities, as this can influence the ability of the separated companies to deliver upon performance expectations described in offering memoranda. While there is no bright line, being miserly when it comes to allocating valuable assets or unfair in allocating liabilities can cause a deal to fail to gain approval to close or to lose tax-free status, opening the potential for shareholder lawsuits.

Transition Services Agreements

A transition services agreement (TSA) is a contract in which a divesting company agrees to continue providing certain services to the divested business after the divestiture.* The purpose of these contracts is to help the divested business maintain business continuity, to ease the process of separating from the divesting company, and in a sale, to support the acquirer in integrating the divested business into its own organization. Depending on their relative capabilities and needs, the divested business may agree to provide certain services to the divesting company, known as a Reverse TSA. TSAs can even operate bilaterally, with the divesting company and the divested business each providing certain services to one another.

TSAs generally address three primary questions:

- Which services will be provided?[†]

- For how long will these services be provided?[‡]

---

* An alternative way for a company to provide services to the divested business is to contract with a third-party service provider until the divested business can handle them on its own. For example, Bayer contracted with Tata Consultancy Services to provide information technology, infrastructure, and business process support for the businesses it sold to BASF (Bayer Chemicals) and Elanco (Bayer Animal Health).

Sources: Tata Consultancy Services. 2018. "TCS' Repeatable Carve-Out Model Helps Bayer Complete Multiple Divestitures on Time." October 29, 2018. https://www.tcs.com/tcs-repeatable-carve-out-model-bayer-complete-multiple-divestitures-on-time.

Elanco. 2020. "Elanco Animal Health Reports 2020 Second Quarter Results." July 30, 2020. https://investor.elanco.com/press-releases/press-releases-details/2020/Elanco-Animal-Health-Reports-2020-Second-Quarter-Results/default.aspx.

† The most common services offered in TSAs are finance, accounting, and IT, each appearing in about 70% of TSAs. At the same time, many divesting companies will exclude certain services like tax, legal, and treasury support from their TSAs given the potential for liability exposure and other reasons. More experienced sellers know to identify excluded services early in the negotiations and to document them clearly in the TSA, allowing for better planning and avoiding fire drills at deal close.

Source: Doyle, Anna Lea, Andrew Wilson, and Ellen Clark. 2014. "It's Not Easy to Say Goodbye: Perspectives on Driving Divestiture and Carve Out Value." Deloitte. https://www2.deloitte.com/content/dam/Deloitte/us/Documents/mergers-acqisitions/us-ma-divestiture-compendium-22315.pdf.

‡ According to one survey, 80% of TSAs last one year or less, of which about half last six months or less.

Source: Doyle, Anna Lea, Andrew Wilson, and Ellen Clark. 2014. "It's Not Easy to Say Goodbye: Perspectives on Driving Divestiture and Carve Out Value." Deloitte. https://www2.deloitte.com/content/dam/Deloitte/us/Documents/mergers-acqisitions/us-ma-divestiture-compendium-22315.pdf.

- How much will it cost to provide these services?

Divestitures in which the divested business relied more intensively on the divesting company or shared more activities with its remaining operations tend to require more detailed, longer-lasting, and more expensive TSAs. As noted earlier, diversified companies benefit from sharing common activities across their businesses. However, these shared activities are exactly what make it more difficult to disentangle the divested business, and hence, what require a more complex TSA.

Divestiture structure also influences TSA characteristics. TSAs tend to be more extensive when a divested business is sold to a financial rather than a strategic acquirer, since financial acquirers may not have the necessary infrastructure to operate the divested business. A strategic acquirer may not need as extensive a TSA, because it may already have many of the relevant functions and services in place to support the divested business once it integrates into that company's operations.[27] By contrast, the scope, duration, and costs of TSAs are often broader in spinoffs than in sales, since spinoffs require the divested business to begin operating as an independent company, but it may not have the necessary capabilities, personnel, or financial capacity to do so at the moment of separation from its former parent company.

Given the duration and costs of TSAs, it is clearly not an insubstantial matter for a divesting company to provide ongoing, post-divestiture support to a business it divests. But significant performance benefits appear to accrue to both divesting companies and divested businesses from having TSAs in place, in large part because these agreements smooth the separation process and allow the divested business to get off to a good start outside of the divesting company's organization. Exhibit 9.1 illustrates this point: the average stock market performance of parent and spinoff companies is higher in spinoffs where a TSA is in place than when one is not, and this performance differential both persists and widens in the months after these transactions. Not only do TSAs make common sense, but they are demonstrably beneficial for the companies that utilize them.

At the same time, a divesting company must structure its TSA to be affordable and of finite duration. After all, the divesting company has its primary operations to run, and it is not (and should not be) in the business of being a service provider to unrelated companies. Exhibit 9.2 shows

EXHIBIT 9.1

Average Value-Weighted Monthly Returns of Parent and Spinoff
Companies in Spinoffs with and Without TSAs[28]

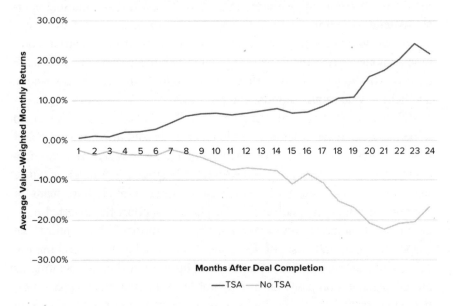

that parent companies experience diminishing returns to TSA duration, in
that their excess shareholder returns are smaller the longer they agree to
provide support to their spinoff companies. Furthermore, Exhibit 9.3 suggests that there is a "sweet spot" for TSA costs, in that parent companies
with the most and the least expensive TSAs have lower excess shareholder
returns than companies with moderately costly TSAs. In other words,
make the TSA too cheap and it may not provide the divested business
with enough support, but make the TSA too expensive and it may become
onerous for the divesting company. These patterns indicate that TSAs can
cause the post-divestiture relationship between the divesting company and
the divested business to persist for longer and perhaps at greater cost than
may be desirable.

EXHIBIT 9.2

Average Cumulative Abnormal Returns of Parent Companies by TSA Duration[29]

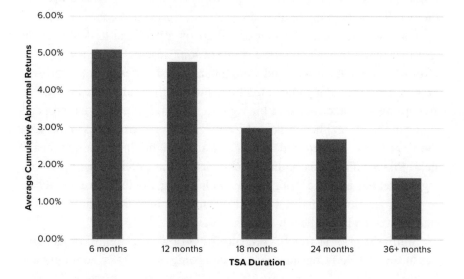

EXHIBIT 9.3

Average Cumulative Abnormal Returns of Parent Companies by Monthly TSA Cost[30]

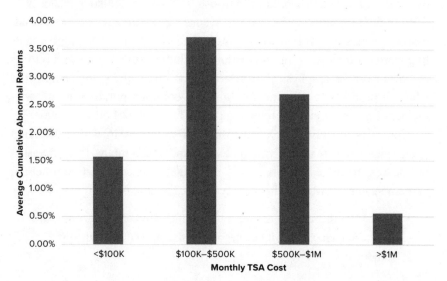

Commercial Arrangements

There are numerous commercial situations in which a divesting company and a divested business may need to continue to transact after their separation, particularly when a historical business connection existed between the two. These ongoing relationships are often governed contractually.

For instance, during its split-off of Zoetis, Pfizer had to deal with the fact that many patents were the result of joint research and development efforts between the human and animal health businesses prior to their separation, and both companies might need to use them after the divestiture. Accordingly, "Pfizer licensed the right to use certain intellectual property rights in the animal health field to Zoetis. Zoetis in turn licensed to Pfizer the right to use certain trademarks and all IP rights in the human health field. Pfizer and Zoetis, although completely independent, set up a strategic research alliance prior to the IPO, giving Zoetis restricted access to the Pfizer library and database to identify compounds that may be of interest to the animal health field."[31]

Similarly, prior to freight company XPO Logistics' spinoff of its logistics business, GXO Logistics, the two companies shared a custom-built and highly complex 3PL (third-party logistics) optimization software. To avoid the lengthy development time, risk, and high cost of GXO building the software anew or buying it from a competitor, XPO granted GXO a "perpetual license for all of XPO's software and technology that it has been building over the years, which would be purpose-built for its logistics business."[32] Even in the separation of Saks Fifth Avenue's e-commerce and bricks-and-mortar businesses, the two companies had nearly 350 licensing agreements to govern all their ongoing interactions, including fulfillments and returns of online orders in physical stores, compensation of in-store employees who sell products to customers online, and common purchasing and pricing decisions that the e-commerce business handles for both companies.[33]

Contracts are also employed to govern situations in which divesting companies need to secure raw materials and other inputs from divested businesses. In these situations, it is important to ensure that commercial agreements are written at third-party terms, for at least three reasons:

- To ensure that each of the separated entities is receiving its fair share of the agreement as if it had negotiated that agreement with any other party

- To avoid undermining the original intention of the divestiture—that is, to allow the divested business to transact with any party, not just its former parent company

- To demonstrate to regulators—and to the IRS—that the divested business is truly independent

For example, when Alcoa split its upstream (new-Alcoa) and downstream (Arconic) aluminum businesses, the two companies signed a minimum three-year deal for new-Alcoa to supply Arconic with raw metal. The deal was a win for Arconic: not only did it secure a minimum of three years' worth of supply, but it retained the flexibility to buy raw materials from other suppliers as well.[34] Similarly, when information services provider CoreLogic sold its India-based captive operations to Cognizant in 2011, the two companies established a long-term service delivery contract under which CoreLogic would continue receiving the services (software product development, analytical modeling, back-office operations, and technology support) its captive unit had previously provided it, as well as a vendor management office to govern the new, arm's-length relationship between the two companies.[35]

In contrast, an insufficient or missing contract can create negative externalities in terms of the divesting company maintaining order volumes, utilization rates, and revenue growth. When Expedia spun off TripAdvisor (its travel planning site), for example, it lost an important marketing channel, since Expedia had previously used TripAdvisor as a major source of leads to which it could sell travel packages. Accordingly, once the spinoff was complete, Expedia found itself "reliant to a great extent on a single, transactional revenue stream" from its own operations, which was diminished now that it had less ability to source leads from TripAdvisor.[36] Expedia eventually bought a majority stake in Trivago to diversify its traffic sources and marketing channels.[37]

Finally, as much as contracts can govern ongoing engagement between a divesting company and a divested business post-divestiture, they can equally be useful in delineating areas where those two entities *may not* interact. For example, one of the features of the eBay–PayPal separation was the fact that the two companies agreed to (renewable) five-year non-compete agreements, in which eBay agreed not to participate in any payment solutions businesses, and PayPal agreed not to develop any e-commerce platforms on which to sell physical goods.[38] As any divorce lawyer worth his salt will tell you, the principle of "what's mine is mine and what's yours is yours" is a good one to abide by in any separation, including a divestiture.

CHAPTER 10

Reconfiguring Internal Processes

INTRODUCTION

Divestitures require companies to adjust to the new reality that their organizations now consist of fewer businesses, with different opportunities, demands, people, and capabilities than they had prior to those transactions. This new reality typically manifests itself in two ways:

- The scale of corporate resources, functions, and services that are retained post-divestiture may be too large relative to the new scope of these companies' operations.

- Certain businesses in these companies' portfolios may have greater future growth prospects and hence, resource needs, than they did pre-divestiture.

Thus, when implementing divestitures, companies need to anticipate and respond to this new reality by reducing their overall cost structures to avoid stranded costs, and by improving their resource allocation processes to support new opportunities.

Consider the industrial products conglomerate Rexnord, which announced in 2020 that it would use a Reverse Morris Trust to spin off and merge its Process Motion Control (PMC) business (accounting for 62% of its sales[1]) with Regal Beloit, creating a new company that would be renamed Regal Rexnord. Rexnord's remaining water management business would be renamed Zurn Water Solutions and would continue operating as an independent—albeit much smaller—publicly traded company. Clearly, Zurn's post-spinoff cost structure would need to shrink to match the smaller size of the new organization, and Rexnord started planning for this outcome early in the divestiture process. Shortly after the divestiture was announced, CEO Todd Adams explained in a quarterly earnings call that while Rexnord had about $40 million of corporate expenses pre-spinoff, less than half of those expenses would be allocated to Zurn post-spinoff due to "a combination of [Zurn] just being smaller, maybe not needing some functions related to international operations and things of the like."[2] The balance of the corporate expenses would be assumed by Regal Rexnord, which was well positioned to do so given the larger size of the merged organization.[3]

During the next two quarterly earnings calls, Mr. Adams elaborated on Zurn's efforts to capture growth and expansion in its remaining water management business. This business had achieved 39% year-over-year sales growth in the second quarter of 2021,[4] and had more than doubled its sales growth in touchless products,[5] fueled in large part by concerns about hand hygiene during the COVID-19 pandemic. He explained: "We've significantly ramped our growth investment spend over the last couple of years to open up new parts of our served markets, drive new markets, drive greater levels of specification and continue to build on the competitive moat we built inside of our water management business" (pun presumably not intended).[6] These efforts culminated in the launch of "BrightShield by Zurn,"[7] a connected ecosystem of products, services, and technologies that would promote touchless, "smart" restrooms. Mr. Adams highlighted the growth initiatives that Zurn was planning in this domain: "There's a lot more to come around BrightShield in the coming months both from a product and capability offering, as well as some adjacent channel opportunities that we see which will greatly enhance our served market."[8]

Consistent with Rexnord's experiences, this chapter considers the two steps that companies must take to reconfigure their internal processes when implementing divestitures:

1. To avoid the burden that "stranded costs" can impose on their ongoing operations, companies must reduce their corporate expenditures in proportion to their smaller scale and minimize their ongoing entanglements with the businesses they have divested.

2. Companies must harness the potential for divestitures to catalyze improvements in their resource allocation processes by reinvesting capital and research and development (R&D) expenditures into the areas of their portfolios that have the strongest future growth prospects.

AVOIDING STRANDED COSTS

As has been discussed throughout this book, two of the main advantages enjoyed by diversified companies are the ability to share corporate functions and services and common resources among their businesses. The provision of corporate functions and services and the sharing of common resources impose both fixed costs (e.g., expenditures on real estate or information technology systems) and variable costs (e.g., hiring personnel to administer finance or human resources functions) on these organizations. In theory, the larger the company, the more it should be able to spread the costs of these common activities and resources across its businesses, and the greater the efficiencies it should gain from doing so.

The reality appears to be somewhat different, however. Selling, general, and administrative (SG&A) expense is an income statement item that includes the central costs of running a company, as well as the indirect costs not associated with the production of goods or services. Thus, SG&A expense is a useful proxy for the costs a company must incur in providing corporate functions and services to its businesses, and in sharing common resources among them. Exhibit 10.1 presents data, broken down by industry, on the average ratio of SG&A expense to revenues (SG&A/Revenue) of different-sized companies. In each industry, the average SG&A/Revenue ratio remains remarkably consistent across company sizes. The fact that larger companies do not have systematically lower average SG&A/Revenue ratios than smaller companies suggests that larger companies do not necessarily leverage the efficiencies that their scale should afford them in sharing activities and resources among their businesses.

How do these insights apply to divestitures? When a company divests, the number of businesses in that organization declines, but the costs of providing corporate functions and services to those businesses, or of sharing resources among them, may remain the same. This problem is known as "stranded costs," which are defined as "any type of cost that does not automatically disappear with the transaction, from costs related to shared services, such as marketing and investor relations, to IT infrastructure."[10] To avoid stranded costs, a divesting company must strive to reduce the costs of any shared activities or resources proportionally to the reduction in company size caused by the divestiture.

EXHIBIT 10.1

Average SG&A/Revenue Ratio by Industry and Company Size[9]

	REVENUES			
Industry	$100m–$500m	$500m–$1b	$1b–$5b	>$5b
Agriculture	14%	22%	12%	14%
Aircraft	16%	15%	17%	16%
Apparel	33%	40%	34%	33%
Automobiles & Trucks	15%	12%	12%	15%
Banking	38%	36%	32%	38%
Beer & Liquor	31%	33%	35%	31%
Business Services	42%	44%	35%	42%
Business Supplies	15%	15%	15%	15%
Candy & Soda	34%	21%	26%	34%
Chemicals	16%	14%	13%	16%
Coal	9%	11%	5%	9%
Communication	27%	36%	25%	27%
Computers	38%	25%	29%	38%
Construction	12%	12%	11%	12%
Construction Materials	20%	17%	18%	20%
Consumer Goods	35%	33%	34%	35%
Defense	20%	21%	10%	20%
Electrical Equipment	29%	21%	19%	29%
Electronic Equipment	31%	27%	22%	31%
Entertainment	24%	21%	18%	24%
Fabricated Products	17%	15%	16%	17%
Food	20%	19%	14%	20%
Healthcare	26%	18%	14%	26%
Insurance	20%	15%	14%	20%
Machinery	26%	22%	20%	26%
Measuring & Control Equipment	37%	14%	33%	37%
Medical Equipment	52%	44%	38%	52%

(continued)

EXHIBIT 10.1 *(continued)*

Industry	REVENUES			
	$100m–$500m	$500m–$1b	$1b–$5b	>$5b
Non-Metallic & Industrial Metal Mining	15%	8%	9%	15%
Other	20%	15%	13%	20%
Personal Services	34%	39%	24%	34%
Petroleum & Natural Gas	16%	11%	9%	16%
Pharmaceutical Products	49%	36%	43%	49%
Precious Metals	14%	8%	9%	14%
Printing & Publishing	39%	38%	40%	39%
Real Estate	27%	35%	22%	27%
Recreation	33%	31%	36%	33%
Restaurants, Hotels, Motels	16%	16%	12%	16%
Retail	28%	32%	26%	28%
Rubber & Plastic Products	21%	17%	22%	21%
Shipbuilding & Railroad Equipment	11%	6%	10%	11%
Shipping Containers	8%	—	9%	8%
Steel Works	9%	10%	9%	9%
Textiles	18%	17%	25%	18%
Tobacco	20%	—	—	20%
Trading	15%	10%	10%	15%
Transportation	15%	9%	13%	15%
Utilities	17%	22%	18%	17%
Wholesale	18%	15%	15%	18%

Consistent with the data presented in Exhibit 10.1, this also does not appear to occur in practice. In a sample of 110 companies that undertook large spinoffs between 2010 and 2019, the revenues of the divesting companies declined by an average of 25% between the year before the announcement of these transactions and the year after their completion, but the SG&A expense of these companies only declined by an average of 20% over the same period. Worse, 60 out of the 110 divesting companies *increased* their SG&A/Revenue ratios in the year after their spinoffs.[11] Far from avoiding stranded costs, these companies may in fact have exacerbated the problem. Providing further evidence in support of these findings, survey data indicate that only 40%[12] to 60%[13] of companies proactively analyze stranded costs before divesting. This suggests that companies may be missing opportunities for value creation, or at least that they may be missing opportunities for avoiding value erosion in these transactions.

There are three major reasons why companies often find themselves burdened with stranded costs after they divest:

1. An inability or unwillingness to cut corporate expenditures after a divestiture

2. An unequal allocation of shared corporate resources and expenses between the divested and non-divested businesses

3. Ongoing commitments to provide certain corporate functions and services to the divested business under a transition services agreement

Inability or Unwillingness to Cut Corporate Expenditures

While divestitures often reduce the overall size of a divesting company, the corporate expenditures that the company must incur to run its remaining, non-divested businesses may not necessarily decline in proportion to the reduction in its scope.* Many corporate expenditures that naturally

---

* The classic example is Macy's Thanksgiving Day Parade, which remained constant throughout Macy's expansions and contractions. Indeed, the late Judge Burton Lifland secured a commitment from the company that it would continue sponsoring the event as a condition to his approving its reorganization.

Source: Altaner, David. 1994. "Macy's Marching Toward Federated." *South Florida Sun-Sentinel*, December 19, 1994. https://www.sun-sentinel.com/news/fl-xpm-1994-12-19-94121 60113-story.html.

Also see: Federated Department Stores, Inc. 1994. "Current Report." October 21, 1994. https://www.sec.gov/Archives/edgar/data/34945/0000950112-94-002774.txt.

belong with the divested business will simply follow it out the door to its new home—to a buyer in the case of a sale, or into an independent company in the case of a spinoff. But, like a recalcitrant college student who stays on his parents' cell phone plan or uses their Netflix subscription after he's left the nest, sometimes a subset of the divesting company's expenditures stubbornly refuses to move out.

For instance, the cost of a company's IT system might remain fixed regardless of the number of businesses in the corporate household. Even if that company were to divest one of its businesses, it simply might not be able to cut the cost of its IT system regardless of the company's smaller scope of operations after the divestiture. As companies grow, moreover, they tend to accumulate layers of staff over time to run their corporate functions. For various reasons, however, companies may find it challenging to lay off corporate staff, leaving these organizations with extra personnel (and their associated costs) relative to the smaller scope of their operations. In some cases, companies may not even be aware of how much "complexity or outright duplication" they have in their corporate functions, especially in heavily matrixed organizations where multiple groups of personnel may provide functions and services to the same product categories or geographic regions.[14] Even when companies are aware of such redundancies, it usually is harder and takes longer to terminate personnel than to hire them,[15] which can further delay the rightsizing of corporate staff.

Unequal Allocation of Shared Corporate Resources and Expenses

As discussed in Chapter 9, a critical part of divestiture implementation is the decision of which shared resources and expenses to allocate to the divested business, versus which ones to keep in the divesting company. As explained in an industry white paper, "corporate and support functions that were previously shared across multiple business units must be separated to serve each of the future businesses. Costs such as senior executive salaries and software licenses are allocated across the entire business. . . . The same situation arises from the costs of corporate staff groups, information technology system maintenance and infrastructure, physical assets such as corporate headquarters and shared contracts and licenses, just to name a few."[16] After a divestiture, these and other shared resources and expenses must be divided and allocated between the divested business and the divesting company's remaining operations.

In certain cases, unequal allocation decisions made by a divesting company may leave it with excessive costs relative to the post-divestiture scale of its operations. For example, a company might elect to keep in its own organization (rather than allocate to the divested business) a factory that previously made products for both the divested and non-divested businesses. After the divestiture, that factory would have excess capacity relative to the existing production needs of the company's non-divested businesses. This would saddle the divesting company with stranded costs from continuing to operate that factory at less than full capacity.

Alternately, the divesting company might choose to allocate a relatively smaller proportion of corporate expenses to the divested business, in the interest of making it attractive to a buyer or of putting it on the strongest possible financial footing after the divestiture. This, too, would create stranded costs in the divesting company by causing it to have excessive overhead expenses relative to its scale. For example, returning to the Motorola separation discussed in Chapter 9, no corporate expenses were allocated to Motorola Mobility. While this decision was well founded from the perspective of making Motorola Mobility attractive to potential acquirers, it likely left Motorola Solutions with corporate overhead expenses that were scaled for a much larger organization.

Ongoing Commitments Under Transition Services Agreements

As described in Chapter 9, transition services agreements (TSAs) are contracts in which the divesting company agrees to continue providing certain functions and services to the divested business after the completion of a divestiture. Although these agreements do not, themselves, impose stranded costs on divesting companies, it is important to recognize that rather, *they delay the ultimate mitigation of stranded costs.* This can create inefficiencies that persist long past the completion of the divestiture in question.

Consider, for example, a hypothetical scenario in which a divesting company has agreed to a TSA in which it will continue providing the divested business with accounting and payroll services for 12 months after the divestiture. To do this, the divesting company would need to keep sufficient assets and employees in place (which it might otherwise have rightsized) to support the divested business along these dimensions for one year after the divestiture. During that year, the divesting company would come out net neutral: even though it would incur the costs of providing accounting and payroll services to the divested business, it would be compensated under the terms of the TSA for doing so. But what about when the TSA ends? To avoid stranded costs appearing at that time, the divesting company would need to cut the resources it had kept in place to support the TSA. A year after the divestiture, though, efforts to eliminate stranded costs will long since have ended. In most cases like this one, the divesting company would simply reabsorb these excess resources into its organization, causing stranded costs to materialize long after the divestiture that caused them in the first place.

* * *

Given the multitude of ways in which stranded costs arise, there are several things that companies can do to avoid them. Most fundamentally, when undertaking divestitures, companies should devote significant upfront planning and attention to their approach to dealing with stranded costs, which are not always readily obvious or easy to eliminate. One study found that companies that started this restructuring process before they divested enjoyed stronger stock market performance and greater revenue and profitability growth from their divestitures than companies that restructured only after they had divested.[17]

To reduce the scale of their corporate expenditures, divesting companies should benchmark their intended cost structures against those of peer companies they will resemble post-divestiture, and they should reconfigure their organizations accordingly. For example, in conjunction with its spinoff of TopBuild (its construction services business), Masco announced plans to cut corporate expenses and headcount by more than 40% to be in line with its peers. Masco CEO Keith Allman explained, "This reflects our adoption of a lean operating model which drives decision-making to our business units and increases our effectiveness as an organization. The reduction of our corporate overhead will result in savings of approximately $35 million to $40 million annually."[18] Mr. Allman's efforts appear to have paid off: Masco's share price rose by 150%, and its return on assets more than doubled in the five years after the TopBuild spinoff and its associated reconfiguration initiatives.[19]

While it is usually straightforward to allocate resources and expenses that are directly attributable to the divested business, the allocation of resources and expenses that are shared between the divested business and the divesting company can be more complex. In these instances, general rules of thumb can serve as guideposts to help companies avoid stranded costs. For example, when Johnson & Johnson divested its consumer health business, it articulated a rule for how to determine whether a given employee would follow the divested business or stay with the pharmaceuticals business. Explained CFO Joseph Wolk: "An employee is considered part of the new consumer-health business if they currently spend at least 51% of their time working in consumer health."[20] Similar approaches could be followed for other shared corporate resources and expenses.

Finally, in situations where the divesting company agrees to continue providing services to its divested business under a TSA, care should be taken at the outset to structure the TSA to avoid the possibility of stranded costs arising in the future. To do this, divesting companies must manage TSA provisions carefully, particularly by limiting the scope of services provided, capping the duration of these agreements, and putting price escalation clauses in place to ensure that they are fully compensated for any extensions of TSA services that may occur.[21] To the extent that allocation decisions or TSAs leave divesting companies with underutilized resources or excessive costs, these organizations should proactively develop future plans for absorbing them into their remaining businesses or eliminating them through cost-cutting or other reconfiguration initiatives.

IMPROVING RESOURCE ALLOCATION PROCESSES

The task of avoiding stranded costs is inherently *retrospective*, requiring divesting companies to adapt their existing cost structures to the fact that they now consist of fewer businesses, with different needs and financial capacities. However, it is important to recognize that divestitures equally create a *prospective* opportunity for companies to improve how they allocate resources to their remaining businesses. In other words, beyond just taking steps to avoid stranded costs, companies should use divestitures as a catalyst to "challenge the status quo and rebuild an organization for the future."[22] To this point, a study found that in a sample of companies that had undertaken large spinoffs, those companies that simultaneously carried out transformation efforts in their remaining businesses outperformed those that did not.[23] As with the task of avoiding stranded costs, however, these kinds of transformation initiatives appear to be underutilized by divesting companies. Survey evidence indicates that nearly two-thirds of divesting companies state that they could have devoted more effort to "reimagining" their remaining organizations by "identifying areas where investment [could] generate greater returns in the core business."[24]

Identifying areas where investment—especially capital and R&D expenditures—can generate the highest returns lies at the heart of the resource allocation process. Capital expenditures are the investments companies make to acquire, upgrade, and maintain the physical assets that are central to their operations, and R&D expenditures are the investments companies make to invent, develop, and commercialize new products and services. As is evident from these definitions, diversified companies must allocate resources—particularly financial capital, but also human and physical resources—to the best investment opportunities among all their businesses. But divestitures change the set of investment opportunities that are available to companies in two ways: not only do divestitures remove certain businesses from companies' portfolios, but more importantly, they also create opportunities for companies to assess whether they have any businesses where scarce resources are being underutilized and to reallocate those resources accordingly.

Capital Expenditures

As discussed in Chapters 2 and 6, diversified companies are notoriously bad at allocating capital to the best investment opportunities among their businesses.[25] Although the supply of capital in these organizations is finite, demand for it is (presumptively) infinite, making internal competition for this resource fierce. This is made worse by political dynamics in which certain divisional managers lobby to receive more capital for their businesses,[26] as well as the fact that capital allocation decisions are often made based on the past prospects of a particular business unit, rather than on its potential future opportunities.[27] As a result, even if certain businesses in a diversified company have better investment opportunities than others, sufficient capital might not be allocated to those businesses. Rather, businesses that have worse investment opportunities may be allocated more capital than might be warranted, while businesses with better prospects may be allocated less capital than they otherwise should.[28]

Divestitures have been shown to improve the efficiency with which capital is allocated to investment opportunities among the divesting company's remaining businesses.[29] After they divest, companies appear to allocate more capital to businesses operating in industries with greater growth potential and less capital to businesses operating in industries with worse prospects than they did before these transactions. Exhibit 10.2 depicts this point graphically: pre-divestiture, the correlation between capital expenditures and investment opportunities is negative, meaning that companies inefficiently invest more capital in businesses that have worse investment opportunities. But post-divestiture, the correlation between capital expenditures and investment opportunities becomes positive, meaning that the same companies start to invest more capital in businesses that have better investment opportunities. These improvements in the efficiency of capital allocation decisions can promote growth in the divesting company's existing product lines, as well as expansions into geographic, customer, and product adjacencies.

EXHIBIT 10.2

Correlation Between Capital Expenditures and Investment Opportunities in Non-Divested Businesses Before and After Spinoffs[30]

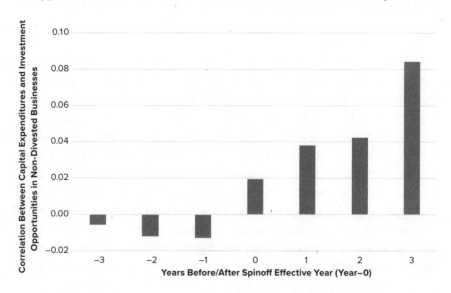

Three divestitures—CBS's split-off of its outdoor billboard advertising division (then CBS Outdoors, now Outfront Media), Saks Fifth Avenue's separation of its bricks-and-mortar and e-commerce businesses, and Masco's spinoff of TopBuild—usefully illustrate these points. In the first of these divestitures, the CEO of CBS Outdoors described the inefficiency of CBS's capital allocation decisions before the split-off: "Within CBS everyone is always fighting for capital, and capital allocation decisions didn't always go exactly the way we wanted,"[31] and "When you are one part of a company and are perceived to be non-core, you have to fight for capital allocation."[32] After the split-off, however, CBS appears to have shifted the capital it had previously allocated to CBS Outdoors to increasing its content library in its remaining media businesses: CBS produced 20% more content in 2015 than in 2014, and production expenses increased by 13% due to "an increased investment in internally developed television series as well as higher costs associated with the mix of titles sold."[33] This $314 million increase in production expense[34] represented about half of CBS's previous expenditures on CBS Outdoors in 2012,[35] underscoring the point that CBS may have reallocated capital from its divested business to capture better growth opportunities in its remaining operations.

Marc Metrick, the former CEO of Saks Fifth Avenue who became the CEO of Saks.com after the company split its e-commerce and bricks-and-mortar businesses, gave an interview with the *Wall Street Journal* in which he cogently described how the separation resolved some of the challenges of inefficient capital allocation in the combined company. " 'I was running an 'or' company. I was either investing in stores or investing online.' He said he can now focus on improving Saks's digital business, and his counterpart . . . can do the same for the bricks-and-mortar business."[36] Consistent with Mr. Metrick's remarks,* after the two businesses separated, each of them was able to direct its capital investments to the opportunities where they were likely to yield the highest returns. "Mr. Metrick said that since the split he has upgraded Saks's website, improving its searchability, among other things. . . . The stores have made their own

---

* A counterpoint to Mr. Metrick's opinion appears in Chapter 2's discussion of several companies that passed the Better Off Test and therefore chose not to divest. For example, Macy's declined to split its bricks-and-mortar and e-commerce businesses in response to activist demands that it do so, arguing that the value of keeping these operations integrated exceeded the value of separating them.

improvements, including the addition of return desks at 18 of Saks's 41 stores."[37] The investments that Saks.com and Saks Fifth Avenue were able to make in their respective businesses appear to have paid off: between 2019 and 2021, quarterly online sales increased by 84% and traffic by 88%, and quarterly in-store sales grew 24%.[38]

Finally, one of the main strategic rationales that Masco articulated for its spinoff of TopBuild was the opportunity for Masco to drive growth in its remaining businesses (plumbing products, decorative architectural products, cabinets, and windows) by increasing capital expenditures in those areas.[39] In an investor call, CEO Keith Allman detailed some of these opportunities: "With regards to capital allocation, investing in that core business growth and plumbing for example, leveraging our brands into category expansion, expanding our global frosted shower market presence, in paint globalizing and further penetrating the pro-market. In windows, we are expanding geographically. We are continuing to build out our global spa business so there are a number of capital allocation investments that we are looking at to drive that full potential growth."[40] Consistent with this statement, Masco increased its overall capital expenditures by $52 million between 2014 and 2016, and capital expenditures as a share of sales rose from 1.8% in 2014 to 2.2% in 2015 to nearly 2.5% in 2016.[41]

R&D Expenditures

As they do with the efficiency of capital allocation decisions, divestitures can equally improve the innovative outcomes that companies realize from their R&D expenditures. The innovation process consists of three steps: (1) invention, the process of finding solutions to complex technical problems; (2) development, the process of converting an invention into a final product; and (3) commercialization, the process of bringing new products to market and capturing value from them.[42] Divestitures have been shown to improve companies' performance along all three of these dimensions:

- Companies produce more novel inventions after undertaking divestitures, because the financial slack that these transactions create promotes risk taking.

- Companies progress more inventions through development after undertaking divestitures, since the capital that these transactions free up enables them to test and scale up more prototype products and to eliminate bottlenecks in production.

- Companies earn higher revenues from their top products after undertaking divestitures due to the improvements in invention quality and development progress that these transactions promote.[43]

Divestitures are highly prevalent in the pharmaceutical industry, a context in which innovation is critically important: deal values rose from $3.9 billion in 2010 to $10.9 billion in 2017, and companies divested more than $25 billion worth of assets, with at least one $5 billion divestiture each year since 2013.[44] This increase in divestiture activity has been explicitly linked to the ability to shift R&D efforts into new therapeutic classes and new technologies after these transactions. According to one commentator who was interviewed in a market intelligence report, "We'll see, I think, more and more divestitures of therapeutic categories as a way to free up capital, prune the tree and focus on the areas [in which companies] want to compete long term. . . . In a market that sees innovative changes to data use and digitization . . . companies are now more likely to divest and be ready to invest in those new technologies."[45]

Takeda Pharmaceuticals provides an excellent example of these trends and tendencies. Takeda divested numerous non-core businesses to promote focus on the therapeutic areas it deemed to be core to its long-term global growth strategy.[46] Having completed these divestitures, CFO Costa Saroukos described Takeda's plans to increase R&D expenditures to promote growth and innovation in the company's remaining businesses: "With the cost-cutting done and the bulk of asset sales closed, we are now pivoting from integration to a phase of accelerating the top line and ramping up investment in our innovative pipeline."[47] CEO Christophe Weber called 2021 an "inflection year" for Takeda "as it starts to marshal new molecules from its pipeline across regulatory finish lines."[48] Mr. Weber further elaborated that Takeda is experiencing "growth momentum on its pipeline, including 12 approvals across key markets. . . . The businesses we have divested are no growth businesses and in many cases declining. That's why we're seeing accelerating of our remaining businesses."[49]

* * *

Taken together, the findings and examples discussed in this section reveal that divestitures can catalyze improvements in how companies allocate capital and R&D expenditures to better opportunities in their non-divested businesses, with significant benefits for these companies' overall strategic direction and performance. Accordingly, a best practice in divestiture implementation is for companies to use divestitures as a prompt to review their strategic priorities, to determine whether resources are being allocated in a way that advances those priorities, and if not, to take proactive steps to improve their resource allocation processes.

CHAPTER 11

Reshaping External Perceptions

INTRODUCTION

This chapter considers the third and final aspect of divestiture implementation, the need for divesting companies to reshape the perceptions that external stakeholders have of their organizations. A company's stakeholders consist of two main groups:

- Financial constituencies, such as shareholders, creditors, prospective investors, securities analysts, and ratings agencies

- Non-financial constituencies, such as customers, suppliers, employees, regulators, the media, and local communities

Clearly, both groups of stakeholders contribute to competitive advantage by providing the goods, services, information, technology, knowledge, money, and other resources that companies need to survive and thrive in their relevant markets. While financial constituencies primarily facilitate the flow of capital that permits companies to function on a day-to-day basis, it is important to recognize the critical contributions of non-financial constituencies as well. They provide specialized and socially complex resources, such as talent, skills, relationships, and capabilities, which, in many cases, contribute more to companies' ability (or inability) to outperform competitors than simple financial resources do. Consider how much value organizations like Pixar, Apple, and Amazon respectively derive from the contributions of their animators, product designers, and suppliers; conversely, consider the prices paid by companies like Wells Fargo, United Airlines, and Monsanto when the opinion of regulators, customers, and the public (appropriately) turned against them. Empirical evidence provides further support for these examples: two studies found that employee satisfaction is positively correlated with long-term stock market performance,[1] and a third study established that companies that consider certain non-financial constituencies' interests during their acquisitions outperform those that do not.[2]

These findings highlight the point that stakeholder perceptions matter a great deal for corporate performance and even survival, especially during the execution of major transactions like divestitures. When stakeholders have favorable perceptions of such transactions, their willingness to continue contributing resources to—and to continue working with—these companies may be heightened, especially over the long term. However, when stakeholders have negative perceptions of certain transactions, they may run for the exits, in some instances threatening companies' very viability. Divestitures have the strong potential to impair stakeholder perceptions by altering companies' financial needs, disrupting employment relationships, harming local communities, or requiring new supplier and customer contracts. Thus, it is imperative that companies carefully manage stakeholders' perceptions of divestitures.

Divestitures influence two aspects of stakeholder perceptions:

1. *Perceptions of strategy.* Divestitures often reflect a change in corporate strategy, but stakeholders may continue to associate the divesting company with the divested business even after these entities separate.

2. *Perceptions of implementation.* Certain implementation decisions (e.g., headcount reductions, plant closures, relocations of corporate headquarters) may harm stakeholders' interests, tarnishing their perceptions of the divesting company.

This chapter describes how these two issues manifest themselves, as well as some of the steps that companies can take to manage them.

PERCEPTIONS OF STRATEGY

Over the past decade, Vivek Shah executed a fundamental transformation of the venerable publishing company, Ziff Davis. As the publisher of *PC Magazine*, Ziff Davis was a leader in the technology print media space at the height of the dot-com bubble, only to fall into bankruptcy after three private equity buyouts as the bubble burst and digital media came to dominate.[3] With backing from private equity firm Great Hill Partners, Mr. Shah bought Ziff Davis out of bankruptcy and turned it into an advertising technology giant. What accounted for Mr. Shah's success after three previous owners and one bankruptcy reorganization? Rather than the typical targeted advertisements, Mr. Shah repositioned Ziff Davis's strategy around the niche of "helping advertisers reach people [like corporate IT managers] that make decisions about buying products—particularly high-end technology products [for their companies]."[4] After achieving triple-digit revenue growth and going on a massive acquisition spree, Mr. Shah sold Ziff Davis to J2 Global in 2012, staying on and eventually becoming CEO of that company in 2018.

Fast forward to 2021: J2 Global announced it would spin off its slower-growing online fax business (eFax) into a new company called Consensus Cloud Solutions, leaving behind a digital media company consisting of its faster-growing assets (such as Mashable, RetailMeNot, and IGN). Guess what name Vivek Shah chose for the remaining company he would continue running? Ziff Davis, of course. "In an interview, Mr. Shah said that the parent company will be renamed Ziff Davis, a nod to the century-old publisher. Mr. Shah said he picked the name—which calls to mind the heyday of the dot-com boom—because that publishing company survived an industry shake-up from print to digital and weathered a 2008 bankruptcy."[5]

Divestitures frequently represent significant changes to corporate strategy. As discussed in Part I, these transactions enable companies to remove underperforming units, to focus on different core businesses, or even to shift into new strategic domains. The significance of the strategic change implied by divestitures is especially pronounced when these transactions remove large businesses or businesses that are linked to companies' past histories.[6] Accordingly, companies may need to convey to their stakeholders the magnitude of strategic change implied by their divestitures, often by changing their corporate names, as highlighted by the Ziff Davis anecdote.

Corporate names and their associated representations, such as logos, corporate colors, and ticker symbols, are critical reflections of a company's strategy since they are readily visible to all stakeholders that interact with it. A company's name can enhance its competitive advantage by distinguishing the unique features of what that company does in comparison to its peers. It can provide direction and purpose to employees, aiding with recruiting and retention. It can boost the brand identities and images of the individual products and services that a company provides, as can be seen from companies like Coca-Cola and Apple. A company's name can even shape the way that the investment community sees it and interprets its message, influencing that company's market valuation and access to capital. Accordingly, corporate name changes can cause stakeholders to alter both their perceptions of a company and their behavior toward it, with significant implications for many aspects of its operations and performance.

Stakeholders react strongly to corporate names and name changes, though at times in ways that prioritize style over substance. For example, research has shown that companies that added ".com" to their names during the tech bubble enjoyed significant increases in their stock prices,[7] as did companies that removed ".com" from their names after the bubble had burst.[8] Individuals looking to invest in Nest (the smart appliances company) after Google acquired it confused that company with Nestor (whose ticker is NEST), causing Nestor's stock price to soar by 1,900%.[9] Similarly, Tweeter Home Entertainment's stock price increased by 685% after Twitter announced its plans for an initial public offering,[10] and the stock price of Zoom Technologies (a defunct Chinese wireless communications company whose ticker is ZOOM) rose by 1,500% as investors sought to buy shares in Zoom Video Communications (the videoconferencing platform) at the onset of the COVID-19 pandemic.[11] Even shares in Canadian materials science company Meta Materials rose by as much as 10% the day after Facebook announced it would rename itself Meta Platforms. The founder and CEO of Meta Materials politely commented on this news: "I applaud Mark Zuckerberg's and Meta Platforms Inc.'s multibillion-dollar commitment to make the metaverse a reality."[12]

Given the importance of corporate names in the eyes of stakeholders, name changes are a valuable technique for reshaping stakeholder perceptions of companies that undertake major transactions. For example, companies that combine in so-called mergers of equals often rename the merged entity and change its associated imagery to reflect that company's new identity as an "equal" product of its predecessor companies (e.g., DaimlerChrysler, AOL Time Warner, and Morgan Stanley Dean Witter

Discover), or to signal a fresh start as a completely new company (e.g., BB&T and SunTrust merged and became Truist Financial). But sometimes these name changes fall flat; for instance, the Truist name change sparked much amusement among commentators, "with one academic wondering if they stole the name from a tube of toothpaste."[13] These quips are quite common, the classic one having been directed at the corporate name Enteron, which was quickly abandoned when the press pointed out that the word "enteron" is a scientific term for the digestive tract.[14] The company's name was then changed to Enron. Similarly, a former shareholder of the newly renamed Aurizon, an Australian railroad, showed the author an email that he sent to the company's public relations department, opining that Aurizon could plausibly be the name of Verizon's hearing aid subsidiary.

The signaling benefits of corporate name changes are more substantial when it comes to divestitures. When a company's current name evokes a connection to the business it is divesting, a name change can help it convey to stakeholders that (1) the divested business will no longer be part of the divesting company, and (2) the focus of the divesting company will be different after that transaction. For example, after divesting Corn Products International (its legacy corn refining business), CPC International renamed itself Bestfoods. The elimination of the letters "CPC" reflected the removal of the corn refining business from the company's portfolio, and the new name signified its intention to focus on branded food products after the divestiture: "Best Foods" was the brand name of the mayonnaise that it sold west of the Rocky Mountains. Similarly, after divesting the Illinois Central Railroad, IC Industries became Whitman Corporation. The removal of the initials "IC" from the company's name reflected the divestiture of the eponymously initialed railroad business, and "Whitman" was a more neutral corporate name associated with the diversified holding company's chocolate candy business. In Kraft Foods' spinoff of its North American grocery business, Kraft assigned its existing name to the grocery business (where it would likely carry more brand equity, a critical consideration in the constant battle for shelf space) and renamed the global snacks business Mondelez International. "Coined by two of Kraft's employees, the name is meant to evoke the global ambitions of the new snack business, which will take on the titan Frito-Lay, and pique the palate as well with its nod to the words for "world" and "delicious" in a variety of romance languages."[15] Having said this, Nelson Peltz (the activist investor who successfully pushed for the Kraft–Mondelez split) commented that the name Mondelez "sounds like a disease."[16]

The signaling benefits of corporate name changes are especially valuable in situations where the divested business carries a stigma from which the divesting company wishes to escape. For example, after divesting American Tobacco, American Brands changed its name to Fortune Brands. The press immediately recognized the wisdom of this name change; an article in *Fortune* proclaimed, "The rechristening itself was a good idea. Even though American Brands had been out of the U.S. tobacco business for two years, its name is still associated with tobacco. The new name should put an end to that source of confusion."[17] In a similar vein, a few years before divesting its international tobacco operations, Philip Morris renamed itself Altria Group, ostensibly also to dissociate the company from its tobacco businesses, to which the Philip Morris name was historically linked. As early as 1989, nearly 15 years before the Altria name change, Philip Morris's branding consultants advocated that " 'the name change alternative offers the possibility of masking the negatives associated with the tobacco business,' thus enabling the company to improve its image and raise its profile without sacrificing tobacco profits."[18]

Consistent with these examples, more than half of companies that undertake divestitures also change their corporate names within five years of those transactions,[19] underscoring the idea that corporate name changes can be a valuable way to convey information to stakeholders about the magnitude of change implied by a divestiture, and to shape their perceptions of what the divesting company's remaining, non-divested businesses will do after that transaction. As evidence of this point, divesting companies appear to enjoy significant performance benefits when they undertake divestitures contemporaneously with corporate name changes: the shareholder returns to companies that change their names within three years of undertaking divestitures are more than double the shareholder returns to companies that divest without changing their corporate names.[20]

Conversely, the failure to change a company's name sufficiently in conjunction with a divestiture can create confusion and harm relations between that company and its stakeholders. For example, Time Warner Inc. spun off its cable business as Time Warner Cable in 2009, yet due to the similarity of their corporate names, stakeholders routinely confuse the two companies more than a decade after their separation. The *Wall Street Journal* reported an amusing anecdote about the name confusion, in which Time Warner Inc. CEO Jeff Bewkes received a vitriolic email from an irate consumer calling him a "f—ing piece of s—." The customer was upset about his cable service and the many failed attempts technicians had made to fix it. Thankfully, Mr. Bewkes was amused; it wasn't the first time that an angry customer had mistaken Time Warner Inc. for Time Warner Cable.[21] Indeed, the fun continued when the Senate mistakenly summoned Time Warner Cable's former CEO, Robert Marcus (rather than Mr. Bewkes), to testify at a Senate Judiciary Antitrust Subcommittee hearing about the then proposed merger between AT&T and Time Warner Inc.[22] AT&T tried to resolve the confusion in a filing with the SEC,[23] but the damage had already been done.*

Just as the Time Warner confusion illustrates the challenges of name changes that do not sufficiently distinguish the divesting company's new identity in the eyes of its stakeholders, name changes that are unappealing to stakeholders can also be ineffective at reflecting the new strategic goals achieved by a divestiture. For example, after spinning off its newspaper publishing business, Tribune Company renamed its remaining broadcasting and digital media assets "tronc" (short for "Tribune online content"). John Oliver (a satirical news host) mocked this name change as resembling "the noise an ejaculating elephant makes or, more appropriately, the sound of a stack of print newspapers being thrown into a dumpster,"[24] and *The Verge* described it as "the sound of a Millennial falling down the stairs."[25] The company was renamed Tribune Publishing just a few years later. Humor aside, the findings and examples discussed in this section imply that (judicious) corporate name changes are a useful tactic to pursue in conjunction with divestitures, given their ability to reflect the extent to which a company is separating from the divested business, and to signal the nature of the divesting company's remaining operations and strategy to stakeholders.

---

* Remarkably, this SEC filing stated: "Time Warner Inc. should not be confused with Time Warner Cable, which is a distinct, independent company owned by Charter Communications. In 2008, Time Warner and Time Warner Cable announced a complete legal and structural separation of the companies. That separation was completed in 2009, and the companies have been completely separate and independent entities ever since."

PERCEPTIONS OF IMPLEMENTATION

In addition to the challenges that divestitures can pose for stakeholders' perceptions of strategy, the decisions that companies make when implementing these transactions can also damage stakeholder interests in certain situations. One of the most common ways in which this occurs is when divestitures are accompanied by headcount reductions or when certain employees must follow the divested business to its new corporate owner. Not only are these decisions costly to the affected employees, but they can also prompt feelings of resentment or fear among the employees that remain with the divesting company, impairing their performance and commitment to that organization. For example, when Masco announced that it would lay off 40% of its corporate staff in conjunction with the spinoff of its construction services business (as described in Chapter 10), CEO Keith Allman acknowledged these challenges: "Allman said he knows the job cuts will be a painful blow to the morale of the workforce, which has already been through several rounds of job cuts in recent years. 'Whenever business decisions cross personal relationships, it is tough, and this is tough. And we are working through it,' Allman said. 'Our focus is on the future.' "[26] In contrast, the New York Times Company took a somewhat different approach when it announced the sale of its Regional Media Group to Halifax Media Holdings just after Christmas 2011, explaining in a memo that Halifax would be making all employee retention (and layoff) decisions. An article in *The Wire* savaged the likely effects of these decisions on both New York Times Company and Regional Media Group employees:

> But let's be honest: Regardless of whether you write articles or sell ads for a Times Company Regional newspaper, Halifax saying you will be notified if you will receive a job offer is a very polite way of saying that you'd better get ready to lose your job. . . . You can just imagine what the other Regional Media Group employees are thinking right now. Maybe: At least The Times waited until after Christmas to break the bad news![27]

Relatedly, companies often change the locations of and/or close facilities (such as corporate headquarters, factories, and plants) in conjunction with divestitures, potentially resulting in further dislocations among employees as well as economic disruptions to local communities. For instance, when ConocoPhillips spun off Phillips 66 (its downstream chemicals and refining business), commentators described the Bartlesville, Oklahoma, community, home to 3,500 shared services jobs for both companies, as being "literally in flux," in that "all employees are being moved to one of the two companies [Phillips 66 or ConocoPhillips], with co-workers who once sat side to side now literally shifted to separate buildings."[28] Similarly, when DowDuPont announced that it would divide the newly merged company into three independent companies (Dow, DuPont, and Corteva), local leaders in Wilmington, Delaware, expressed serious concerns about the consolidation of facilities and personnel that would accompany these divestitures. After the deal was announced, the *Philadelphia Inquirer* reported:

> [CEO Ed Breen] quickly began consolidating staff jobs and gutting corporate offices in Wilmington. Most DuPont Central Research scientists were laid off or transferred to business units. Admirers of the old DuPont howled. . . . Union representatives appealed to Breen to leave enough people at the plants to get work done safely. Residents of areas near aging and blighted former DuPont plants worry about the poisons left behind.[29]

While the decisions a company must make in terms of these and other contentious issues may be necessary for it to realize value from a divestiture, they are clearly not always easy ones. Accordingly, the way that companies handle divestiture implementation decisions has the potential either to enhance or to erode stakeholders' perceptions of those organizations. There are three best practices that companies should follow to manage stakeholder perceptions of divestiture implementation decisions:

- Actively communicating with stakeholders as to how implementation decisions will affect them

- Exhibiting sensitivity and compassion when making implementation decisions that might harm stakeholders' interests

- Taking responsibility for and helping to mitigate or resolve any non-legal problems that occurred prior to or during those transactions

Active Communication

As underscored by the previous discussion, divestitures can cause stakeholders to question why certain businesses were divested and how those decisions might come to affect them. Absent clear answers to such questions, stakeholders often assume the worst, causing them to act in ways that erode the value-creation potential of these divestitures. However, active communication with stakeholders can promote buy-in and avoid negative and costly surprises. One study showed that communications from management that helped employees understand the events surrounding divestitures (i.e., layoffs) improved employees' perceptions of the "procedural justice" of those transactions and promoted their commitment to their companies after the divestitures were complete.[30]

For example, in Acxiom's sale of Acxiom Marketing Services (AMS) to Interpublic Group, CEO Warren Jemson emphasized the avoidance of uncertainty among stakeholders as an important goal of the company's communication strategy about the divestiture: "Our end-to-end communications about the divestiture were completely transparent. In February of 2018, we publicly announced that we were beginning a process to explore strategic alternatives for AMS. We explained to employees how we intended to map various roles across both entities and communicate with those affected by the divestiture of AMS—in such situations, no solution is perfect, but we tried to eliminate as much uncertainty as possible."[31]

Similarly, in ServiceMaster's sale of its Management Services business to Aramark in 2003, it anticipated significant concerns among its employees about the reason for the divestiture and how it would affect them, especially among the employees that would follow the Management Services business to Aramark. As a result, the company hired Dome Communications to help manage a strategic communications program to educate internal audiences about these issues. Dome described some of the approaches it took to achieve this goal:

> [Helping] divested employees feel comfortable that the values and culture of acquirer Aramark would be compatible with their own principles and philosophy . . . was imperative. . . . Dome conducted a series of meetings with the Aramark management to discuss opportunities for employee growth within the new company as well as gather information regarding Aramark's corporate citizenship program that would ultimately help the

divested employees feel comfortable and positive about integration into the new corporate structure.[32]

Sensitivity and Compassion

In addition to communicating with stakeholders, companies must also exhibit sensitivity and compassion when making and executing divestiture implementation decisions that might damage stakeholders' interests. Research has established that in situations where corporate decisions harm stakeholders' interests (e.g., when a manufacturing process pollutes the local environment), companies that have collaborative relationships with their stakeholders and that work together to mitigate or share the burden of those problems outperform companies that do not.[33] This suggests that when companies make divestiture implementation decisions that impair stakeholder interests, an approach that seeks to offset some of the damage of those decisions may be valuable.

For example, just before Altria spun off Philip Morris International (its international tobacco business), it closed its Cabarrus plant in North Carolina and consolidated its remaining North American cigarette production into its facility in Richmond, Virginia. Rather than simply laying off all the Cabarrus employees, Altria carefully managed employee relations and community perceptions by offering positions in Richmond to "most North Carolina hourly employees and many salaried employees," which brought "several hundred" jobs to Richmond and bolstered Altria's reputation there.[34] To avoid damaging the economic interests of the employees that were not transferred to Richmond, Altria decided that "other workers at the North Carolina plant [would] be eligible for between three and 20 months of severance pay and benefits, depending on length of service, plus outplacement counseling."[35] Although these implementation decisions likely reduced the financial benefits to Altria of the Cabarrus plant closure, the company's humane treatment of its employees during this aspect of the divestiture process might still have been a net positive by improving stakeholder perceptions of the transaction.

When DowDuPont announced that it would split itself into three new companies (Dow, DuPont, and Corteva) in 2018, local leaders expressed reservations about how various implementation decisions would affect their communities—particularly the decision to keep DuPont's and Corteva's headquarters in Wilmington, Delaware, rather than to relocate them to midwestern cities. However, the three companies' collaborative approaches to community relations during the divestiture process turned out to be a resounding success. For example, DuPont and Corteva sought to maintain good relations with the midwestern farming communities where their operations were based by creating two "global business sites" in Johnston, Iowa, and Indianapolis, Indiana.[36] While these decisions were undoubtedly partially driven by the need to maintain physical proximity to the farmers that were and would continue to be customers of the two companies, there was also an important perceptual component to them, in that the optics of severing ties (or impairing relations) with stakeholders in Iowa and Indiana would have been quite negative for DuPont and Corteva. Additionally, in retaining its corporate headquarters in Midland, Michigan, Dow "reaffirmed its commitment to Michigan and promised to honor its philanthropic obligations. 'Dow will continue to have a leading presence in the region and we will continue to provide our resources, time, talents and people to the Great Lakes Bay Region,' Dow CEO James Fitterling said in a statement. 'We will continue to partner with our community organizations that make our region a great place to live and work.'"[37] DuPont equally poured significant effort into developing strong community relations in Midland by contributing to numerous volunteer projects and educational initiatives.[38]

Taking Responsibility

A final aspect of managing stakeholder perceptions of divestiture implementation is a willingness to take responsibility for and to help rectify any non-legal problems that occurred prior to or during those transactions. Even though a divestiture separates the divested business from its former parent, this does not absolve the divesting company from taking responsibility for damage the divested business may have caused to stakeholders. The divesting company must still do the right thing vis-à-vis those stakeholders.

To bring this point to life, consider Rio Tinto's approach to stakeholder relations in its 2016 transfer of its 53.8% stake in Bougainville Copper Ltd. (the operating company that ran the Panguna mine in Papua New Guinea) to the Bougainville and Papua New Guinea governments.[39] Panguna was one of the world's largest open-pit copper and gold mines and was extremely important to the local economy, even as it generated significant pollution. Rio Tinto's decision to exit its stake in Bougainville Copper was attributed to commodity price declines and investor risks,[40] yet Rio Tinto initially refused to take any responsibility for the environmental impact the mine had had on the local community or to contribute to its estimated billion dollar remediation cost.[41] One member of the local parliament poignantly explained, "Our rivers are poisoned with copper, our homes get filled with dust from the tailings mounds, our kids get sick from the pollution. . . . These are not problems we can fix with our bare hands. We urgently need Rio Tinto to do what's right and deal with the disaster they have left behind."[42] After significant bad press and backlash from stakeholders about this and other community violations (Rio Tinto's CEO resigned in 2020 after the destruction of a 46,000-year-old sacred indigenous site to expand an iron mine in Australia,[43] prompting a former Australian prime minister to dub the company "Rio TNT"[44]), Rio Tinto softened its stance and agreed to engage in settlement talks to address its financial liabilities and human rights responsibilities at Panguna. But the damage was done, and Rio Tinto is widely described as facing a long road to rebuilding its tarnished reputation.[45]

* * *

This chapter concludes Part III, which has analyzed the three main aspects of divestiture implementation: the separation of the divested business from the divesting company's remaining operations, the reconfiguration of internal processes within the divesting company, and the need to reshape external perceptions of the divesting company. These steps are summarized in Exhibit 11.1.

Summary of Steps in Divestiture Implementation

Steps in Divestiture Implementation	Required Activities
Separate the Divested Business	• Define the scope of the divested business by identifying which resources will follow the divested business and which ones will not
	• Divide common resources, expenses, and liabilities the divested business previously shared with the non-divested units
	• Use transition services agreements and other contracts to govern ongoing interactions between the divested business and the divesting company
Reconfigure Internal Processes	• Avoid stranded costs by reducing corporate expenditures in proportion to the smaller scale of the divesting company's operations
	• Improve resource allocation processes by reinvesting capital and R&D expenditures into businesses that have the strongest future growth potential
Reshape External Perceptions	• Convey the magnitude of strategic change implied by a divestiture to stakeholders through corporate name changes
	• Mitigate negative perceptions of divestiture implementation decisions by actively communicating with and exhibiting compassion and social responsibility toward stakeholders

CONCLUSION

In an article in *The Atlantic*, author, musician, and businessman Ted Gioia cited two interesting statistics: as of January 2022, "old songs" represented 70% of the current U.S. music market, and the 200 most popular new tracks accounted for less than 5% of total streams.[1] Opining on the causes of the dearth of good new music relative to the hits of yore, Mr. Gioia remarked:

> I learned the danger of excessive caution long ago, when I consulted for huge Fortune 500 companies. The single biggest problem I encountered—shared by virtually every large company I analyzed—was investing too much of their time and money into defending old ways of doing business, rather than building new ones. We even had a proprietary tool for quantifying this misallocation of resources. . . . Senior management hated hearing this, and always insisted that defending the old business units was their safest bet.[2]

Nowhere are these sentiments more apt than when it comes to divestitures. One of the main insights of this book is that divestitures are not affirmatively utilized as extensively, or as readily, as they should be. The causes of this imbalance are manifold, but they all ultimately lead back to Mr. Gioia's comments about embedded mindsets, risk aversion, and defending old ways of doing business. Just as he explained, the inertia against divestitures is usually quite costly, leading to underperformance at best and failure at worst.

Fundamentally, divestitures empower companies to change. Market conditions, consumer preferences, technologies, industry trajectories, regulatory environments, macroeconomic cycles, and even social mores constantly evolve, and companies must act to capture the value of dynamic circumstances and avoid being left behind. While mergers and acquisitions can certainly contribute to the realization of these objectives, expansionary initiatives are often insufficient and sometimes counterproductive, especially when they are poorly conceived and/or executed and so fail to yield the anticipated returns. This book has established that divestitures can foundationally reshape the businesses in which companies operate, and in the process, change their very strategies and identities as well. Accordingly, divestitures should be a central part of any company's strategic toolbox, in that they can create significant value when executives undertake them proactively, structure them efficiently, and implement them effectively.

At the same time, it is crucial to recognize that divestitures are not a panacea to be used by all companies in all situations. The Introduction to this book invoked General Electric as an example of a company *not divesting even though the circumstances clearly demanded that it divest.* Accordingly, it is only fitting that this Conclusion invoke another corporate titan, Berkshire Hathaway, to illustrate the opposite: *not divesting when it is wholly appropriate not to divest.* Consider the following excerpt from a letter to shareholders written by Warren Buffett in 2015, the Golden Anniversary of his (and Charles Munger's) tenure at Berkshire Hathaway:

> Sometimes pundits propose that Berkshire spin-off certain of its businesses. . . . Voluntary spin-offs, though, make no sense for us: We would lose control value, capital-allocation flexibility and, in some cases, important tax advantages. The CEOs who brilliantly run our subsidiaries now would have difficulty in being as effective if running a spun-off operation, given the operating and financial advantages derived from Berkshire's ownership. Moreover, the parent and the spun-off operations, once separated, would likely incur moderately greater costs than existed when they were combined.[3]

Berkshire Hathaway's diversification strategy has clearly generated incredible shareholder returns over the decades (a 2,810,526% overall gain in the company's per-share market value from 1965 to 2020, as compared to a 23,454% overall gain in the S&P 500 over the same period),[4] and Mr. Buffett convincingly explains how divestitures would run counter to that strategy in his letter. But, as documented in the Introduction to this book, General Electric equally destroyed significant shareholder value by remaining diversified and not divesting GE Capital 10 years sooner than it did. So, which of these companies is correct? Does diversification create or destroy value? Should executives embrace or eschew divestitures? How does one explain the corporate dissolutions of so many other conglomerates?

As with many difficult questions, the answers to these are, "It depends." The job this leaves for executives is to develop a strategic mindset that enables them to recognize the value of both diversification *and* focus—with the latter being what is too often underappreciated and sometimes missed altogether. In other words, when it comes to divestitures, executives must identify, seize, and occupy the ground between General Electric and Berkshire Hathaway: being able to recognize the value-creation potential of keeping a set of businesses together as part of the same corporate household, but at the same time, being able to see—and to act on—the handwriting on the wall once it becomes apparent that one or more of the company's businesses is no longer adding value to the portfolio. This, ultimately, is the core message of this book.

Minor Divestiture Structures

This appendix briefly summarizes the main features of three minor divestiture structures: like-kind exchanges, rights offerings, and exchangeable securities.

Like-Kind Exchanges

If one thinks of a simple exchange as the swapping of one asset for another, a like-kind exchange is the swapping of one asset for another *identical* asset. Subject to very strict tax regulations, a like-kind exchange can be tax-free, except to the extent that cash, indebtedness, or other liabilities are part of the exchange. Moreover, taxes will only be deferred until the new property is sold.

Like-kind exchanges are still reasonably common in the real estate industry, and they once occurred with some regularity in connection with broadcast licenses. Although like-kind exchanges could in theory be used to swap businesses, it's difficult to envision a situation in which such a swap could occur, especially in view of the many alternative structures in the divestiture toolbox.

Rights Offerings

In a rights offering, a company will grant subscription rights to its stockholders, such that the holders of the rights may use them to purchase their aliquot shares of stock in the granting entity. The recipients of such rights have three alternatives: (1) they can exercise them by tendering the rights together with cash to acquire the shares being offered;[*] (2) they can sell them if a market exists for the rights; or (3) they can let them expire.

Obviously, rights offerings are a means for a company to raise cash. A rights offering is typically used by a company that is about to engage in a dilutive transaction; it permits stockholders to engage in anti-dilutive purchases of that company's shares. However, there is nothing to prevent a company from using a rights offering to divest a subsidiary. Instead of granting a right to buy its own equity, the company could simply grant a right to buy its subsidiary's equity. Indeed, the ever-evolving world of corporate reorganizations has become the principal arena for rights offerings to be used to raise cash and divest business units.[1]

Exchangeable Securities

An exchangeable security of an issuer (typically a bond or a preferred stock) can be *exchanged* for the shares of a *different company*. Therefore, it is similar to a convertible security of an issuer (also, typically a bond or a preferred stock), which can be *converted* into shares of that *same company*.

Northern Natural Gas (one of the major predecessors of Enron) divested a subsidiary in a merger into Mobil Oil in 1964, in which Mobil became the owner of the subsidiary and Northern Natural Gas received a large block of Mobil's shares.[2] Later, the gas company raised $200 million from the sale of newly issued debentures that were *exchangeable* into those shares.[3] Both the merger and the bond issuance were tax-free; taxes were only incurred upon each actual exchange of the bonds.

---

* There have been instances in which rights could be tendered with cash or *with the issuer's debt securities*. The package of a right with a debt security is known as a "synthetic convertible bond." Warrants (i.e., rights) were given to the former stockholders in the 1993 reorganization of LTV Corporation. Those warrants were exercisable with the tender of either cash or certain debt securities, which marginally increased their value.

Sources: Harper, Peter Alan. 1993. "LTV Files Reorganization Plan." *AP News*, January 20, 1993. https://apnews.com/article/21233c2200257c698af9796c824babc4.

Sloan, Allan. 1993. "What LTV Securities Are Really Worth." *The Morning Call*, February 7, 1993. https://www.mcall.com/news/mc-xpm-1993-02-07-2903854-story.html.

Representative Divesting Joint Ventures (>$1 Billion)

Representative Divesting Joint Ventures (>$1 Billion)[4]

Year Announced	Divesting Company	Divested Business	Independent Counterparty	Resulting Joint Venture	% of JV Initially Owned by Divesting Company	% of JV Initially Owned by Independent Counterparty
1994	U.S. West	Domestic Cellular Assets	Airtouch Communications (Domestic Cellular Assets)	Wireless Management Company	30.0%	70.0%
1997	Ashland Petroleum	Downstream Operations	Marathon Oil (Downstream Operations)	Marathon Ashland Petroleum LLC	38.0%	62.0%
2002	IBM	Hard Disk Drive Business	Hitachi (Hard Disk Drive Business)	Hitachi Global Storage Technologies	30.0%	70.0%
2003	Vivendi Universal	Vivendi Universal Entertainment	General Electric (NBC)	NBC Universal (NBCU)	20.0%	80.0%
2004	IBM	PC Business	Lenovo	Lenovo	18.9%	81.1%
2007	Molson Coors Brewing Co	U.S. Operations	SABMiller PLC (U.S., Puerto Rican Ops)	MillerCoors	42.0%	58.0%
2011	General Electric	NBC Universal (NBCU)	Comcast	NBCUniversal	49.0%	51.0%
2014	Novartis	Over-the-Counter Business	GlaxoSmithKline (Cons. Healthcare Business)	GSK Consumer Healthcare	36.5%	63.5%

(continued)

Representative Divesting Joint Ventures (>$1 Billion) *(continued)*

Year Announced	Divesting Company	Divested Business	Independent Counterparty	Resulting Joint Venture	% of JV Initially Owned by Divesting Company	% of JV Initially Owned by Independent Counterparty
2015	Mondelez International	Coffee Business	Acorn Holdings (D.E. Master Blenders 1753)	Jacobs Douwe Egberts	44.0%	56.0%
2016	Nestlé	Ice Cream Business	PAI Partners (R&R Ice Cream)	Froneri	50.0%	50.0%
2016	General Electric	GE Oil & Gas	Baker Hughes	Baker Hughes, a GE Company	62.5%	37.5%
2017	Fujitsu	Global PC Business (Fujitsu Client Computing Ltd)	Lenovo Development Bank of Japan	Fujitsu Client Computing Ltd	44.0%	51% (Lenovo) 5% (DBJ)
2019	Newmont Mining	Nevada Mining Operations	Barrick Gold (Nevada Mining Operations)	Nevada Mining Operations	38.5%	61.5%
2021	General Electric	GE Capital Aviation Services	AerCap	AerCap	46.0%	54.0%
2021	PepsiCo	Juice Business	PAI Partners	Juice Business	39.0%	61.0%

NOTES

INTRODUCTION

1. Derived from data gathered from Refinitiv (formerly Thomson One) and Compustat. Accessed: January 2, 2021, and January 26, 2022.
2. KPMG CEO Survey conducted in conjunction with Gerson Lehrman Group. September 2019.
3. Derived from data gathered from Refinitiv (formerly Thomson One). Accessed: January 2, 2021, and January 26, 2022.
4. Ibid.
5. Derived from data gathered from Refinitiv (formerly Thomson One) and CRSP. Accessed: January 2, 2021, and February 9, 2022.
6. Ibid.
7. Derived from data gathered from Compustat. Accessed: January 8, 2022.
8. Gryta, Thomas, and Ted Mann. 2018. "GE Powered the American Century—Then It Burned Out." *Wall Street Journal*, December 14, 2018. https://www.wsj.com/articles/ge-powered-the-american-centurythen-it-burned-out-11544796010.
9. Colvin, Geoff. 2015. "For GE, Breaking up Is Hard to Do." *Fortune*, August 21, 2015. https://fortune.com/2015/08/21/general-electric-end-of-conglomerates/.
10. Gryta, Thomas, and Ted Mann. 2018. "GE Powered the American Century—Then It Burned Out." *Wall Street Journal*, December 14, 2018. https://www.wsj.com/articles/ge-powered-the-american-centurythen-it-burned-out-11544796010.
11. Ibid.
12. Anonymous executive, personal interview with author, January 12, 2018.
13. Feldman, Emilie R. 2021. "Restructuring and Divestitures." In: *Strategic Management: State of the Field and Its Future*, edited by Irene Duhaime, Michael Hitt, and Marjorie Lyles, 153–166. New York: Oxford University Press.

CHAPTER 1

1. FitzGerald, Drew, Joe Flint, and Benjamin Mullin. 2021. "AT&T's Hollywood Ending Erased Billions in Value." *Wall Street Journal*, May 17, 2021. https://www.wsj.com/articles/att-hollywood-ending-erased-billions-value-hbo-discovery-warner-11621297279?mod=series_attdiscover.
2. Krouse, Sarah, and Micah Maidenberg. 2018. "Verizon Takes $4.5 Billion Charge Related to Digital Media Business." *Wall Street Journal*, 2018. https://www.wsj.com/articles/verizon-takes-4-6-billion-charge-related-to-digital-media-business-11544538587?mod=article_inline.
3. Derived from data analyzed in Feldman, Emilie R. 2014. "Legacy Divestitures: Motives and Implications." *Organization Science* 25, no. 3 (May–June 2014): 815–832.
4. Derived from data analyzed in Miller, Alex, Todd Dubner, Tom Mayor, Rick Harpster, Ramahi Sarma-Rupavtarm, and Emilie R. Feldman. 2020. "Think Like an Activist: To Maximize Value, CEOs Can Borrow from the Activist Playbook." KPMG LLP. https://advisory.kpmg.us/content/dam/advisory/en/pdfs/2020/think-like-an-activist.pdf.
5. Kaplan, Steven N., and Michael S. Weisbach. 1992. "The Success of Acquisitions: Evidence from Divestitures." *Journal of Finance* 47, no. 1 (March 1992): 107–138.
   Ravenscraft, David J., and Frederic M. Scherer. 1987. *Mergers, Selloffs, and Economic Efficiency*. Washington, DC: Brookings Institution Press.
   Porter, Michael E. 1987. "From Competitive Advantage to Corporate Strategy." *Harvard Business Review* 65, no. 3 (May–June): 43–59.
6. Feldman, Emilie R. 2014. "Legacy Divestitures: Motives and Implications." *Organization Science* 25, no. 3 (May–June 2014): 815–832.
7. Kaplan, Steven N., and Michael S. Weisbach. 1992. "The Success of Acquisitions: Evidence from Divestitures." *Journal of Finance* 47, no. 1 (March 1992): 107–138.
8. Chen, Siwen, and Emilie R. Feldman. 2018. "Activist-Impelled Divestitures and Shareholder Value." *Strategic Management Journal* 39, no. 10 (October 2018): 2726–2744.
9. Unpublished research conducted by the author.
10. Kaplan, Steven N., and Michael S. Weisbach. 1992. "The Success of Acquisitions: Evidence from Divestitures." *Journal of Finance* 47, no. 1 (March 1992): 107–138.
11. Ernst & Young. 2021. "2021 Global Corporate Divestment Study." https://www.ey.com/en_us/divestment-study.
12. Unpublished research conducted by the author.
13. Buchholtz, Ann K., Michael Lubatkin, and Hugh M. O'Neill. 1999. "Seller Responsiveness to the Need to Divest." *Journal of Management* 25, no. 5 (1999): 633–652.

14. Porter, Michael E. 1979. "How Competitive Forces Shape Strategy." *Harvard Business Review* 57, no. 2 (March–April 1979): 137–145.

15. Saul, Stephanie. 2008. "New York's Tisch Family Eases Away from Cigarettes." *New York Times*, June 10, 2008. https://www.nytimes.com/2008/06/10/business/worldbusiness/10iht-menthol.4.13614794.html.

16. Ibid.

17. Stynes, Tess, and John W. Miller. 2016. "Alcoa Results Hurt by Weak Aluminum Prices." *Wall Street Journal*, April 11, 2016. https://www.wsj.com/articles/alcoa-hurt-by-weak-aluminum-prices-1460408314.

18. Miller, John W., and David Benoit. 2016. "Alcoa Reaches Deal with Elliott on Board Members." *Wall Street Journal*, February 1, 2016. https://www.wsj.com/articles/SB10421484055275154434404581514362872337854.

19. Mitchell, Russ, and Andrea Chang. 2014. "EBay Agrees to Spin Off PayPal After Pressure from Activist Investors." *Los Angeles Times*, October 1, 2014. https://www.latimes.com/business/la-fi-ebay-paypal-20141001-story.html.

20. Chen, Siwen, and Emilie R. Feldman. 2018. "Activist-Impelled Divestitures and Shareholder Value." *Strategic Management Journal* 39, no. 10 (October 2018): 2726–2744.

21. Christofferson, Scott A., Robert S. McNish, and Diane L. Sias. 2004. "Where Mergers Go Wrong." *McKinsey Quarterly*, May 1, 2004. https://www.mckinsey.com/business-functions/strategy-and-corporate-finance/our-insights/where-mergers-go-wrong.

22. Deighton, John. 2002. "How Snapple Got Its Juice Back." *Harvard Business Review* 80, no. 1 (January 2002): 47–53.

23. Bertolucci, Jeff. 2009. "Skype, eBay Divorce: What Went Wrong." *PCWorld*, September 1, 2009. https://www.pcworld.com/article/171267/skype_ebay_divorce_what_went_wrong.html.

24. Jamerson, Joshua. 2017. "Xerox Stock Climbs After Splitting with Business-Services Unit." *Wall Street Journal*, January 3, 2017. https://www.wsj.com/articles/xerox-stock-climbs-after-splitting-with-business-services-unit-1483461921.

25. Knowledge@Wharton. 2016. "Will Xerox's Spinoff Unlock Value for Investors?" February 10, 2016. https://knowledge.wharton.upenn.edu/article/will-xeroxs-spinoff-unlock-value-for-investors/.

26. Brew, Alan. 2014. "Why Corporate Mergers of Equals Almost Never Work." *Forbes*, June 5, 2014. https://www.forbes.com/sites/forbesleadershipforum/2014/06/05/why-corporate-mergers-of-equals-almost-never-work/#650bf5a44176.

27. Stoll, John D. 2019. "In 'Mergers of Equals,' One Side Is Always a Bit More Equal." *Wall Street Journal*, June 14, 2019. https://www.wsj.com/articles/in-mergers-of-equals-one-side-is-always-a-bit-more-equal-11560528068.

28. St. Jean, Dianne C., and Cohen, Allan R. 2000. "DaimlerChrysler Merger: The Quest to Create 'One Company.'" Babson Case BAB041.

29. Isidore, Chris. 2007. "Daimler Pays to Dump Chrysler." *CNN Money*, May 14, 2007. https://money.cnn.com/2007/05/14/news/companies/chrysler_sale/.

30. McGrath, Rita Gunther. 2015. "15 Years Later, Lessons from the Failed AOL-Time Warner Merger." *Fortune*, January 10, 2015. https://fortune.com /2015/01/10/15-years-later-lessons-from-the-failed-aol-time-warner-merger/.

31. Ibid.

32. Feloni, Richard. 2018. "Billionaire Investor Steve Case Says the Failure of the 2000 AOL Time Warner Mega Merger Taught Him a Crucial Lesson About Execution." *Business Insider*, October 13, 2018. https://www.businessinsider .com/steve-case-lesson-aol-time-warner-merger-2018-10.

33. Truell, Peter. 1997. "Morgan Stanley and Dean Witter Agree to Merge." *New York Times*, February 6, 1997. https://www.nytimes.com/1997/02/06 /business/morgan-stanley-and-dean-witter-agree-to-merge.html.

34. Chaudhuri, Saikat, and David Way. 2007. "Forming a Financial Services Goliath: The Morgan Stanley-Dean, Witter & Discover, Co. Merger." Wharton Teaching Case.

35. Anonymous executive, personal interview with author, December 2014.

36. Yeats, William Butler. 1916. *Responsibilities and Other Poems*. New York: Macmillan Company.

37. Porter, Michael E. 1976. "Please Note Location of Nearest Exit: Exit Barriers and Planning." *California Management Review* 19, no. 2 (Winter 1976): 21–33. Harrigan, Kathryn Rudie. "Deterrents to Divestiture." *Academy of Management Journal* 24, no. 2 (June 1981): 306–323.

38. Aguilar, Francis J., Dwight B. Crane, and Florence Langford. 1984. "American Can Company, 1984." Harvard Business School Case 284-095.

39. Cruz, Ernesto. 1982. Esmark, Inc. (A). Harvard Business School Case 9-283-013.

40. Yulico, Nicholas. 2007. "More Trouble Ahead for Builders." *TheStreet*, January 4, 2007. https://www.thestreet.com/personal-finance/insurance/more -trouble-ahead-for-builders-10330500.

41. Etiorre, Barbara. 1978. "Avon Plans to Take Over Tiffany for $104 Million." *New York Times*, November 22, 1978. https://www.nytimes.com/1978/11/22 /archives/avon-plans-to-take-over-tiffany-for-104-million-cosmetics-concern .html.

42. Wayne, Leslie, and John Duka. 1983. "At Tiffany, A Troubled Transition." *New York Times*, October 16, 1983. https://www.nytimes.com/1983/10/16 /business/at-tiffany-a-troubled-transition.html.

43. Vise, David A. 1984. "Tiffany Returning to Its Past." *Washington Post*, September 6, 1984. https://www.washingtonpost.com/archive/business/1984/09 /06/tiffany-returning-to-its-past/04e9ed0b-420b-474f-9670-9056e81fbe8d/.

44. Ibid.

45. Wayne, Leslie, and John Duka. 1983. "At Tiffany, A Troubled Transition." *New York Times*, October 16, 1983. https://www.nytimes.com/1983/10/16 /business/at-tiffany-a-troubled-transition.html.

46. Kapner, Suzanne. 2021. "Tiffany's New French Owner Brings a Makeover— and a Culture Clash." *Wall Street Journal*, December 23, 2021. https:// www.wsj.com/articles/tiffanys-new-french-owner-brings-a-makeoverand -a-culture-clash-11640264191.
47. Feldman, Emilie R. 2014. "Legacy Divestitures: Motives and Implications." *Organization Science* 25, no. 3 (May–June 2014): 815–832.
48. Flint, Jerry. 1987. "Take the High Ground: Pet Inc." *Forbes*, June 15, 1987.
49. Feldman, Emilie R. 2014. "Legacy Divestitures: Motives and Implications." *Organization Science* 25, no. 3 (May–June 2014): 815–832.
50. Ibid.
51. Villalonga, Belén, and Raphael Amit. 2006. "How Do Family Ownership, Control and Management Affect Firm Value?" *Journal of Financial Economics* 80, no. 2 (May 2006): 385–417.
52. Feldman, Emilie R., Raphael Amit, and Belén Villalonga. 2016. "Corporate Divestitures and Family Control." *Strategic Management Journal* 37, no. 3 (March 2016): 429–446.
53. Bercovici, Jeff. 2012. "Nice Guy, Finishing Last: How Don Graham Fumbled the Washington Post Co." *Forbes*, February 8, 2012. https://www.forbes .com/sites/jeffbercovici/2012/02/08/don-graham-washington-post/?sh= 1eec07ac7383.
54. Farhi, Paul. 2013. "Washington Post to Be Sold to Jeff Bezos, the Founder of Amazon." *Washington Post*, August 5, 2013. https://www.washingtonpost .com/national/washington-post-to-be-sold-to-jeff-bezos/2013/08/05 /ca537c9e-fe0c-11e2-9711-3708310f6f4d_story.html.

CHAPTER 2

1. Spain, William, and Alistair Barr. 2010. "Pershing May Push for Fortune Brands Split." *MarketWatch*, October 8, 2010. https://www.marketwatch.com /story/pershing-may-push-for-fortune-brands-split-2010-10-08.
2. Ibid.
3. Ashworth, Will. 2013. "Fortune Brands: A Great-but-Not-Perfect Moment for Ackman." *InvestorPlace*, May 9, 2013. https://investorplace.com/2013/05 /fortune-brands-a-great-but-not-perfect-moment-for-ackman/.
4. Ibid.
5. Ovide, Shira. 2010. "Bill Ackman's $300 Million Profit on the Fortune Brands Breakup." *Wall Street Journal*, December 8, 2010. https://www.wsj .com/articles/BL-DLB-29609.
6. Porter, Michael E. 1987. "From Competitive Advantage to Corporate Strategy." *Harvard Business Review* 65, no. 3 (May–June): 43–59.
7. Ibid.
8. Fund Letters. 2019. "Third Point Investor Letter—A Stronger Sony." *Seeking Alpha*, June 24, 2019. https://static.seekingalpha.com/uploads/sa _presentations/419/43419/original.pdf.

9. Sony Corporation. 2019. "Letter from the CEO to Sony's Shareholders and All Stakeholders." September 17, 2019. https://www.sony.net/SonyInfo/IR /news/20190917_E.pdf?mod=article_inline.

10. Ibid.

11. United Technologies. 2020. "United Technologies Board of Directors Approves Separation of Carrier and Otis and Declares Spin Off Distribution of Carrier and Otis Shares." March 11, 2020. https://www.prnewswire.com /news-releases/united-technologies-board-of-directors-approves-separation -of-carrier-and-otis-and-declares-spin-off-distribution-of-carrier-and-otis -shares-301021893.html.

12. Trentmann, Nina. 2019. "Otis Names New CFO as It Preps for Separation from United Technologies." *Wall Street Journal*, September 16, 2019. https:// www.wsj.com/articles/otis-names-new-cfo-as-it-preps-for-separation-from -united-technologies-11568666713?mod=searchresults&page=1&pos=1.

13. Trentmann, Nina. 2019. "Carrier's New CFO to Guide Spinoff from United Technologies." *Wall Street Journal*, September 13, 2019. https:// www.wsj.com/articles/carriers-new-cfo-to-guide-spinoff-from-united- technologies-11568409546?mod=searchresults&page=1&pos=9.

14. Teece, David J., Richard Rumelt, Giovanni Dosi, and Sidney Winter. 1994. "Understanding Corporate Coherence: Theory and Evidence." *Journal of Economic Behavior & Organization* 23, no. 1 (January 1994): 1–30.

15. Collis, David J., and Cynthia A. Montgomery. 1998. "Creating Corporate Advantage." *Harvard Business Review* 76, no. 3 (May–June 1998): 70–83.

16. Teece, David J., Richard Rumelt, Giovanni Dosi, and Sidney Winter. 1994. "Understanding Corporate Coherence: Theory and Evidence." *Journal of Economic Behavior & Organization* 23, no. 1 (January 1994): 1–30.

17. Prahalad, C. K., and Gary Hamel. 1990. "The Core Competence of the Cor- poration." *Harvard Business Review* 68, no. 3 (May–June 1990): 79–91.

18. Collis, David J., and Cynthia A. Montgomery. 2008. "Competing on Resources." *Harvard Business Review* 86, no. 7–8 (July–August 2008): 140–150.

19. Greenberg, Julia. 2015. "How Disney Is Making Sure You'll Never Be Able to Escape *Star Wars*." *Wired*, November 17, 2015. https://www.wired.com/2015 /11/how-disney-is-making-sure-youll-never-be-able-to-escape-star-wars/.

20. Comment, Robert, and Gregg A. Jarrell. 1995. "Corporate Focus and Stock Returns." *Journal of Financial Economics* 37, no. 1 (January 1995): 67–87. John, Kose, and Eli Ofek. 1995. "Asset Sales and Increase in Focus." *Journal of Financial Economics* 37, no. 1 (January 1995): 105–126. Markides, Constantinos C. 1992. "Consequences of Corporate Refocusing: Ex Ante Evidence." *Academy of Management Journal* 35 no. 2 (June 1992): 398–412. Markides, Constantinos C. 1995. "Diversification, Restructuring and Eco- nomic Performance." *Strategic Management Journal* 16, no. 2 (1995): 101–118.

21. Reingold, Jennifer. 2015. "Everybody Hates Pearson." *Fortune*, January 21, 2015. https://fortune.com/2015/01/21/everybody-hates-pearson/.

22. Pearson PLC. 2019. "Pearson PLC Disposal." December 18, 2019. https://markets.ft.com/data/announce/full?dockey=1323-14353304 -3UDK5O8634V3ABMH9G2INSI81D.

23. Goold, Michael, Andrew Campbell, and Marcus Alexander. 1994. *Corporate-Level Strategy: Creating Value in the Multibusiness Company*. New York: Wiley.

 Porter, Michael E. 1987. "From Competitive Advantage to Corporate Strategy." *Harvard Business Review* 65, no. 3 (May–June): 43–59.

24. Rawley, Evan. 2010. "Diversification, Coordination Costs, and Organizational Rigidity: Evidence from Microdata." *Strategic Management Journal* 31, no. 8 (August 2010): 873–891.

 Zhou, Yue Maggie. 2011. "Synergy, Coordination Costs, and Diversification Choices." *Strategic Management Journal* 32, no. 6 (June 2011): 624–639.

25. Duchin, Ran, Amir Goldberg, and Denis Sosyura. 2017. "Spillovers Inside Conglomerates: Incentives and Capital." *Review of Financial Studies* 30, no. 5 (May 2017): 1696–1743.

26. Shaw, Jason D., Nina Gupta, and John E. Delery. 2002. "Pay Dispersion and Workforce Performance: Moderating Effects of Incentives and Interdependence." *Strategic Management Journal* 23, no. 6 (June 2002): 491–512.

27. Card, David, Alexandre Mas, Enrico Moretti, and Emmanuel Saez. 2012. "Inequality at Work: The Effect of Peer Salaries on Job Satisfaction." *American Economic Review* 102, no. 6 (October 2012): 2981–3003.

 Obloj, Tomasz, and Todd Zenger. 2017. "Organization Design, Proximity, and Productivity Responses to Upward Social Comparison." *Organization Science* 28, no. 1 (January–February 2017): 1–18.

28. Carnahan, Seth, Rajshree Agarwal, and Benjamin A. Campbell. 2012. "Heterogeneity in Turnover: The Effect of Relative Compensation Dispersion of Firms on the Mobility and Entrepreneurship of Extreme Performers." *Strategic Management Journal* 33, no. 12 (December 2012): 1411–1430.

 Kacperczyk, Aleksandra, and Chanchal Balachandran. 2018. "Vertical and Horizontal Wage Dispersion and Mobility Outcomes: Evidence from the Swedish Microdata." *Organization Science* 29, no. 1 (January–February 2018): 17–38.

29. Feldman, Emilie R., Claudine Gartenberg, and Julie Wulf. 2018. "Pay Inequality and Corporate Divestitures." *Strategic Management Journal* 39, no. 11 (November 2018): 2829–2858.

30. Lucchetti, Aaron, and Daniel Machalaba. 1999. "Of Two Spinoff Plans, Janus Is Facing the Undesired One." *Wall Street Journal*, October 6, 1999. https://www.wsj.com/articles/SB939164734838623298.

31. Ibid.

32. Trefis Team. 2015. "Understanding GE Capital's Exit Plan." *Forbes*, June 2, 2015. https://www.forbes.com/sites/greatspeculations/2015/06/02/understanding-ge-capitals-exit-plan/#6498f5ad70c1.
33. Ibid.
34. Berger, Philip G., and Eli Ofek. 1995. "Diversification's Effect on Firm Value." *Journal of Financial Economics* 37, no. 1 (January 1995): 39–65.
35. Dubner, Todd, Emilie R. Feldman, Tom Pernsteiner, Eric Shapiro, and Ramahi Sarma-Rupavtarm. 2018. "Can Your Valuation Be Improved?" KPMG LLP. https://advisory.kpmg.us/content/dam/advisory/en/pdfs/can-your-valuation-be-improved.pdf.
36. Zuckerman, Ezra W. 1999. "The Categorical Imperative: Securities Analysts and the Illegitimacy Discount." *American Journal of Sociology* 104, no. 5 (March 1999): 1398–1438.
    Gilson, Stuart C., Paul M. Healy, Christopher F. Noe, and Krishna G. Palepu. 2001. "Analyst Specialization and Conglomerate Stock Breakups." *Journal of Accounting Research* 39, no. 3 (December 2001): 565–582.
37. Feldman, Emilie R. 2016. "Corporate Spinoffs and Analysts' Coverage Decisions: The Implications for Diversified Firms." *Strategic Management Journal* 37, no. 7 (July 2016): 1196–1219.
38. Ibid.
39. Baker, Stephen. 1996. "Who's Really Out from Under at Westinghouse?" *BusinessWeek*, November 25, 1996.
40. Trachtenberg, Jeffrey A. 2014. "Corporate News: B&N to Carve Off Its Nook Business: Retailer is Splitting in Two, with Underperforming E-book and E-reader Unit as a New Company." *Wall Street Journal*, June 26, 2014.
41. Cruz, Ernesto. 1982. Esmark, Inc. (A). Harvard Business School Case 9-283-013.
42. Ibid.
43. Cruz, Ernesto. 1982. Esmark, Inc. (B). Harvard Business School Case 9-283-014.
44. Hayes, Thomas C. 1980. "Esmark Puts Value on Offer; $55-60 Range Is Below Estimates Part of Sweeping Divestiture 'Worth More Than $30' for Years." *New York Times*, July 1, 1980. https://www.nytimes.com/1980/07/01/archives/esmark-puts-value-on-offer-5560-range-is-below-estimates-part-of.html.
45. Jensen, Michael C., and Kevin J. Murphy. 1990. "Performance Pay and Top-Management Incentives." *Journal of Political Economy* 98, no. 2 (April 1990): 225–264.
46. Buchholtz, Ann K., Michael Lubatkin, and Hugh M. O'Neill. 1999. "Seller Responsiveness to the Need to Divest." *Journal of Management* 25, no. 5 (1999): 633–652.

47. Jensen, Michael C. 1986. "Agency Costs of Free Cash Flow, Corporate Finance, and Takeovers." *American Economic Review* 76, no. 2 (May 1986): 323–329.

Stulz, René M. 1990. "Managerial Discretion and Optimal Financing Policies." *Journal of Financial Economics* 26, no. 1 (July 1990): 3–27.

Amihud, Yakov, and Baruch Lev. 1981. "Risk Reduction as a Managerial Motive for Conglomerate Mergers." *Bell Journal of Economics* (Autumn 1981): 605–617.

Shleifer, Andrei, and Robert W. Vishny. 1989. "Management Entrenchment: The Case of Manager-Specific Investments." *Journal of Financial Economics* 25, no. 1 (November 1989): 123–139.

48. Jensen, Michael C., and William H. Meckling. 1976. "Theory of the Firm: Managerial Behavior, Agency Costs and Ownership Structure." *Journal of Financial Economics* 3, no. 4 (October 1976): 305–360.

Jensen, Michael C. 1986. "Agency Costs of Free Cash Flow, Corporate Finance, and Takeovers." *American Economic Review* 76, no. 2 (May 1986): 323–329.

49. Jakab, Spencer. 2018. "Turning GE's Sacred Cows into Hamburger." *Wall Street Journal*, May 23, 2018. https://www.wsj.com/articles/turning-ges -sacred-cows-into-hamburger-1527109360.

50. "Power Failure: John Flannery Gets Down to Business Restructuring General Electric." *The Economist*, June 30, 2018. https://www.economist.com/business /2018/06/28/john-flannery-gets-down-to-business-restructuring-general -electric.

51. Dranikoff, Lee, Tim Koller, and Antoon Schneider. 2002. "Divestiture: Strategy's Missing Link." *Harvard Business Review* 80, no. 5 (May 2002): 74–83.

52. Ernst & Young. 2021. "2021 Global Corporate Divestment Study." https:// www.ey.com/en_us/divestment-study.

53. Chen, Siwen, and Emilie R. Feldman. 2018. "Activist-Impelled Divestitures and Shareholder Value." *Strategic Management Journal* 39, no. 10 (October 2018): 2726–2744.

54. Lazard's Capital Markets Advisory Group. 2022. "2021 Review of Shareholder Activism." https://www.lazard.com/media/451963/lazards-q4-2021 -review-of-shareholder-activism_vf.pdf.

55. Honeywell. 2017. "Honeywell Announces Planned Portfolio Changes." October 11, 2017. https://www.honeywell.com/us/en/press/2017/10/honeywell -announces-planned-portfolio-changes.

56. Chen, Siwen, and Emilie R. Feldman. 2018. "Activist-Impelled Divestitures and Shareholder Value." *Strategic Management Journal* 39, no. 10 (October 2018): 2726–2744.

57. Ibid.

58. Miller, Alex, Todd Dubner, Tom Mayor, Rick Harpster, Ramahi Sarma-Rupavtarm, and Emilie R. Feldman. 2020. "Think Like an Activist: To

Maximize Value, CEOs Can Borrow from the Activist Playbook." KPMG LLP. https://advisory.kpmg.us/content/dam/advisory/en/pdfs/2020/think-like -an-activist.pdf.

CHAPTER 3

1. Baird, Les, David Harding, Andrei Vorobyov, and Shikha Dhar. 2020. "Corporate M&A Report 2020: Disrupt or Be Disrupted? More Companies Choose to Play Offense with Scope M&A." Bain & Company, 2020. https:// www.bain.com/globalassets/noindex/2020/bain_report_corporate_m_and _a_report_2020.pdf.

2. Derived from data gathered from Refinitiv (formerly Thomson One) and CRSP. Accessed: January 2, 2021.

3. IBM. 2020. "IBM to Accelerate Hybrid Cloud Growth Strategy and Execute Spin-Off of Market-Leading Managed Infrastructure Services Unit." October 8, 2020. https://newsroom.ibm.com/2020-10-08-IBM-To-Accelerate -Hybrid-Cloud-Growth-Strategy-And-Execute-Spin-Off-Of-Market-Leading -Managed-Infrastructure-Services-Unit.

4. Ibid.

5. Ibid.

6. Hesseldahl, Arik. 2016. "Hewlett Packard Enterprise Will Spin Off Its Troubled Services Business in an $8.5 Billion Deal." *Vox*, May 24, 2016. https:// www.vox.com/2016/5/24/11763362/hpe-spins-off-services-deal-csc.

7. Hewlett Packard Enterprise. 2021. "Acquisitions." https://investors.hpe.com /financial/acquisitions.

8. Hewlett Packard Enterprise. 2016. "Why the 'Spin-Merge' of HPE's Enterprise Services with CSC is the Right Next Step." https://www.hpe.com /us/en/newsroom/blog-post/2017/03/why-the-spin-merge-of-hpes-enterprise -services-with-csc-is-the-right-next-step.html.

9. Ibid.

10. Rooney, Ben. 2009. "Sea World, Busch Gardens Sold for $2.7 Billion." *CNN Money*, October 7, 2009. https://money.cnn.com/2009/10/07/news/companies /blackstone_anheuser_busch_inbev/.

11. Leonard-Barton, Dorothy, and Gary Pisano. 1990. "Monsanto's March into Biotechnology." Harvard Business School Case 9-690-009.

12. Chiem, Phat X. 2000. "Monsanto Sells Off Sweetener Business." *Chicago Tribune*, February 5, 2000. https://www.chicagotribune.com/news/ct-xpm -2000-02-05-0002050176-story.html.

13. Patel, Sahil. 2020. "Disney Sells Ad-Tech Firm TrueX to Gimbal." *Wall Street Journal*, September 28, 2020. https://www.wsj.com/articles/disney -sells-ad-tech-firm-truex-to-gimbal-11601317342.

14. Ibid.

15. Maksimovic, Vojislav, Gordon Phillips, and Nagpurnanand R. Prabhala. 2011. "Post-Merger Restructuring and the Boundaries of the Firm." *Journal of Financial Economics* 102, no. 2 (November 2011): 317–343.

16. Ibid.

17. Kaplan, Steven N., and Michael S. Weisbach. 1992. "The Success of Acquisitions: Evidence from Divestitures." *Journal of Finance* 47, no. 1 (March 1992): 107–138.

18. Capron, Laurence, Will Mitchell, and Anand Swaminathan. 2001. "Asset Divestiture Following Horizontal Acquisitions: A Dynamic View." *Strategic Management Journal* 22, no. 9 (September 2001): 817–844.

19. Reuters Staff. 2015. "J.M. Smucker to Sell U.S. Canned Milk Business." *Reuters*, November 3, 2015. https://www.reuters.com/article/j-m-smucker -divestiture-cannedmilk/update-2-j-m-smucker-to-sell-u-s-canned-milk -business-idUSL3N12Y3QZ20151103.

20. Reuters Staff. 2020. "J.M. Smucker to Sell Crisco Business in $550 Million Cash Deal." *Reuters*, October 26, 2020. https://www.reuters.com/article /us-j-m-smucker-divestiture-b-g-foods/j-m-smucker-to-sell-crisco-business -in-550-million-cash-deal-idUSKBN27B2PG.

21. The J.M. Smucker Company. 2018. "The J.M. Smucker Company Completes the Divestiture of its U.S. Baking Business." August 31, 2018. https:// www.prnewswire.com/news-releases/the-j-m-smucker-company-completes -the-divestiture-of-its-us-baking-business-300705428.html.

22. Fusaro, Dave. 2018. "Smucker to Acquire Rachael Ray Nutrish Pet Food, Maybe Sell its Baking Business." *Food Processing*, April 5, 2018. https:// www.foodprocessing.com/industrynews/2018/smucker-rachael-ray-nutrish/.

23. Tyler, Jordan. 2021. "Smucker's Closes Sale of Natural Balance for $50 Million." *Pet Food Processing*, February 2, 2021. https://www.petfoodprocessing .net/articles/14305-smucker-to-sell-off-natural-balance-for-50-million.
The J.M. Smucker Company. 2018. "The J.M. Smucker Company to Acquire Ainsworth Pet Nutrition, LLC, Maker of Rachael Ray Nutrish Pet Food; Company to Explore Strategic Options for U.S. Baking Business." April 4, 2018. https://www.prnewswire.com/news-releases/the-j-m-smucker-company-to -acquire-ainsworth-pet-nutrition-llc-maker-of-rachael-ray-nutrish-pet-food -company-to-explore-strategic-options-for-us-baking-business-300624569 .html.

24. Tyler, Jordan. 2021. "Smucker's Closes Sale of Natural Balance for $50 Million." *Pet Food Processing*, February 2, 2021. https://www.petfoodprocessing .net/articles/14305-smucker-to-sell-off-natural-balance-for-50-million.

25. Treasury Wine Estates. 2015. "TWE Announces Acquisition of Diageo's Wine Business for US$600 Million and Entitlement Offer." October 14, 2015. https://www.tweglobal.com/-/media/Files/Global/Retail-Entitlement-Offer /Announcement-14-October-2015.ashx.

26. Jasper, Clint. 2016. "Treasury Wine Estates Dumps Cheaper US Brands." *ABC Rural*, July 3, 2016. https://www.abc.net.au/news/rural/rural-news/2016 -07-04/treasury-wine-estates-dumps-cheaper-us-brands/7566328.

27. House, Alana. 2017. "TWE's New Zealand Shake-Up Continues." *Drinks Trade*, April 3, 2017. https://www.drinkstrade.com.au/twes-new-zealand -shake-up-continues.
Swindell, Bill. 2015. "Gallo to Buy Asti Winery, Souverain Brand." *Press Democrat*, July 20, 2015. https://www.pressdemocrat.com/article/business/gallo-to -buy-asti-winery-souverain-brand/?sba=AAS.

28. Jasper, Clint. 2016. "Treasury Wine Estates Dumps Cheaper US Brands." *ABC Rural*, July 3, 2016. https://www.abc.net.au/news/rural/rural-news/2016 -07-04/treasury-wine-estates-dumps-cheaper-us-brands/7566328.

29. Van Bronkhorst, Erin. 2013. "Umpqua Will Buy Sterling in $2 Billion Bank Merger." *Puget Sound Business Journal*, September 11, 2013. https://www .bizjournals.com/seattle/news/2013/09/11/umpqua-sterling-bank-companies -merge.html.

30. Giegerich, Andy. 2014. "Umpqua to Consolidate Branches as Sterling Merger Effects Take Shape." *Portland Business Journal*, June 23, 2014. https://www .bizjournals.com/portland/morning_call/2014/06/umpqua-to-consolidate -branches-as-sterling-merger.html.

31. Tri-City Herald Staff. 2014. "Banner Bank Buys Branches of Umpqua." *Tri-City Herald*, June 24, 2014. https://www.tri-cityherald.com/news/business /article32184801.html.

32. Giegerich, Andy. 2014. "Umpqua to Consolidate Branches as Sterling Merger Effects Take Shape." *Portland Business Journal*, June 23, 2014. https://www .bizjournals.com/portland/morning_call/2014/06/umpqua-to-consolidate -branches-as-sterling-merger.html.

33. Phillips, Don. 1995. "Union Pacific to Merge with Southern Pacific." *Washington Post*, August 4, 1995. https://www.washingtonpost.com/archive/business /1995/08/04/union-pacific-to-merge-with-southern-pacific/8eded38e-d307 -4c2f-8738-bce411d10e43/.

34. Staff and Wire Reports. 1995. "BN Santa Fe to Buy Track from Rivals." *Spokesman-Review*, September 27, 1995. https://www.spokesman.com /stories/1995/sep/27/bn-santa-fe-to-buy-track-from-rivals/

35. Phillips, Don. 1995. "Union Pacific to Merge with Southern Pacific." *Washington Post*, August 4, 1995. https://www.washingtonpost.com/archive/business /1995/08/04/union-pacific-to-merge-with-southern-pacific/8eded38e-d307 -4c2f-8738-bce411d10e43/.

36. Hammes, Paul, and Steve Krouskos. 2016. "Global Corporate Divestment Study. Learning from Private Equity: Experts at Extracting Hidden Value." Ernst & Young, 2016. https://cdn.ey.com/echannel/gl/en/services/transactions /GDS-2016-01/pdf/EY_Global-Corporate-Divestment-Study_2016.pdf.

37. Bunge, Jacob. 2016. "Cargill Says Revamp Showing Results." *Wall Street Journal*, August 11, 2016. https://www.wsj.com/articles/cargill-records-loss-amid-weak-grains-operations-1470836094.
38. Cargill. 2017. "Metal One Corporation to Acquire Cargill's U.S. Metals Business." December 29, 2017. https://www.cargill.com/2017/metal-one-to-acquire-cargills-us-metals-business.
39. Painter, Kristen Leigh. 2017. "Cargill to Sell Power and Gas Business to Macquarie." *Star Tribune*, June 9, 2017. https://www.startribune.com/cargill-to-sell-power-and-gas-business-to-macquarie/427537273/.
40. Bunge, Jacob, and Dominic Chopping. 2015. "Cargill Buys Norwegian Fish-Feed Producer EWOS for $1.5 Billion." *Wall Street Journal*, August 17, 2015. https://www.wsj.com/articles/cargill-buys-norwegian-fish-feed-producer-ewos-for-1-5-billion-1439798406.
41. Kiernan, Lynda. 2017. "Cargill Acquires First Animal Feed Company in Brazil." *Global Ag Investing*, October 31, 2017. http://www.globalaginvesting.com/cargill-acquires-first-animal-feed-company-brazil/.
42. Bunge, Jacob. 2016. "Cargill Says Revamp Showing Results." *Wall Street Journal*, August 11, 2016. https://www.wsj.com/articles/cargill-records-loss-amid-weak-grains-operations-1470836094.
43. Nanda, Vikram, and M. P. Narayanan. 1999. "Disentangling Value: Financing Needs, Firm Scope, and Divestitures." *Journal of Financial Intermediation* 8, no. 3 (July 1999): 174–204.
    Lang, Larry, Annette Poulsen, and René Stulz. 1995. "Asset Sales, Firm Performance, and the Agency Costs of Managerial Discretion." *Journal of Financial Economics* 37, no. 1 (January 1995): 3–37.
44. BP plc. 2010. "BP Establishes $20 Billion Claims Fund for Deepwater Horizon Spill and Outlines Dividend Decisions." June 16, 2010. https://www.bp.com/en/global/corporate/news-and-insights/press-releases/bp-establishes-20-billion-claims-fund-for-deepwater-horizon-spill-and-outlines-dividend-decisions.html.
45. Wearden, Graeme. 2010. "BP Credit Rating Downgraded." *The Guardian*, June 3, 2010. https://www.theguardian.com/business/2010/jun/03/bp-credit-rating-downgraded
46. Ernst & Young. 2021. "2021 Global Corporate Divestment Study." https://www.ey.com/en_us/divestment-study.
47. Recording of in-class visit of Hugh Connerty, President of Outback Steakhouse International, November 14, 2000.
48. Bennett, Victor Manuel, and Emilie R. Feldman. 2017. "Make Room! Make Room! A Note on Sequential Spinoffs and Acquisitions." *Strategy Science* 2, no. 2 (June 2017): 100–110.

49. Heneghan, Carolyn. 2015. "Treasury Wine to Acquire Diageo's US, UK Wine Assets for $552M." *FoodDive*, October 14, 2015. https://www.fooddive .com/news/treasury-wine-to-acquire-diageos-us-uk-wine-assets-for-552m /407300/.

50. Bennett, Victor Manuel, and Emilie R. Feldman. 2017. "Make Room! Make Room! A Note on Sequential Spinoffs and Acquisitions." *Strategy Science* 2, no. 2 (June 2017): 100–110.

51. Cornell, Joe. 2016. "ConAgra Foods to Spin-Off Lamb Weston." *Forbes*, October 12, 2016. https://www.forbes.com/sites/joecornell/2016/10/12 /conagra-foods-to-spin-off-lamb-weston-on-november-9-2016/?sh= 3d4976bd4b43.

52. Gasparro, Annie. 2015. "ConAgra to Sell Private Brands to Tree-House for $2.7 Billion." *Wall Street Journal*, November 2, 2015. https:// www.wsj.com/articles/conagra-to-sell-private-brands-to-treehouse-for-2-7- billion-1446468508.

53. ConAgra Foods, Inc. 2016. "ConAgra Foods to Sell JM Swank to Platinum Equity." June 8, 2016. https://www.businesswire.com/news /home/20160608006422/en/ConAgra-Foods-to-Sell-JM-Swank-to-Platinum -Equity.

54. Trotter, Greg. 2016. "ConAgra to Sell Spice Business for $340 Million." *Chicago Tribune*, May 24, 2016. https://www.chicagotribune.com/business/ct -conagra-spicetec-sale-0524-biz-20160523-story.html.

55. Byington, Lillianna. 2019. "How Conagra Uses M&A to Stay Ahead in the Snacking Sector." *FoodDive*, March 7, 2019. https://www.fooddive.com/news /how-conagra-uses-ma-to-stay-ahead-in-the-snacking-sector/549888/.
Hirsch, Lauren. 2018. "Conagra Brands to Acquire Pinnacle Foods for About $8.1 Billion." *CNBC*, June 27, 2018. https://www.cnbc.com/2018/06 /27/conagra-brands-to-acquire-pinnacle-foods-for-10point9-billion-in-cash -and.html.

56. Conagra Brands. "Company Milestones." https://www.conagrabrands.com /our-company/overview/company-milestones.

57. Doering, Christopher. 2021. "Let's Make a Deal: How Nestlé Is Using M&A and Multibillion-Dollar Divestitures to Shape its Portfolio." *FoodDive*, March 1, 2021. https://www.fooddive.com/news/lets-make-a-deal-how-nestle -is-using-ma-and-multibillion-dollar-divestit/593601/.

58. Nestlé. 2021. "Nestlé Continues Strategic Transformation of Water Business, Agrees on Sale of Nestlé Waters North America Brands." February 17, 2021. https://www.nestle.com/media/pressreleases/allpressreleases/agreement-sale -nestle-waters-north-america-brands.

59. Nestlé. 2021. "Nestlé Acquires Essentia, Expands Presence in Premium Functional Water Segment." March 5, 2021. https://www.nestle.com/media /news/nestle-acquires-essentia.

60. Nestlé. 2021. "Nestlé Health Science to Acquire Nuun, Entering the Fast-Growing Functional Hydration Market." May 10, 2021. https://www.nestle.com/media/news/nestle-health-science-acquire-nuun-entering-functional-hydration-market.

61. Doering, Christopher. 2021. "Let's Make a Deal: How Nestlé Is Using M&A and Multibillion-Dollar Divestitures to Shape its Portfolio." *FoodDive*, March 1, 2021. https://www.fooddive.com/news/lets-make-a-deal-how-nestle-is-using-ma-and-multibillion-dollar-divestit/593601/.

62. Crawford, Elizabeth. 2020. "Nestlé Is Ready to Buy After 18 Months of Divesting Brands, But It Will Do So Cautiously, CFO Says." *Food Navigator-USA*, September 11, 2020. https://www.foodnavigator-usa.com/Article/2020/09/11/Nestle-is-ready-to-buy-after-18-months-of-divesting-brands-but-it-will-do-so-cautiously-CFO-says.

CHAPTER 4

1. Montgomery, Cynthia A., Ann R. Thomas, and Rajan Kamath. 1984. "Divestiture, Market Valuation, and Strategy." *Academy of Management Journal* 27, no. 4 (December 1984): 830–840.

2. Trefis Team. 2016. "Here's How AB InBev Trimmed Business to Make Room for SABMiller." *Forbes*, December 22, 2016. https://www.forbes.com/sites/greatspeculations/2016/12/22/heres-how-ab-inbev-trimmed-business-to-make-room-for-sabmiller/?sh=117cb7473b93.

3. Esterl, Mike. 2016. "AB InBev, SABMiller Deal Expected to Face Global Antitrust Grilling." *Wall Street Journal*, September 16, 2015. https://www.wsj.com/articles/a-global-antitrust-grilling-is-expected-1442442266.

4. Ibid.

5. Drozdiak, Natalia, and Tripp Mickle. 2016. "EU Clears AB InBev's $108 Billion SABMiller Takeover." *Wall Street Journal*, May 24, 2016. https://www.wsj.com/articles/eu-clears-ab-inbevs-108-billion-sabmiller-takeover-1464107386.

6. Trefis Team. 2016. "Here's How AB InBev Trimmed Business to Make Room for SABMiller." *Forbes*, December 22, 2016. https://www.forbes.com/sites/greatspeculations/2016/12/22/heres-how-ab-inbev-trimmed-business-to-make-room-for-sabmiller/?sh=117cb7473b93.

7. Department of Justice. 2016. "Justice Department Requires Anheuser-Busch InBev to Divest Stake in MillerCoors and Alter Beer Distributor Practices as Part of SABMiller Acquisition." July 20, 2016. https://www.justice.gov/opa/pr/justice-department-requires-anheuser-busch-inbev-divest-stake-millercoors-and-alter-beer.

8. Trefis Team. 2016. "Here's How AB InBev Trimmed Business to Make Room for SABMiller." *Forbes*, December 22, 2016. https://www.forbes.com/sites/greatspeculations/2016/12/22/heres-how-ab-inbev-trimmed-business-to-make-room-for-sabmiller/?sh=117cb7473b93.

9. Federal Trade Commission. "The Antitrust Laws." https://www.ftc.gov/tips
   -advice/competition-guidance/guide-antitrust-laws/antitrust-laws.
10. Ibid.
11. Law Library—American Law and Legal Information. "Sherman Antitrust
    Act: What Happened Next . . ." https://law.jrank.org/pages/12387/Sherman
    -Antitrust-Act-What-happened-next.html.
12. Reed, Brad. 2007. "U.S. Department of Justice vs. AT&T." *NetworkWorld*,
    October 26, 2007. https://www.networkworld.com/article/2287512/u-s-
    -department-of-justice-vs--at-t.html.
13. Federal Trade Commission. "The Antitrust Laws." https://www.ftc.gov/tips
    -advice/competition-guidance/guide-antitrust-laws/antitrust-laws.
14. Ibid.
15. U.S. Department of Justice & the Federal Trade Commission. 2020. "Verti-
    cal Merger Guidelines." https://www.ftc.gov/system/files/documents/reports
    /us-department-justice-federal-trade-commission-vertical-merger-guidelines
    /vertical_merger_guidelines_6-30-20.pdf.
16. Federal Trade Commission. "Competitive Effects." https://www.ftc.gov
    /tips-advice/competition-guidance/guide-antitrust-laws/mergers/competitive
    -effects.
17. Department of Justice. 2013. "Justice Department Requires US Airways and
    American Airlines to Divest Facilities at Seven Key Airports to Enhance
    System-wide Competition and Settle Merger Challenge." November 12, 2013.
    https://www.justice.gov/opa/pr/justice-department-requires-us-airways-and
    -american-airlines-divest-facilities-seven-key.
18. Department of Justice. 2018. "The Walt Disney Company Required to Divest
    Twenty-Two Regional Sports Networks in Order to Complete Acquisition
    of Certain Assets from Twenty-First Century Fox." June 27, 2018. https://
    www.justice.gov/opa/pr/walt-disney-company-required-divest-twenty-two
    -regional-sports-networks-order-complete.
19. Federal Trade Commission. 2017. "FTC Requires Mars to Divest 12 Vet-
    erinary Clinics as a Condition of Acquiring Pet Care Company VCA Inc."
    August 30, 2017. https://www.ftc.gov/news-events/press-releases/2017/08/ftc
    -requires-mars-divest-12-veterinary-clinics-condition.
20. Kendall, Brent. 2019. "U.S. Appeals Court Rejects Justice Department
    Antitrust Challenge to AT&T-Time Warner Deal." *Wall Street Journal*, Feb-
    ruary 26, 2019. https://www.wsj.com/articles/u-s-appeals-court-rejects-justice
    -department-antitrust-challenge-to-at-t-time-warner-deal-11551194524.
21. Goovaerts, Diana. 2018. "AT&T Resists Divestitures in Time Warner
    Merger." *Mobile World Live*. May 4, 2018. https://www.mobileworldlive.com
    /featured-content/top-three/att-resists-divestitures-in-time-warner-merger.
22. Baird, Les, David Harding, Andrei Vorobyov, and Shikha Dhar. 2020.
    "Corporate M&A Report 2020: Disrupt or Be Disrupted? More Companies

Choose to Play Offense with Scope M&A." Bain & Company, 2020. https://www.bain.com/globalassets/noindex/2020/bain_report_corporate_m_and_a_report_2020.pdf.

23. Milloy, Meghan, and Jacqueline Varas. 2018. "CFIUS: A Primer." April 13, 2018. https://www.americanactionforum.org/insight/cfius-a-primer/.

24. U.S. Treasury Department. "Executive Order 11858 (As Amended by Executive Order 13456): Foreign Investment in the United States." https://www.treasury.gov/resource-center/international/foreign-investment/Documents/EO-11858-Amended.pdf.

25. Sanger, David E. 1987. "Japanese Purchase of Chip Maker Canceled After Objections in U.S." *New York Times*, March 17, 1987. https://www.nytimes.com/1987/03/17/business/japanese-purchase-of-chip-maker-canceled-after-objections-in-us.html.

26. Markheim, Daniella, and James Carafano. 2006. "After Dubai Ports: Getting CFIUS Reforms Right." *Heritage Foundation*, May 17, 2006. https://www.heritage.org/defense/report/after-dubai-ports-getting-cfius-reforms-right.

27. Sanger, David E. 2006. "Under Pressure, Dubai Company Drops Port Deal." *New York Times*, March 10, 2006. https://www.nytimes.com/2006/03/10/politics/under-pressure-dubai-company-drops-port-deal.html.

28. U.S. Congress. 2007. "Foreign Investment and National Security Act of 2007." Public Law 110–49, July 26, 2007. https://www.congress.gov/110/plaws/publ49/PLAW-110publ49.pdf.

29. Lee, Judith Alison, Jose Fernandez, and Stephanie Connor. 2019. "CFIUS Developments: Notable Cases and Key Trends." Gibson, Dunn, & Crutcher, LLP, April 24, 2019. https://www.gibsondunn.com/cfius-developments-notable-cases-and-key-trends/.

30. Ibid.

31. Milloy, Meghan, and Jacqueline Varas. 2018. "CFIUS: A Primer." April 13, 2018. https://www.americanactionforum.org/insight/cfius-a-primer/.

32. Ibid.

33. Bush, George. 1990. "Message to the Congress on the China National Aero-Technology Import and Export Corporation Divestiture of MAMCO Manufacturing, Incorporated." February 1, 1990. https://fas.org/nuke/guide/china/contractor/90020112.html.

34. Associated Press. 2019. "Obama Blocks Chinese Purchase of Small Oregon Wind Farm Project." *The Oregonian*, January 10, 2019. https://www.oregonlive.com/environment/2012/09/oregon_wind_farm_purchase_by_c.html.

35. Leiter, Michael, Ivan Schlager, and Donald Vieira. 2018. "Broadcom's Blocked Acquisition of Qualcomm." Harvard Law School Forum on Corporate Governance, April 3, 2018. https://corpgov.law.harvard.edu/2018/04/03/broadcoms-blocked-acquisition-of-qualcomm/.

36. Lippman, Thomas W. 1981. "Kuwait Assures U.S. on Santa Fe." *Washington Post*, October 23, 1981. https://www.washingtonpost.com/archive/business /1981/10/23/kuwait-assures-us-on-santa-fe/a7083d67-d780-40fa-a63c -42c474491aef/.

   U.S. House of Representatives. 1981. "Federal Response to OPEC Country Investments in the United States: Hearings Before a Subcommittee of the Committee on Government Operations." September 22 and 23, 1981. https:// www.google.com/books/edition/Federal_Response_to_OPEC_Country _Investm/JhHKlFzAgugC?hl=en&gbpv=1&dq=%22Federal+Response+ to+OPEC+Country+Investments+in+the+United+States+%22&printsec= frontcover).

37. Tkacik, John. 2008. "Magnequench: CFIUS and China's Thirst for U.S. Defense Technology." *Heritage Foundation*, May 2, 2008. https://www .heritage.org/asia/report/magnequench-cfius-and-chinas-thirst-us-defense -technology.

38. Bradsher, Keith. 2010. "Amid Tension, China Blocks Vital Exports to Japan." *New York Times*, September 22, 2010. https://www.nytimes.com/2010/09/23 /business/global/23rare.html.

39. Farrah, Jeff. 2019. "Another Day, Another U.S. Company Forced to Divest of Chinese Investors." *TechCrunch*, April 15, 2019. https://techcrunch.com /2019/04/15/another-day-another-u-s-company-forced-to-divest-of-chinese -investors/.

40. Restuccia, Andrew, and Jing Yang. 2020. "Trump Executive Orders Target TikTok, WeChat Apps." *Wall Street Journal*, August 7, 2020. https://www .wsj.com/articles/senate-votes-to-ban-tiktok-on-government-issued-phones -11596760843.

41. McKinnon, John D., and Alex Leary. 2021. "TikTok Sale to Oracle, Walmart Is Shelved as Biden Reviews Security." *Wall Street Journal*, February 10, 2021. https://www.wsj.com/articles/tiktok-sale-to-oracle-walmart-is-shelved -as-biden-reviews-security-11612958401.

42. Ziobro, Paul. 2021. "Biden Seeks Review of Foreign-Owned Apps Beyond TikTok, WeChat. Here's What You Need to Know." *Wall Street Journal*, June 10, 2021. https://www.wsj.com/articles/biden-seeks-review-of-foreign-owned -apps-beyond-tiktok-wechat-heres-what-you-need-to-know-11623356392.

43. Rubio, Marco. 2022. "Rubio, Colleagues Call on Biden Administration to Provide Plan to Combat Security Risks Posed by TikTok." Marco Rubio, U.S. Senator for Florida, June 27, 2022. https://www.rubio.senate.gov/public/index .cfm/2022/6/rubio-colleagues-call-on-biden-administration-to-provide-plan -to-combat-security-risks-posed-by-tiktok.

44. Sanger, David E. 1987. "Japanese Purchase of Chip Maker Canceled After Objections in U.S." *New York Times*, March 17, 1987. https://www.nytimes .com/1987/03/17/business/japanese-purchase-of-chip-maker-canceled-after -objections-in-us.html.

45. Sanger, David E. 2006. "Under Pressure, Dubai Company Drops Port Deal." *New York Times*, March 10, 2006. https://www.nytimes.com/2006/03/10 /politics/under-pressure-dubai-company-drops-port-deal.html.
46. Restuccia, Andrew, and Jing Yang. 2020. "Trump Executive Orders Target TikTok, WeChat Apps." *Wall Street Journal*, August 7, 2020. https://www .wsj.com/articles/senate-votes-to-ban-tiktok-on-government-issued-phones -11596760843.
47. Milloy, Meghan, and Jacqueline Varas. 2018. "CFIUS: A Primer." April 13, 2018. https://www.americanactionforum.org/insight/cfius-a-primer/.
48. Skadden, Arps, Slate, Meagher, & Flom, LLP. "CFIUS." https://www .skadden.com/capabilities/practices/cfius-national-security-international -trade/cc/cfius-and-foreign-investment-reviews.
49. Lee, Judith Alison, Jose Fernandez, and Stephanie Connor. 2019. "CFIUS Developments: Notable Cases and Key Trends." Gibson, Dunn, & Crutcher, LLP, April 24, 2019. https://www.gibsondunn.com/cfius-developments -notable-cases-and-key-trends/.
50. Feldman, Emilie R. 2006. "A Basic Quantification of the Competitive Implications of the Demise of Arthur Andersen." *Review of Industrial Organization* 29, no. 3 (October 2006): 193–212.
51. Enrich, David, Ben Casselman, and Deborah Solomon. 2009. "How Occidental Scored Citi Unit Cheaply." *Wall Street Journal*, October 12, 2009. https://www.wsj.com/articles/SB125509326073375979.
52. Dash, Eric, and Jack Healy. 2009. "Citigroup Sheds Energy Unit and Its $100 Million Trader." *New York Times*, October 9, 2009. https://www.nytimes.com /2009/10/10/business/10citi.html.
53. Feldman, Emilie R. 2006. "A Basic Quantification of the Competitive Implications of the Demise of Arthur Andersen." *Review of Industrial Organization* 29, no. 3 (October 2006): 193–212.
54. Forbes. 2005. "Was Arthur Andersen A Mistake?" *Forbes*, June 1, 2005. https://www.forbes.com/2005/06/01/cx_da_0601topnews.html?sh= 735793c849a0.
Marotta, Michael E. 2014. "The Wrongful Conviction of Arthur Andersen LLC." ResearchGate, November 20, 2014. https://www.researchgate.net /publication/341757348_The_Wrongful_Conviction_of_Arthur_Andersen _LLC.

CHAPTER 5

1. Sorkin, Andrew Ross. 2014. "The Mergers and Acquisitions Cycle: Buy. Divide. Conquer." *New York Times*, December 10, 2014. https://dealbook .nytimes.com/2014/12/10/the-mergers-and-acquisitions-cycle-buy-divide -conquer/.
2. Miller, Alex, Todd Dubner, Tom Mayor, Rick Harpster, Ramahi Sarma-Rupavtarm, and Emilie R. Feldman. 2020. "Think Like an Activist: to

Maximize Value, CEOs Can Borrow from the Activist Playbook." KPMG LLP. https://advisory.kpmg.us/content/dam/advisory/en/pdfs/2020/think-like -an-activist.pdf.

3. Derived from data gathered from Refinitiv (formerly Thomson One). Accessed: February 14, 2022.

4. Lombardo, Cara, and Dana Cimilluca. 2019. "Huntsman to Sell Two Units for $2.1 Billion." *Wall Street Journal*, August 7, 2019. https://www.wsj.com /articles/huntsman-to-sell-two-units-for-2-1-billion-11565219997.

5. Hays, Kristen. 2020. "Indorama Ventures Closes $2 Billion Acquisition of Huntsman Assets." *S&P Global Platts*, January 6, 2020. https://www .spglobal.com/platts/en/market-insights/latest-news/petrochemicals/010620 -indorama-ventures-closes-2-billion-acquisition-of-huntsman-assets.

6. Huntsman Corporation. 2019. "Huntsman Agrees to Sell its Chemical Inter-mediates and Surfactants Businesses to Indorama Ventures for $2.1 Billion." August 7, 2019. https://www.huntsman.com/news/media-releases/detail/415 /huntsman-agrees-to-sell-its-chemical-intermediates-and.

7. Powers, Eric A. 2001. "Spinoffs, Selloffs and Equity Carveouts: An Analysis of Divestiture Method Choice." (January 2001). http://dx.doi.org/10.2139/ssrn .257600.

8. Ravenscraft, David J., and Frederic M. Scherer. 1991. "Divisional Sell-off: A Hazard Function Analysis." *Managerial and Decision Economics* 12, no. 6 (December 1991): 429–438.

9. Eccles, Robert G., Kersten L. Lanes, and Thomas C. Wilson. 1999. "Are You Paying Too Much for that Acquisition?" *Harvard Business Review* 77, no. 4 (July–August 1999): 136–136.

10. Bargeron, Leonce L., Frederik P. Schlingemann, René M. Stulz, and Chad J. Zutter. 2008. "Why Do Private Acquirers Pay So Little Compared to Public Acquirers?" *Journal of Financial Economics* 89, no. 3 (September 2008): 375–390.

11. Wong, Jacky. 2020. "7-Eleven's $21 Billion Deal Could Be a Marathon." *Wall Street Journal*, August 3, 2020. https://www.wsj.com/articles/7-elevens -21-billion-deal-could-be-a-marathon-11596451820.

12. Lombardo, Cara, Miriam Gottfried, and Rebecca Elliott. 2020. "Marathon Petroleum in Talks with Potential Buyers of Speedway Gas-Station Unit." *Wall Street Journal*, June 18, 2020. https://www.wsj.com/articles/marathon -petroleum-in-talks-with-potential-buyers-of-speedway-gas-station-unit -11592515818?mod=article_inline.

13. Elliott, Rebecca. 2020. "Marathon Petroleum to Sell Gas-Station Chain to 7-Eleven Owners for $21 Billion." *Wall Street Journal*, August 3, 2020. https://www.wsj.com/articles/marathon-petroleum-to-sell-gas-station-chain -to-7-eleven-owners-for-21-billion-11596409261.

14. Reuters Staff. 2020. "Marathon Petroleum Sells Speedway to 7-Eleven Owner for $21 Billion." *Reuters*, August 2, 2020. https://www.reuters.com /article/us-marathon-ptrlum-speedway-seven-i-hldg-idCAKBN24Y0RT.
15. Wong, Jacky. 2020. "7-Eleven's $21 Billion Deal Could Be a Marathon." *Wall Street Journal*, August 3, 2020. https://www.wsj.com/articles/7-elevens -21-billion-deal-could-be-a-marathon-11596451820.
16. Kress, Melissa. 2020. "Marathon Petroleum CEO: Speedway Sale Is a 'Win-Win' for Both Sides." *Convenience Store News*, August 4, 2020. https:// csnews.com/marathon-petroleum-ceo-speedway-sale-win-win-both-sides.
17. Powers, Eric A. 2001. "Spinoffs, Selloffs and Equity Carveouts: An Analysis of Divestiture Method Choice." (January 2001). http://dx.doi.org/10.2139/ssrn .257600.
18. Harrigan, Kathryn Rudie, and Brian M. Wing. 2021. "Corporate Renewal and Turnaround of Troubled Businesses: The Private Equity Advantage." *Strategic Management Review* 2, no. 2 (September 2021): 363–390.
19. Kaul, Aseem, Paul Nary, and Harbir Singh. 2018. "Who Does Private Equity Buy? Evidence on the Role of Private Equity from Buyouts of Divested Businesses." *Strategic Management Journal* 39, no. 5 (May 2018): 1268–1298.
20. Buttigieg, Kevin. 2015. "Symantec Veritas Sale Avoids Spinoff." *Barron's*, August 12, 2015. https://www.barrons.com/articles/symantec-veritas-sale -avoids-spinoff-1439391461.
21. Garcia, Tonya. 2020. "Nutrisystem Parent Tivity Health Shares Plummet 44% After Earnings Miss and Downgrade." *MarketWatch*, February 22, 2020. https://www.marketwatch.com/story/nutrisystem-parent-tivity-health -shares-plummet-42-after-earnings-miss-and-downgrade-2020-02-20.
22. De Lombaerde, Geert. 2020. "Tivity May Shed Nutrisystem." *Nashville Post*, May 7, 2020. https://www.nashvillepost.com/business/health-care/article /21132176/tivity-may-shed-nutrisystem.
23. White, Martin. 2020. "Kainos Capital to Acquire Nutrisystem from Tivity Health for $575m." *FoodBev Media*, October 20, 2020. https://www.foodbev .com/news/kainos-capital-to-acquire-nutrisystem-from-tivity-health-for -575m.
24. Lang, Larry, Annette Poulsen, and René Stulz. 1995. "Asset Sales, Firm Performance, and the Agency Costs of Managerial Discretion." *Journal of Financial Economics* 37, no. 1 (January 1995): 3–37.
25. Powers, Eric A. 2001. "Spinoffs, Selloffs and Equity Carveouts: An Analysis of Divestiture Method Choice." (January 2001). http://dx.doi.org/10.2139/ssrn .257600.
26. Nanda, Vikram, and M. P. Narayanan. 1999. "Disentangling Value: Financing Needs, Firm Scope, and Divestitures." *Journal of Financial Intermediation* 8, no. 3 (July 1999): 174–204.

Lang, Larry, Annette Poulsen, and René Stulz. 1995. "Asset Sales, Firm Performance, and the Agency Costs of Managerial Discretion." *Journal of Financial Economics* 37, no. 1 (January 1995): 3–37.

27. Linnane, Ciara. 2018. "Is Campbell Soup Making a Bad Decision to Sell Its Fresh Foods Business?" *MarketWatch*, September 9, 2018. https://www .marketwatch.com/story/is-campbell-soup-making-a-bad-decision-to-sell-its -fresh-food-business-2018-08-30.

28. Rose, Kennedy. 2019. "Campbell Soup Co. sells off last part of its international business for $2.2B." *Philadelphia Business Journal*, December 23, 2019. https://www.bizjournals.com/philadelphia/news/2019/12/23/campbell -soup-co-sells-off-last-part-international.html.

29. Liu, Angus. 2020. "Bayer, Elanco Get FTC's Final Antitrust Go-Ahead for $7.6B Animal Health Merger After Divestitures." *Fierce Pharma*, July 16, 2020. https://www.fiercepharma.com/pharma/ftc-gives-elanco-s-7-6b-bayer -animal-health-merger-final-antitrust-go-ahead-after.

30. Bender, Ruth. 2018. "Bayer to Cut 12,000 Jobs, Shed Coppertone and Dr. Scholl's Brands." *Wall Street Journal*, November 29, 2018. https://www.wsj .com/articles/bayer-plans-to-sell-brands-including-coppertone-and-dr-scholl -1543500418.

31. Kantchev, Georgi. 2022. "Roundup Owner Bayer Divests Pest-Control Unit in $2.6 Billion Deal." *Wall Street Journal*, March 10, 2022. https://www.wsj .com/articles/roundup-owner-bayer-divests-pest-control-unit-in-2-6-billion -deal-11646908242.

32. "Asset Purchase Agreement among Newsweek, Inc., the Washington Post Company, Harman Media, LLC and Sidney Harman, Ph.D." August 2, 2010. https://www.sec.gov/Archives/edgar/data/104889/000119312510224885 /dex21.htm.

33. Baron, Michael. 2010. "Washington Post Sold Newsweek for $1." *TheStreet*, October 6, 2010. https://www.thestreet.com/investing/stocks/washington -post-sold-newsweek-for-1-10882203.
Pompeo, Joe. 2010. "Newsweek Sells For $1 to Stereo Equipment Mogul Sidney Harman." *Business Insider*, August 2, 2010. https://www.businessinsider .com/its-official-newsweek-will-be-sold-to-former-stereo-equipment-mogul -sidney-harman-who-reportedly-bid-1-in-excha-2010-8.

34. Stableford, Dylan. 2010. "Filing: Newsweek Sold for $1." *The Wrap*, October 7, 2010. https://www.thewrap.com/filing-newsweek-sold-1-dollar-21523/.

35. Huntsman Corporation. 2020. "Huntsman Agrees to Sell its Remaining Interest in Venator Materials PLC." August 28, 2020. https://www.huntsman .com/news/media-releases/detail/451/huntsman-agrees-to-sell-its-remaining -interest-in-venator.

36. "Huntsman Completes the Sale of Shares in Venator." *European Coatings*, January 6, 2021. https://www.european-coatings.com/articles/huntsman -completes-the-sale-of-shares-in-venator.

37. Huntsman Corporation. 2020. "Huntsman Agrees to Sell its Remaining Interest in Venator Materials PLC." August 28, 2020. https://www.huntsman .com/news/media-releases/detail/451/huntsman-agrees-to-sell-its-remaining -interest-in-venator.

38. Knutson, Ryan. 2017. "Why Verizon Decided to Stick with Yahoo Deal After Big Data Breaches." *Wall Street Journal*, February 21, 2017. https://www .wsj.com/articles/why-verizon-decided-to-still-buy-yahoo-after-big-data -breaches-1487679768.

39. Schmidt, Ann. 2020. "Bed Bath & Beyond, 1-800-Flowers Settle Lawsuit Over PersonalizationMall.com." *Fox Business*, July 21, 2020. https://www .foxbusiness.com/lifestyle/bed-bath-beyond-1-800-flowers-settle-lawsuit.

40. Bahreini, Dariush, Roerich Bansal, Gerd Finck, and Marjan Firouzgar. 2019. "Done Deal? Why Many Large Transactions Fail to Cross the Finish Line." McKinsey & Company, August 5, 2019. https://www.mckinsey.com/business -functions/strategy-and-corporate-finance/our-insights/done-deal-why-many -large-transactions-fail-to-cross-the-finish-line.

41. Chin, Kimberly. 2020. "L Brands, Sycamore Agree to Scrap Victoria's Secret Deal." *Wall Street Journal*, May 4, 2020. https://www.wsj.com/articles /l-brands-sycamore-agree-to-scrap-victorias-secret-deal-11588633861.

42. Safdar, Khadeeja, and Cara Lombardo. 2020. "Victoria's Secret Buyer Seeks to Cancel Takeover After Coronavirus." *Wall Street Journal*, April 22, 2020. https://www.wsj.com/articles/sycamore-partners-cancels-plan-to-buy -victoria-s-secret-11587568843.

43. Sebastian, Dave. 2021. "L Brands to Spin Off Victoria's Secret." *Wall Street Journal*, May 11, 2021. https://www.wsj.com/articles/l-brands-to-spin-off -victorias-secret-11620737102.

44. González, Angel. 2015. "Haggen's Expansion in Southwest Fraught with Legal Problems, Layoffs." *Seattle Times*, July 28, 2015. https://www .seattletimes.com/business/retail/haggens-expansion-in-southwest-fraught -with-legal-problems-layoffs/.

45. Ibid.

46. Li, Shan. 2015. "Haggen Accuses Albertsons of Sabotaging Store Takeover, Sues for $1 Billion." *Los Angeles Times*, September 1, 2015. https://www .latimes.com/business/la-fi-haggen-albertsons-lawsuit-20150901-story.html.

47. Stewart, Ashley. 2015. "Haggen Sues Albertsons for $1 Billion, Claims Larger Chain Sabotaged Deal." *Puget Sound Business Journal*, September 2, 2015. https://www.bizjournals.com/seattle/morning_call/2015/09/haggen -sues-albertsons-for-1-billion-claims-larger.html.

48. Banse, Tom. 2016. "Conspiracy? Albertsons Buys Back Grocery Stores at A Bargain." *NW News Network*, March 29, 2016. https://www.nwnewsnetwork .org/post/conspiracy-albertsons-buys-back-grocery-stores-bargain.

49. Williamson, Mark D., B. Scott Burton, and Andrew Diaz-Matos. 2012. "M&A Transition Services Agreements: Negotiating and Drafting Key Terms to

Preserve Business Value and Mitigate Risk." *Strafford*, August 9, 2012. http:// media.straffordpub.com/products/m-and-a-transition-services-agreements -2012-08-09/presentation.pdf.
50. Ibid.

CHAPTER 6

1. Derived from data gathered from Refinitiv (formerly Thomson One). Accessed: February 14, 2022.
2. Sorkin, Andrew Ross. 2015. "Barry Diller's Business Model Bears Fruit." *New York Times*, November 23, 2015. https://www.nytimes.com/2015/11/24 /business/dealbook/barry-dillers-business-model-bears-fruit.html.
3. Ibid.
4. Vimeo. 2021. "IAC Completes Spin-Off of Vimeo." May 25, 2021. https:// www.prnewswire.com/news-releases/iac-completes-spin-off-of-vimeo -301298522.html.
5. McCann, David. 2019. "Buy, Build, Spin: How IAC Supercharges Share-holder Value." *CFO*, December 19, 2019. https://www.cfo.com/ma/2019/12 /buy-build-spin-how-iac-supercharges-shareholder-value/.
6. Vimeo. 2021. "IAC Completes Spin-Off of Vimeo." May 25, 2021. https:// www.prnewswire.com/news-releases/iac-completes-spin-off-of-vimeo -301298522.html.
7. Birkeland, Cathy A., Mark D. Gerstein, and Laurence J. Stein. 2019. "Spin-offs Unraveled." Harvard Law School Forum on Corporate Governance, October 31, 2019. https://corpgov.law.harvard.edu/2019/10/31/spin-offs -unraveled/.
8. Birkeland, Cathy A., Mark D. Gerstein, and Laurence J. Stein. 2019. "Spin-offs Unraveled." Harvard Law School Forum on Corporate Governance, October 31, 2019. https://corpgov.law.harvard.edu/2019/10/31/spin-offs -unraveled/.
   Bodoh, Devon, Graham Magill, and Joseph Pari. 2021. "Spinoffs in the Uncertain Environment." Weil, Gotshal, and Manges LLP, January 27, 2021. https://www.weil.com/~/media/mailings/2021/q1/part-i--spinoffs-in-the-current-uncertain-environment.pdf.
9. Farrell Fritz, P.C. 2019. "Corporate Spin-Offs: The 'Active Trade or Business' and the Collection of Income." July 8, 2019. https://www.taxlawforchb.com /2019/07/corporate-spin-offs-the-active-trade-or-business-and-the-collection -of-income/.
10. Wachtell, Lipton, Rosen & Katz. 2020. "Spin-Off Guide." April 2020. https:// www.wlrk.com/wp-content/uploads/2020/05/Spin-Off-Guide-2020.pdf.
11. Ibid.
12. Inelegant Investor. 2015. "From Y To AA—Meet Aabaco Holdings, Yahoo's Spinco." *Stock Spinoffs*, July 21, 2015. https://www.stockspinoffs.com/2015 /07/21/from-y-to-aa-meet-aabaco-holdings-yahoos-spinco/.

13. Inelegant Investor. 2015. "Yahoo Plunges in Last Minute Trade on Word That IRS Will Review Spinoffs." *Stock Spinoffs*, May 19, 2015. https://www .stockspinoffs.com/2015/05/19/yahoo-plunges-in-last-minute-trade-on-word -that-irs-will-review-spinoffs/.
Inelegant Investor. 2015. "Yahoo's Aabaco Spinoff Faces Major Setback as IRS Refuses To Rule On Taxable Status." *Stock Spinoffs*, September 8, 2015. https://www.stockspinoffs.com/2015/09/08/yahoos-aabaco-spinoff-faces -major-setback-as-irs-refuses-to-rule-on-taxable-status/.

14. Nitti, Tony. 2015. "How to Talk About the Yahoo Spin-Off Without Embar-rassing Yourself." *Forbes*, September 9, 2015. https://www.forbes.com /sites/anthonynitti/2015/09/09/how-to-talk-about-the-yahoo-spin-off-without -embarassing-yourself/?sh=385e55d5694f.

15. Spin Doctor. 2016. "Starboard Threatens War on Yahoo—Are They Part of the Problem Though?" *Stock Spinoffs*, January 8, 2016. https://www .stockspinoffs.com/2016/01/08/starboard-threatens-war-on-yahoo/.

16. Spin Doctor. 2015. "Yahoo Takes on the Tax Man—Will Move Forward with Aabaco Spin without Private Letter Ruling." *Stock Spinoffs*, October 1, 2015. https://www.stockspinoffs.com/2015/10/01/yahoo-takes-on-the-tax-man-will -move-forward-with-aabaco-spin-without-private-letter-ruling/.

17. Spin Doctor. 2016. "Starboard Threatens War on Yahoo—Are They Part of the Problem Though?" *Stock Spinoffs*, January 8, 2016. https://www .stockspinoffs.com/2016/01/08/starboard-threatens-war-on-yahoo/.

18. Russell, John. 2019. "Yahoo Spin-Out Altaba Is Selling its Entire Alibaba Stake and Closing Down." *TechCrunch*, April 3, 2019. https://techcrunch .com/2019/04/03/altaba-alibaba-sale/.
Inelegant Investor. 2019. "Altaba, the Spin That Never Happened, Will Become the Company That Isn't." *Stock Spinoffs*, April 8, 2019. https://www .stockspinoffs.com/2019/04/08/altaba-the-spin-that-never-happened-will -become-the-company-that-isnt/.

19. Krishnaswami, Sudha, and Venkat Subramaniam. 1999. "Information Asymmetry, Valuation, and the Corporate Spin-Off Decision." *Journal of Financial Economics* 53, no. 1 (July 1999): 73–112.
Zuckerman, Ezra W. 2000. "Focusing the Corporate Product: Securities Analysts and De-Diversification." *Administrative Science Quarterly* 45, no. 3 (September 2000): 591–619.
Gilson, Stuart C., Paul M. Healy, Christopher F. Noe, and Krishna G. Palepu. 2001. "Analyst Specialization and Conglomerate Stock Breakups." *Journal of Accounting Research* 39, no. 3 (December 2001): 565–582.
Feldman, Emilie R., Stuart C. Gilson, and Belén Villalonga. 2014. "Do Ana-lysts Add Value When They Most Can? Evidence from Corporate Spin-Offs." *Strategic Management Journal* 35, no. 10 (October 2014): 1446–1463.

20. McConnell, John J., Steven E. Sibley, and Wei Xu. 2015. "The Stock Price Performance of Spin-Off Subsidiaries, Their Parents, and the Spin-Off

ETF, 2001–2013." *Journal of Portfolio Management* 42, no. 1 (Fall 2015): 143–152.

21. Grant, Charley. 2021. "To Spin or Not to Spin? Disposals Create Fortunes and Headaches." *Wall Street Journal*, April 2, 2021. https://www.wsj.com/articles/to-spin-or-not-to-spin-disposals-create-fortunes-and-headaches-11617375871.

22. Ibid.

23. Speights, Keith. 2020. "Better Buy: Abbott Laboratories vs. AbbVie." *The Motley Fool*, January 19, 2020. https://www.fool.com/investing/2020/01/19/better-buy-abbott-laboratories-vs-abbvie.aspx.

24. Cornell, Joe. 2012. "How to Play the Kraft Spinoff." *Spin-Off Research*, October 3, 2012. http://www.spinoffresearch.com/in-the-news/oct-2012-Articles.html.

25. Caplinger, Dan. 2013. "Why Has Kraft Stock Soared After Its Spinoff?" *The Motley Fool*, June 19, 2013. https://www.fool.com/investing/general/2013/06/19/why-has-kraft-stock-soared-after-its-spinoff.aspx.

26. Gertner, Robert, Eric Powers, and David Scharfstein. 2002. "Learning About Internal Capital Markets from Corporate Spin-Offs." *Journal of Finance* 57, no. 6 (December 2002): 2479–2506.
Feldman, Emilie R. 2016. "Corporate Spin-Offs and Capital Allocation Decisions." *Strategy Science* 1, no. 4 (December 2016): 256–271.

27. Bennett, Victor Manuel, and Emilie R. Feldman. 2017. "Make Room! Make Room! A Note on Sequential Spinoffs and Acquisitions." *Strategy Science* 2, no. 2 (June 2017): 100–110.

28. Feldman, Emilie R. 2016. "Managerial Compensation and Corporate Spinoffs." *Strategic Management Journal* 37, no. 10 (October 2016): 2011–2030.

29. Comment, Robert, and Gregg A. Jarrell. 1995. "Corporate Focus and Stock Returns." *Journal of Financial Economics* 37, no. 1 (January 1995): 67–87.
Daley, Lane, Vikas Mehrotra, and Ranjini Sivakumar. 1997. "Corporate Focus and Value Creation: Evidence from Spinoffs." *Journal of Financial Economics* 45, no. 2 (August 1997): 257–281.
Desai, Hemang, and Prem C. Jain. 1999. "Firm Performance and Focus: Long-Run Stock Market Performance Following Spinoffs." *Journal of Financial Economics* 54, no. 1 (October 1999): 75–101.

30. Deloitte. 2011. "Spin Cycle: The Rise of Technology Sector 'De-Mergers.'" https://www2.deloitte.com/content/dam/Deloitte/us/Documents/mergers-acqisitions/us-ma-tech-spinoff.pdf.

31. JDS Uniphase Corporation. 2015. "Information Statement." https://www.sec.gov/Archives/edgar/data/1633978/000119312515251781/d870553dex991.htm#toc870553_1.

32. Feldman, Emilie R. 2016. "Corporate Spin-Offs and Capital Allocation Decisions." *Strategy Science* 1, no. 4 (December 2016): 256–271.

Gertner, Robert, Eric Powers, and David Scharfstein. 2002. "Learning About Internal Capital Markets from Corporate Spin-Offs." *Journal of Finance* 57, no. 6 (December 2002): 2479–2506.

33. Exelis, Inc. 2011. "Information Statement." October 5, 2011. https://www.sec .gov/Archives/edgar/data/1524471/000095012311088751/y91928a5exv99w1 .htm#Y91928104.

34. Bennett, Victor Manuel, and Emilie R. Feldman. 2017. "Make Room! Make Room! A Note on Sequential Spinoffs and Acquisitions." *Strategy Science* 2, no. 2 (June 2017): 100–110.

35. Feldman, Emilie R. 2016. "Managerial Compensation and Corporate Spinoffs." *Strategic Management Journal* 37, no. 10 (October 2016): 2011–2030.

36. Glover, Stephen, Robert A. Klyman, Kristin A. Linsley, Sabina Jacobs Margot. 2017. "Spinning Out of Control: Potential Pitfalls and Liabilities in Spin-Off Transactions." Gibson, Dunn & Crutcher, LLP, October 31, 2017. https://www.gibsondunn.com/wp-content/uploads/2017/11/WebcastSlides -Potential-Pitfalls-and-Liabilities-in-Spin-Off-Transactions-31-October-2017 .pdf.

37. McCue, Dan. 2010. "Verizon's Idearc Spinoff Called a Put-Up Job." *Courthouse News Service*, September 17, 2010. https://www.courthousenews.com /verizons-idearc-spinoff-called-a-put-up-job/.

38. Ibid.

39. "Verizon Wins Ruling in $9.5 Billion Lawsuit over Idearc Spinoff." *Impact Trial*, January 23, 2013. https://impacttrial.com/news/verizon-wins-ruling-in -9-5-billion-lawsuit-over-idearc-spinoff/.

40. U.S. Environmental Protection Agency. 2013. "Case Summary: Court Decision in Tronox Bankruptcy Fraudulent Conveyance Case Results in Largest Environmental Bankruptcy Award Ever." https://www.epa.gov/enforcement /case-summary-court-decision-tronox-bankruptcy-fraudulent-conveyance -case-results-largest.

41. Ibid.

42. Department of Justice. 2014. "United States Announces $5.15 Billion Settlement of Litigation Against Subsidiaries of Anadarko Petroleum Corp. to Remedy Fraudulent Conveyance Designed to Evade Environmental Liabilities." April 3, 2014. https://www.justice.gov/opa/pr/united-states-announces -515-billion-settlement-litigation-against-subsidiaries-anadarko.

43. Simpson, Stephen. 2020. "Garrett Motion Upping the Stakes in its Asbestos Battle with Honeywell." *Seeking Alpha*, August 28, 2020. https:// seekingalpha.com/article/4371329-garrett-motion-upping-stakes-in-asbestos -battle-honeywell.

44. Ibid.

45. Garrett Motion, Inc. 2020. "Garrett Motion Files Complaint Against Honeywell in Asbestos Indemnity Suit." January 16, 2020. https://www

.businesswire.com/news/home/20200116005467/en/Garrett-Motion-Files
-Complaint-Against-Honeywell-in-Asbestos-Indemnity-Suit.

46. Honeywell. 2021. "Honeywell Resolves Claims with Garrett Motion Inc."
January 11, 2021. https://www.honeywell.com/us/en/press/2021/1/honeywell
-resolves-claims-with-garrett-motion-inc.

47. Wachtell, Lipton, Rosen & Katz. 2020. "Spin-Off Guide." April 2020. https://
www.wlrk.com/wp-content/uploads/2020/05/Spin-Off-Guide-2020.pdf.

48. Unpublished research conducted by the author.

49. Garrett Motion, Inc. 2020. "Garrett Motion Files Complaint Against
Honeywell in Asbestos Indemnity Suit." January 16, 2020. https://www
.businesswire.com/news/home/20200116005467/en/Garrett-Motion-Files
-Complaint-Against-Honeywell-in-Asbestos-Indemnity-Suit.

50. Offshore Energy Today Staff. 2017. "Paragon Sues Noble Over 'Fraudulent
Corporate Spin-Off.'" *Offshore Energy Today*, December 18, 2017. https://
www.offshore-energy.biz/paragon-sues-noble-over-fraudulent-corporate
-spin-off/.

51. United States Bankruptcy Court District of Delaware. 2019. "Paragon Offshore vs. Noble Corporation et al., Chapter 11 Case No. 16-10386 (CSS)."
https://www.docketbird.com/court-documents/Paragon-Litigation-Trust
-v-Noble-Corporation-PLC-et-al/Amended-Complaint/deb-1:2017-ap-51882
-00265.

52. FitzGerald, Drew. 2022. "AT&T Sets WarnerMedia Spinoff Plan and Lowers
Its Dividend." *Wall Street Journal*, February 1, 2022. https://www.wsj.com
/articles/at-t-to-slash-dividend-after-spinoff-of-warnermedia-11643716166.

CHAPTER 7

1. Birkeland, Cathy A., Mark D. Gerstein, and Laurence J. Stein. 2019. "Spinoffs Unraveled." Harvard Law School Forum on Corporate Governance,
October 31, 2019. https://corpgov.law.harvard.edu/2019/10/31/spin-offs
-unraveled/.

2. Ibid.

3. Derived from data gathered from Refinitiv (formerly Thomson One).
Accessed: April 12, 2021, and February 10, 2022.

4. Miles, James A., and J. Randall Woolridge. 1999. *Spin-Offs and Equity
Carve-Outs: Achieving Faster Growth and Better Performance*. Morristown,
NJ: Financial Executives Research Foundation.

5. Eli Lilly. 2019. "Registration Statement: Eli Lilly and Company Offer to
Exchange Up to 293,290,000 Shares of Common Stock of Elanco Animal
Health Incorporated which are Owned by Eli Lilly and Company for Outstanding Shares of Common Stock of Eli Lilly and Company." https://www
.sec.gov/Archives/edgar/data/1739104/000104746919000413/a2237651zs
-4.htm.

6. O'Neal, Lydia. 2019. "Eli Lilly Saves Up to $2 Billion in Taxes in Elanco 'Split-Off.'" *Bloomberg Tax*, February 13, 2019. https://news.bloombergtax .com/daily-tax-report/eli-lilly-saves-up-to-2-billion-in-taxes-in-elanco-split -off?context=article-related.

7. Baxter International Inc. 2016. "Annual Report." https://www.sec.gov /Archives/edgar/data/0000010456/000156459017002240/bax-10k_20161231 .htm.

8. Annema, André, William C. Fallon, and Marc H. Goedhart. 2001. "Do Carve-Outs Make Sense? Yes, But Not for the Reasons You Might Think." McKinsey & Company, September 2001. https://www.mckinsey.com/ ~/media/McKinsey/Business%20Functions/Strategy%20and%20Corporate %20Finance/Our%20Insights/Do%20carve%20outs%20make%20sense/Do %20carve%20outs%20make%20sense%20Yes%20but%20not%20for%20the %20reasons%20you%20might%20think.pdf.

9. Powers, Eric A., Spinoffs, Selloffs and Equity Carveouts: An Analysis of Divestiture Method Choice (January 2001). http://dx.doi.org/10.2139/ssrn .257600.

10. Lashinsky, Adam. 2007. "The Next Big Silicon Valley IPO." *CNN Money*, May 31, 2007. https://money.cnn.com/magazines/fortune/fortune_archive /2007/06/11/100060833/index.htm.

11. Ryan, Vincent. 2008. "'Partial' Success: In the Current IPO Market, Carve-Outs Are Poised for a Revival." *CFO*, February 1, 2008. https://www.cfo.com /banking-capital-markets/2008/02/partial-success/.

12. Bray, Chad. 2014. "Finding It an Odd Fit, Fiat Chrysler Will Spin Off Ferrari." *New York Times*, October 29, 2014. https://dealbook.nytimes.com/2014 /10/29/fiat-chrysler-to-spin-off-sports-car-brand-ferrari/.

13. Sharman, Andy. 2015. "Ferrari Files for New York IPO." *Financial Times*, July 23, 2015. https://www.ft.com/content/62a6e9d2-3127-11e5-8873-775ba7 c2ea3d.

14. Ibid.

15. Automotive Industry Portal Marklines. 2014. "Fiat Chrysler's new five-year plan: Sales target of 7 million units by 2018." June 9, 2014. https://www .marklines.com/en/report/rep1299_201405.

16. Miles, James A., and J. Randall Woolridge. 1999. *Spin-Offs and Equity Carve-Outs: Achieving Faster Growth and Better Performance*. Morristown, NJ: Financial Executives Research Foundation.

17. Lamont, Owen A., and Richard H. Thaler. 2003. "Can the Market Add and Subtract? Mispricing in Tech Stock Carve-Outs." *Journal of Political Economy* 111, no. 2 (April 2003): 227–268.

18. England, Robert Stowe. 1999. "Take Part of My IPO: How Companies Are Unlocking Value by Carving Out Pieces of Their Business." *CFO*, March 1, 1999. https://www.cfo.com/strategy/1999/03/take-part-of-my-ipo/.

19. Corporate Finance Institute. "Reverse Morris Trust: A Tax-Free Spin-Off with a Pre-Arranged Merger." https://corporatefinanceinstitute.com/resources /knowledge/deals/reverse-morris-trust/.

20. Ibid.

21. Willens, Robert. 2002. "Reviving the Reverse Morris Trust for Mergers." *CFO*, July 3, 2002. https://www.cfo.com/accounting-tax/2002/07/reviving -the-reverse-morris-trust-for-mergers/.

22. Derived from data gathered from Refinitiv (formerly Thomson One). Accessed: April 27, 2021, and February 10, 2022.

23. Hoffman, Liz. 2015. "What's a 'Reverse Morris Trust' and Why Is Every-body Doing One?" *Wall Street Journal*, March 27, 2015. https://www.wsj .com/articles/BL-MBB-34994.

24. Ibid.

25. Derived from data gathered from Refinitiv (formerly Thomson One). Accessed: April 27, 2021, and February 10, 2022.

26. Sloan, Allan. 2015. "For Tax Techies, P&G's Deal with Coty is a Thing of Beauty." *Washington Post*, July 16, 2015. https://www.washingtonpost.com /business/economy/for-tax-techies-pandgs-deal-with-coty-is-a-thing-of -beauty/2015/07/16/6944bb5e-2c11-11e5-a250-42bd812efc09_story.html.

27. Monk, Dan. 2016. "Procter & Gamble Fell $1 Billion Short on Coty Deal and Made Everyone Happy." *WCPO Cincinnati*, October 7, 2016. https://www .wcpo.com/news/insider/procter-gamble-fell-1-billion-short-on-coty-deal-and -made-everyone-happy.

28. The Dow Chemical Company. 2015. "Dow and Olin Corporation Create an Industry Leader in Chlor-Alkali and Derivatives with Revenues Approach-ing $7 Billion." March 27, 2015. https://www.businesswire.com/news/home /20150327005208/en/Dow-and-Olin-Corporation-Create-an-Industry-Leader -in-Chlor-Alkali-and-Derivatives-with-Revenues-Approaching-7%C2 %A0Billion.

29. "Here's Why the Olin Deal Is a Positive For Dow Shareholders." *Trefis Team*, June 19, 2015. https://www.trefis.com/stock/dow/articles/301720/heres-why -the-olin-deal-is-a-positive-for-dow-shareholders/2015-06-19.

30. AT&T Inc. 2021. "AT&T's WarnerMedia and Discovery, Inc. Creating Stand-alone Company by Combining Operations to Form New Global Leader in Entertainment." May 17, 2021. https://about.att.com/story/2021/warnermedia _discovery.html.

31. FitzGerald, Drew. 2022. "AT&T Sets WarnerMedia Spinoff Plan and Lowers Its Dividend." *Wall Street Journal*, February 1, 2022. https://www.wsj.com /articles/at-t-to-slash-dividend-after-spinoff-of-warnermedia-11643716166.

32. "AT&T Is Overpaying for Time Warner." *Real Money*, October 23, 2016. https://realmoney.thestreet.com/articles/10/23/2016/att-overpaying-time -warner.

33. Dittmar, Amy. 2004. "Capital Structure in Corporate Spin-Offs." *Journal of Business* 77, no. 1 (January 2004): 9–43.

34. Kastiel, Koby. 2015. "Using Spin-offs to Raise Cash, Reduce Debt and Recapitalize." Harvard Law School Forum on Corporate Governance, January 3, 2015. https://corpgov.law.harvard.edu/2015/01/03/using-spin-offs-to -raise-cash-reduce-debt-and-recapitalize/.

    The Timken Company. 2014. "Information Statement: TimkenSteel Corporation." May 15, 2014. https://www.sec.gov/Archives/edgar/data/1598428 /000119312514201428/d721860dex991.htm.

    Sears Holdings. 2014. "Information Statement: Land's End." January 31, 2014. https://www.sec.gov/Archives/edgar/data/799288/000119312514030430 /d632333dex991.htm.

    Sears Holdings. 2014. "Information Statement: Land's End." March 14, 2014. https://www.sec.gov/Archives/edgar/data/799288/000119312514100537 /d632333dex991.htm.

35. Dittmar, Amy. 2004. "Capital Structure in Corporate Spin-Offs." *Journal of Business* 77, no. 1 (January 2004): 9–43.

36. Honeywell International. 2018. "Tax Matters Agreement between Honeywell and Resideo." October 2, 2018. https://www.sec.gov/Archives/edgar/data /1740332/000119312518290883/d601987dex23.htm.

37. Honeywell International. 2018. "Indemnification and Reimbursement Agreement by and among New Hapi Inc. and Honeywell International Inc." October 14, 2018. https://www.sec.gov/Archives/edgar/data/773840 /000119312518298884/d625197dex21.htm.

CHAPTER 8

1. Comcast. 2009. "Comcast and GE to Create Leading Entertainment Company." December 3, 2009. https://corporate.comcast.com/news-information /news-feed/comcast-and-ge-to-create-leading-entertainment-company.

2. Goldman, David, and Julianne Pepitone. 2009. "GE, Comcast Announce Joint NBC Deal." *CNN Money*, December 3, 2009. https://money.cnn.com /2009/12/03/news/companies/comcast_nbc/.

3. Flint, Joe. 2009. "Comcast in Deal Talks with NBC Universal." *Los Angeles Times*, September 30, 2009. https://latimesblogs.latimes.com /entertainmentnewsbuzz/2009/09/comcast-wants-nbc-universal-.html.

4. General Electric. 2009. "Conference Call Transcript: GE Investor Webcast Regarding NBC Universal." December 3, 2009. https://www.ge.com/sites /default/files/ge_transcript_nbcu_12032009_0.pdf.

5. GlaxoSmithKline plc. 2014. "GlaxoSmithKline plc Proposed Major Transaction with Novartis AG: Circular to Shareholders and Notice of General Meeting." November 24, 2014. https://www.sec.gov/Archives/edgar/data /1131399/000119312514422633/d788516d6k.htm.

6. General Electric. 2021. "GE Announces Combination of GECAS and AerCap." March 10, 2021. https://www.ge.com/news/press-releases/ge -announces-combination-of-gecas-and-aercap.

7. Josephs, Leslie. 2021. "GE to Merge Aircraft Leasing Unit with Rival Aer- Cap in a \$30 Billion Deal as Industry Faces More Pandemic Turmoil." *CNBC*, March 10, 2021. https://www.cnbc.com/2021/03/10/general-electric -aercap-aircraft-leasing-merger.html.

8. Cimilluca, Dana, Dana Mattioli, and David Benoit. 2016. "GE to Combine Oil and Gas Business With Baker Hughes." *Wall Street Journal*, October 31, 2016. https://www.wsj.com/articles/ge-to-combine-oil-and-gas-business-with -baker-hughes-1477908407.

9. Mann, Joshua. 2017. "GE, Baker Hughes Structured Deal with Clause for Potential Early Exit." *Houston Business Journal*, November 21, 2017. https:// www.bizjournals.com/houston/news/2017/11/21/ge-baker-hughes-structured -deal-with-clause-for.html.

10. Hampton, Liz. 2018. "The Culture Clash Behind GE's Quick Exit from Baker Hughes Stake." *Reuters*, June 26, 2018. https://www.reuters.com/article /us-baker-hughes-ge-future-insight/the-culture-clash-behind-ges-quick-exit -from-baker-hughes-stake-idUSKBN1JM312.

11. Ibid.

12. General Electric. 2018. "GE Focuses Portfolio for Growth and Shareholder Value Creation." June 26, 2018. https://www.ge.com/news/press-releases/ge -focuses-portfolio-growth-and-shareholder-value-creation.

13. Gryta, Thomas. 2019. "GE to Give Up Majority Control of Baker Hughes." *Wall Street Journal*, September 10, 2019. https://www.wsj.com/articles/ge-to -give-up-majority-control-of-baker-hughes-11568154610.

14. Pulsinelli, Olivia. 2018. "Baker Hughes, GE Announce Agreements to Accel- erate Separation." *Houston Business Journal*, November 13, 2018. https:// www.bizjournals.com/houston/news/2018/11/13/baker-hughes-ge-announce -agreements-to-accelerate.html.

15. Chapa, Sergio. 2019. "Independent Again: Baker Hughes Rolls Out New Look." *Houston Chronicle*, October 8, 2019. https://www.chron.com /business/energy/article/Independent-Again-Baker-Hughes-rolls-out-new -look-14500658.php.

16. Derived from data gathered from Bloomberg. Accessed: April 13, 2021, and February 10, 2022.

17. Tuna, Ayse Irem. 2003. "Determinants and Consequences of Equity Restruc- turing Transactions: How Are Tracking Stocks Different from Equity Carveouts and Spinoffs?" PhD Diss., University of Michigan.

18. Cauley, Leslie. 2000. "John Malone's Prescription for AT&T: New Tracking Stock, Focus on Content." *Wall Street Journal*, July 12, 2000. https://www .wsj.com/articles/SB963357225995727588.

19. Banham, Russ. 1999. "Track Stars." *Journal of Accountancy* 188, no. 1 (July 1999): 45.
20. Campbell, Doug. 2001. "Loews May Create Lorillard Tracking Stock." *Triad Business Journal*, October 18, 2001. https://www.bizjournals.com/triad /stories/2001/10/15/daily35.html.
21. Borland, John. 2002. "Tracking Stocks Take on the Telecom World." *CNET*, January 2, 2002. https://www.cnet.com/news/tracking-stocks-take-on-the -telecom-world/.
22. Deogun, Nikhil. 1999. "Pittston Plans to Sell Coal Business and Scuttle Tracking-Stock Effort." *Wall Street Journal*, December 6, 1999. https://www .wsj.com/articles/SB944438577766576580.
23. Ibid.
24. Fidelity National Financial, Inc. 2016. "FNFV Announces Fidelity National Financial, Inc. Tax-Free Plan to Redeem and Exchange Shares of FNFV Tracking Stock, With End Result Being an Independent, Publicly-Traded FNFV Common Stock." December 7, 2016. https:// www.investor.fnf.com/news-releases/news-release-details/fnfv-announces- fidelity-national-financial-inc-tax-free-plan.
25. Fidelity National Financial, Inc. 2016. "Fidelity National Financial, Inc. Announces Tax-Free Plan to Distribute Shares of Black Knight Financial Services Common Stock and Redeem and Exchange Shares of FNFV Tracking Stock; Following Distributions, FNF Will Revert to a Common Stock and Become Index Eligible." December 7, 2016. https://www.prnewswire .com/news-releases/fidelity-national-financial-inc-announces-tax-free-plan -to-distribute-shares-of-black-knight-financial-services-common-stock-and -redeem-and-exchange-shares-of-fnfv-tracking-stock-following-distributions -fnf-will-revert-to-a-co-300374250.html.
26. Matthews, Robert Guy. 2000. "USX Rethinks Tracking Stocks on Signs Share Price Is Lagging." *Wall Street Journal*, December 1, 2000. https:// www.wsj.com/articles/SB975629336405750073.
27. Bloomberg Business News. 2002. "Carolina Group's Shares Debut: The Sale of 35 Million Shares at $28 Each Gives Loews Corp. Needed Cash." *Greensboro News & Record*, February 1, 2002. https://greensboro.com/carolina -groups-shares-debut-the-sale-of-35-million-shares-at-28-each-gives-loews /article_38b7571f-17e6-5777-abac-764186267f1e.html.
28. Bary, Andrew. 2020. "Atlanta Braves Owner John Malone Has a Great Investing Record. Here's How to Play Along." *Barron's*, May 15, 2020. https://www .barrons.com/articles/bigger-bargains-to-be-found-in-john-malones-liberty -media-stocks-51589579637.
29. Banham, Russ. 1999. "Track Stars." *Journal of Accountancy* 188, no. 1 (July 1999): 45.
30. Ibid.

31. "Human Genome race Tweaked by Celera's Stock Offer." *Forbes*, April 29, 1999. https://www.forbes.com/1999/04/29/feat2.html?sh=5cb8c9974213.

32. Pollack, Andrew. 2002. "Sequencer of Genome to Change Focus." *New York Times*, April 22, 2002. https://www.nytimes.com/2002/04/22/business /sequencer-of-genome-to-change-focus.html.

33. GM Heritage Center. "The Origins of OnStar." https://www.gmheritagecenter .com/featured/OnStar.html.

34. Bary, Andrew. 2020. "Atlanta Braves Owner John Malone Has a Great Investing Record. Here's How to Play Along." *Barron's*, May 15, 2020. https://www .barrons.com/articles/bigger-bargains-to-be-found-in-john-malones-liberty -media-stocks-51589579637.

35. Drucker, Jesse. 2003. "Sprint Highlights the Pitfalls of Tracking-Stock Structure." *Wall Street Journal*, March 7, 2003. https://www.wsj.com/articles /SB104699971768830900.

36. Ibid.

37. Banham, Russ. 1999. "Track Stars." *Journal of Accountancy* 188, no. 1 (July 1999): 45.

38. Drucker, Jesse. 2003. "Sprint Highlights the Pitfalls of Tracking-Stock Structure." *Wall Street Journal*, March 7, 2003. https://www.wsj.com/articles /SB104699971768830900.

39. Ibid.

40. Banham, Russ. 1999. "Track Stars." *Journal of Accountancy* 188, no. 1 (July 1999): 45.

41. Hennessey, Raymond. 2002. "First Deal of the New Year Is Tracking Stock Carolina." *Wall Street Journal*, January 28, 2002. https://www.wsj.com /articles/SB1012167131527733520.

CHAPTER 9

1. Twentyman, Jessica. 2020. "Clean Break: How Resideo Decoupled Core IT from Parent Honeywell—Even as Covid Hit." *CIO*, December 2020. https:// www.i-cio.com/innovation/it-infrastructure/item/a-clean-break-how-resideo -decoupled-core-it-from-former-parent-honeywell-even-as-covid-19-hit.

2. Resideo Technologies. 2020. "Presentation Details: Summary of Certain Honeywell Agreements." February 26, 2020. https://investor.resideo.com /events-and-presentations/presentations/presentation-details/2020/Summary -of-Certain-Honeywell-Agreements/default.aspx.
Honeywell International Inc. 2018. "Form of Trademark License Agreement by and between Honeywell International Inc. and Resideo Technologies, Inc." https://www.sec.gov/Archives/edgar/data/0001740332/00011931251825 5566/d601987dex26.htm.

3. Koenig, Jamie, Anthony Luu, and Steve Miller. 2020. "Three Degrees of Separation: How to Successfully Execute Divestitures." McKinsey & Company, June 12, 2020. https://www.mckinsey.com/business-functions/strategy

-and-corporate-finance/our-insights/three-degrees-of-separation-how-to -successfully-execute-divestitures.

4. Castillo, Alan. 2019. "Key Operational Carve-Out Considerations for Sellers." BDO USA LLP, April 2019. https://www.bdo.com/insights/business -financial-advisory/m-a-and-transaction-advisory/key-operational-carve-out -considerations-for-selle.

5. Yu, Douglas. 2018. "Nutella owner Ferrero acquires Nestlé's US candy business for $2.8bn." *ConfectioneryNews.com*, January 16, 2018. https://www .confectionerynews.com/Article/2018/01/16/Nutella-owner-Ferrero-acquires -Nestle-s-US-candy-business.

6. De Meester, Sjiva, Shantanu Bhattacharya, and Sameer Hasija. 2015. "Zoetis, Pfizer's Animal Health Spin-off (B)." INSEAD Teaching Case IN1092.

7. Fabris, Peter. 2019. "A Successful Spinoff." *Modern Counsel*, February 11, 2019. https://modern-counsel.com/2019/jared-richardson-trinity-industries/.

8. Reuters Staff. 2015. "Armstrong World to Spin Off Floorings Business to Focus on Ceilings Unit." *Reuters*, February 23, 2015. https://www.reuters .com/article/us-armstrong-world-divestiture/armstrong-world-to-spin-off -floorings-business-to-focus-on-ceilings-unit-idUSKBN0LR16P20150223.

9. Guillot, Craig. 2019. "As Old Navy and Gap Split, So Do Their Supply Chains." *Supply Chain Dive*, May 14, 2019. https://www.supplychaindive .com/news/old-navy-gap-split-supply-chains/554686/.

10. "Body Shop bought by Brazil's Natura." *BBC*, June 27, 2019. https://www .bbc.com/news/business-40417961.

11. "L'Oreal sells Body Shop." *BV World*, September 6, 2017. https://bv.world /blue-sky/business-brands/2017/09/loreal-sells-body-shop/.

12. Maurer, Mark. 2021. "Johnson & Johnson Prepares to Untangle Finances Ahead of Planned Split." *Wall Street Journal*, December 6, 2021. https:// www.wsj.com/articles/johnson-johnson-prepares-to-untangle-finances-ahead -of-planned-split-11638786602.

13. Kovar, Joseph F. 2015. "Symantec Selling Veritas: End of an Acquisition That Never Lived Up to Promises." *CRN*, August 11, 2015. https://www.crn.com /news/storage/300077766/symantec-selling-veritas-end-of-an-acquisition -that-never-lived-up-to-promises.htm.

14. Wabha, Phil. 2020. "Why Gap Inc. Torpedoed Its Old Navy Spinoff." *Fortune*, January 17, 2020. https://fortune.com/2020/01/17/gap-inc-old-navy-spin -off/.

15. Twentyman, Jessica. 2020. "Clean Break: How Resideo Decoupled Core IT from Parent Honeywell—Even as Covid Hit." *CIO*, December 2020. https:// www.i-cio.com/innovation/it-infrastructure/item/a-clean-break-how-resideo -decoupled-core-it-from-former-parent-honeywell-even-as-covid-19-hit.

16. Fabris, Peter. 2019. "A Successful Spinoff." *Modern Counsel*, February 11, 2019. https://modern-counsel.com/2019/jared-richardson-trinity-industries/.

17. Harrigan, Kathryn Rudie. 2012. "Motorola's Spin-Off of its Cell Phone Business." Columbia CaseWorks ID# CU129.
18. "Abusing Chapter 11: Corporate Efforts to Side-Step Accountability Through Bankruptcy." https://www.judiciary.senate.gov/meetings/abusing-chapter-11 -corporate-efforts-to-side-step-accountability-through-bankruptcy.
19. Gleit, Jeffrey R., and Matthew R. Bentley. 2021. "When the Music Stops: The Texas Two-Step and Forecasting Its Future Application." *American Bankruptcy Institute*, December 1, 2021. https://www.abi.org/abi-journal /when-the-music-stops-the-texas-two-step-and-forecasting-its-future -application.
20. Gilson, Stuart C. 2014. "Humana Inc.: Managing in a Changing Industry." Harvard Business School Case 9-294-062.
21. Harrigan, Kathryn Rudie. 2012. "Motorola's Spin-Off of its Cell Phone Business." Columbia CaseWorks ID# CU129.
22. Fitzgerald, Patrick, Daniel Gilbert, and Andrew Grossman. 2014. "Anadarko Settles Tronox Lawsuit for $5.15 Billion." *Wall Street Journal*, April 3, 2014. https://www.wsj.com/articles/anadarko-settles-tronox-lawsuit-for-5-15-billion -1396551743.
23. Henes, Jonathan S. 2008. "Solutia Inc.'s Chapter 11 Cases." The Heyman Center on Corporate Governance Third Annual Perspectives in Corporate Restructurings Conference, April 9, 2008. https://www.kirkland.com /siteFiles/News/93BEEB1EDC8EBC149F4247C5CEC9AE44.pdf.
24. "Paragon Sues Noble Over 'Fraudulent Corporate Spin-Off.'" *Offshore Energy Today*, December 18, 2017. https://www.offshore-energy.biz/paragon -sues-noble-over-fraudulent-corporate-spin-off/.
25. Garrett Motion Inc. 2020. "Garrett Motion Files Complaint Against Honeywell in Asbestos Indemnity Suit." January 16, 2020. https://www .businesswire.com/news/home/20200116005467/en/Garrett-Motion-Files -Complaint-Against-Honeywell-in-Asbestos-Indemnity-Suit.
26. Alaix, Juan Ramón. 2014. "The CEO of Zoetis on How He Prepared for the Top Job." *Harvard Business Review* 92, no. 6 (June 2014): 41–44.
27. Keienburg, Georg, Jens Kengelbach, Felix Stellmaszek, Jacqueline Govers, Quentin Decouvelaere, Marc-André Drillose, Neal Srivastava, Karthik Valluru, and Dominik Degen. 2021. "Don't Let Carve-Out Costs Compromise Value Creation." Boston Consulting Group, June 3, 2021. https://mkt -bcg-com-public-pdfs.s3.amazonaws.com/prod/beware-of-separation-costs -compromise-value-creation.pdf.
28. Unpublished research conducted by the author.
29. Ibid.
30. Ibid.
31. De Meester, Sjiva, Shantanu Bhattacharya, and Sameer Hasija. 2015. "Zoetis, Pfizer's Animal Health Spin-off (B)." INSEAD Teaching Case IN1092.

32. Berman, Jeff. 2021. "XPO Logistics Announces GXO As Name of Logistics Spin-Off." *Logistics Management*, March 18, 2021. https://www.logisticsmgmt.com/article/xpo_logistics_announces_gxo_as_name_of_logistics_spin_off.

33. Kapner, Suzanne. 2021. "Should Retailers Split E-Commerce from Stores? A High-Level Debate." *Wall Street Journal*, December 29, 2021. https://www.wsj.com/articles/should-retailers-split-e-commerce-from-stores-a-high-level-debate-11640779202?mod=mhp.

34. Carey, Nick. 2016. "Alcoa Spins Off Smelting Business; Aero Auto Unit Now 'Arconic.'" *Reuters*, June 29, 2016. https://www.reuters.com/article/us-alcoa-divestiture-idUSKCN0ZF17U.

35. Doyle, Anna Lea, Andrew Wilson, and Ellen Clark. 2014. "It's Not Easy to Say Goodbye: Perspectives on Driving Divestiture and Carve Out Value." Deloitte. https://www2.deloitte.com/content/dam/Deloitte/us/Documents/mergers-acqisitions/us-ma-divestiture-compendium-22315.pdf.

36. Schaal, Dennis. 2013. "Does Expedia Have TripAdvisor Spinoff Remorse?" *Skift*, October 3, 2013. https://skift.com/2013/10/03/does-expedia-have-tripadvisor-spinoff-remorse/.

37. May, Kevin. 2012. "Expedia Pays $632 Million for Majority Stake in Trivago, Let the Search Games Begin." *PhocusWire*, December 21, 2012. https://www.phocuswire.com/Expedia-pays-632-million-for-majority-stake-in-Trivago-let-the-travel-search-games-begin.

38. eBay Inc. 2015. "Information Statement: PayPal Holdings, Inc." April 9, 2015. https://www.sec.gov/Archives/edgar/data/1633917/000119312515124337/d877527dex991.htm.

CHAPTER 10

1. Rexnord Corporation. 2021. "4Q CY20 December Quarter Financial Results." February 16, 2021. https://www.sec.gov/Archives/edgar/data/1439288/000143928821000014/ex992123120earningscalls.htm.

2. Motley Fool Transcribers. 2021. "Rexnord Corp (RXN) Q4 2020 Earnings Call Transcript." *The Motley Fool*, February 19, 2021. https://www.fool.com/earnings/call-transcripts/2021/02/19/rexnord-corp-rxn-q4-2020-earnings-call-transcript/.

3. Ibid.

4. Rexnord Corporation. 2021. "Second Quarter 2021 Financial Results." July 21, 2021. https://s1.q4cdn.com/233624116/files/doc_financials/2021/q2/Q2-Final-Earnings-Call-Slides.pdf.

5. Rexnord Corporation. 2021. "4Q CY20 December Quarter Financial Results." February 16, 2021. https://www.sec.gov/Archives/edgar/data/1439288/000143928821000014/ex992123120earningscalls.htm.

6. Motley Fool Transcribers. 2021. "Rexnord Corporation (RXN) Q2 2021 Earnings Call Transcript." *The Motley Fool*, July 21, 2021. https://www.fool .com/earnings/call-transcripts/2021/07/21/rexnord-corporation-rxn-q2-2021 -earnings-call-tran/.

7. Rexnord Corporation. 2021. "Second Quarter 2021 Financial Results." July 21, 2021. https://s1.q4cdn.com/233624116/files/doc_financials/2021/q2/Q2 -Final-Earnings-Call-Slides.pdf.

8. Motley Fool Transcribers. 2021. "Rexnord Corporation (RXN) Q2 2021 Earnings Call Transcript." *The Motley Fool*, July 21, 2021. https://www.fool .com/earnings/call-transcripts/2021/07/21/rexnord-corporation-rxn-q2-2021 -earnings-call-tran/.

9. Derived from data gathered from Compustat. Accessed: December 12, 2021.

10. Fubini, David, Michael Park, and Kim Thomas. 2013. "Profitably Parting Ways: Getting More Value from Divestitures." *McKinsey on Finance* 45 (Winter 2013): 14–21. https://www.mckinsey.com/~/media/McKinsey/dotcom /client_service/Corporate%20Finance/MoF/PDF%20issues/PDFs%20Issue %2045/MoF45_3_Divestitures.ashx.

11. Derived from data gathered from Compustat and Refinitiv (formerly Thomson One). Accessed: December 12, 2021.

12. Doyle, Anna Lea, Andrew Wilson, and Ellen Clark. 2014. "It's Not Easy to Say Goodbye: Perspectives on Driving Divestiture and Carve Out Value." Deloitte. https://www2.deloitte.com/us/en/pages/mergers-and-acquisitions/articles /divestiture-compendium.html.

13. Hammes, Paul. 2019. "Will You Set the Divestment Pace, or Try to Keep Up with It? Global Corporate Divestment Study 2019." Ernst & Young. https:// assets.ey.com/content/dam/ey-sites/ey-com/en_gl/topics/divestment/2019 /global_divestment_study_report.pdf.

14. Fubini, David, Michael Park, and Kim Thomas. 2013. "Profitably Parting Ways: Getting More Value from Divestitures." *McKinsey on Finance* 45 (Winter 2013): 14–21. https://www.mckinsey.com/~/media/McKinsey/dotcom /client_service/Corporate%20Finance/MoF/PDF%20issues/PDFs%20Issue %2045/MoF45_3_Divestitures.ashx.

15. Freeman, John, and Michael T. Hannan. 1975. "Growth and Decline Processes in Organizations." *American Sociological Review* 40, no. 2 (April 1975): 215–228.

16. Feibelman, Alan, Curt Underwood, and Marie-Pierre Belanger. 2015. "Successfully Managing Major Utility Business Spin-Offs and Divestitures." Oliver Wyman, January 2015. https://www.oliverwyman.de/content/dam /oliver-wyman/global/en/2015/jan/2015_UTL_Divestitures.pdf.

17. Ezekoye, Obi, and Anthony Luu. 2019. "A case for restructuring before spin-off." McKinsey & Company, July 23, 2019. https://www.mckinsey.com /business-functions/strategy-and-corporate-finance/our-insights/a-case-for -restructuring-before-spin-off.

18. Thomson Reuters StreetEvents. 2014. "Masco Corp Conference Call to Discuss Strategic Initiatives to Drive Shareholder Value." September 30, 2014. https://s1.q4cdn.com/387119661/files/doc_events/archive/MAS-Transcript-2014-09-30T12_30.pdf.

19. Franz, Matt. 2020. "Masco's Shrink to Grow Transformation Looks Complete." Eagle Point Capital, May 15, 2020. https://www.eaglepointcap.com/blog/mascos-shrink-to-grow-transformation-looks-complete.

20. Maurer, Mark. 2021. "Johnson & Johnson Prepares to Untangle Finances Ahead of Planned Split." *Wall Street Journal*, December 6, 2021. https://www.wsj.com/articles/johnson-johnson-prepares-to-untangle-finances-ahead-of-planned-split-11638786602.

21. Kleinguetl, Ed. 2018. "Value Creation through Divestitures: Interdependency Assessment is the Starting Point." Grant Thornton. https://www.grantthornton.com/-/media/content-page-files/financial-services/pdfs/2018/BK/TAS_Value_creation_through_divestitures_article_v2.ashx?la=en&hash=C87DB0CE1A4C70065CD51B9FF8377717CF6A8BCA.
Castillo, Alan. 2019. "Key Operational Carve-Out Considerations for Sellers." BDO USA LLP, April 2019. https://www.bdo.com/insights/business-financial-advisory/m-a-and-transaction-advisory/key-operational-carve-out-considerations-for-selle.

22. Mills, Rich. 2021. "Global Corporate Divestment Study 2021: Can Divesting What Holds You Back Move Your Strategy Forward? CEOs Are Using Divestments to Reimagine Their Organization." Ernst & Young. https://assets.ey.com/content/dam/ey-sites/ey-com/en_gl/topics/divestment/2021/pdfs/ey-global-corporate-divestment-study-2021-report.pdf.

23. Berlin, Mitch, Akshat Dubey, and Nikhil Singh. 2020. "Four reasons to transform RemainCo during a significant spin-off." Ernst & Young, June 1, 2020. https://www.ey.com/en_us/divestment-study/four-reasons-to-transform-remainco-during-significant-spin-off.

24. Mills, Rich. 2021. "Global Corporate Divestment Study 2021: Can Divesting What Holds You Back Move Your Strategy Forward? CEOs Are Using Divestments to Reimagine Their Organization." Ernst & Young. https://assets.ey.com/content/dam/ey-sites/ey-com/en_gl/topics/divestment/2021/pdfs/ey-global-corporate-divestment-study-2021-report.pdf.

25. Rajan, Raghuram, Henri Servaes, and Luigi Zingales. 2000. "The Cost of Diversity: The Diversification Discount and Inefficient Investment." *Journal of Finance* 55, no. 1 (February 2000): 35–80.
Lamont, Owen. 1997. "Cash Flow and Investment: Evidence from Internal Capital Markets." *Journal of Finance* 52, no. 1 (March 1997): 83–109.

26. Meyer, Margaret, Paul Milgrom, and John Roberts. 1992. "Organizational Prospects, Influence Costs, and Ownership Changes." *Journal of Economics & Management Strategy* 1, no. 1 (March 1992): 9–35.

Scharfstein, David S., and Jeremy C. Stein. 2000. "The Dark Side of Internal Capital Markets: Divisional Rent-Seeking and Inefficient Investment." *Journal of Finance* 55, no. 6 (2000): 2537–2564.

27. Arrfelt, Mathias, Robert M. Wiseman, and G. Tomas M. Hult. 2013. "Looking Backward Instead of Forward: Aspiration-Driven Influences on the Efficiency of the Capital Allocation Process." *Academy of Management Journal* 56, no. 4 (August 2013): 1081–1103.

28. Ozbas, Oguzhan, and David S. Scharfstein. 2010. "Evidence on the Dark Side of Internal Capital Markets." *Review of Financial Studies* 23, no. 2 (February 2010): 581–599.
Rajan, Raghuram, Henri Servaes, and Luigi Zingales. 2000. "The Cost of Diversity: The Diversification Discount and Inefficient Investment." *Journal of Finance* 55, no. 1 (February 2000): 35–80.

29. Feldman, Emilie R. 2016. "Corporate Spin-Offs and Capital Allocation Decisions." *Strategy Science* 1, no. 4 (December 2016): 256–271.

30. Derived from data analyzed in Feldman, Emilie R. 2016. "Corporate Spin-Offs and Capital Allocation Decisions." *Strategy Science* 1, no. 4 (December 2016): 256–271.

31. Sharma, Amol. 2014. "CBS Outdoor: A Poster Child for Old Media." *Wall Street Journal*, March 28, 2014. https://www.wsj.com/articles/cbs-outdoor -a-poster-for-old-media-1395979560.

32. Gelles, David. 2014. "I.P.O. to Cut Ill-Fitting Ad Business from CBS." *New York Times*, March 27, 2014. https://dealbook.nytimes.com/2014/03/27/cbs -outdoor-prices-shares-at-28-apiece/.

33. CBS Corporation. 2016. "2015 Annual Report." February 16, 2016. https:// www.sec.gov/Archives/edgar/data/813828/000081382816000065/cbs_10k -123115.htm.

34. Ibid.

35. CBS Corporation. 2013. "2012 Annual Report." February 12, 2013. https://www.sec.gov/Archives/edgar/data/813828/000104746913001192 /a2212776z10-k.htm.

36. Kapner, Suzanne. 2021. "Should Retailers Split E-Commerce from Stores? A High-Level Debate." *Wall Street Journal*, December 29, 2021. https://www .wsj.com/articles/should-retailers-split-e-commerce-from-stores-a-high-level -debate-11640779202?mod=mhp.

37. Ibid.

38. Ibid.

39. Masco Corporation. 2014. "Unlocking Shareholder Value: Strategic Review Update." September 30, 2014. https://www.slideshare.net/Masco_Investors /masco-investor-presentation-september-2014.

40. Thomson Reuters StreetEvents. 2014. "Masco Corp Conference Call to Discuss Strategic Initiatives to Drive Shareholder Value." September 30, 2014.

https://s1.q4cdn.com/387119661/files/doc_events/archive/MAS-Transcript -2014-09-30T12_30.pdf.

41. Masco Corporation. 2017. "2016 Annual Report." March 2017. https://s1 .q4cdn.com/387119661/files/doc_financial/annual/AR2016-10k.pdf.

42. Garud, Raghu, Philipp Tuertscher, and Andrew H. Van de Ven. 2013. "Perspectives on Innovation Processes." *Academy of Management Annals* 7, no. 1 (June 2013): 775–819.

43. Unpublished research conducted by the author.

44. Copp, Josh, Ruth De Backer, Gerti Pellumbi, and Julia Samorezov. 2019. "Divestiture in Medtech: Are You the Natural Owner of Your Businesses?" McKinsey & Company, March 18, 2019. https://www.mckinsey.com /industries/pharmaceuticals-and-medical-products/our-insights/divestiture-in -medtech-are-you-the-natural-owner-of-your-businesses.

45. Gibney, Michael, and Jason Woleben. 2020. " 'Tidal Wave' of Science Leads Pharma Giants to Shed Slow-Growing Units." *S&P Global Market Intelligence*, February 28, 2020. https://www.spglobal.com/marketintelligence /en/news-insights/latest-news-headlines/tidal-wave-of-science-leads-pharma -giants-to-shed-slow-growing-units-57244389.

46. Takeda Pharmaceutical Company Limited. 2020. "Takeda Continues Divestiture Strategy with Sale of Select OTC and Non-Core Assets in Europe to Orifarm for up to Approximately $670M USD." April 24, 2020. https:// www.businesswire.com/news/home/20200424005106/en/Takeda-Continues -Divestiture-Strategy-Sale-Select-OTC.

47. Garcia, Mauricio Holguin. 2021. "Takeda Pivoting to Growth Amid Renewed Focus on 'Core Assets.' " *Pharma Boardroom*, May 20, 2021. https:// pharmaboardroom.com/articles/takeda-pivoting-to-growth-amid-re-focusing -on-core-assets/.

48. Liu, Angus. 2021. "With Cost Cuts and Asset Sales Largely Wrapped, Takeda Gears Up for Growth: CEO." *Fierce Pharma*, May 11, 2021. https:// www.fiercepharma.com/pharma-asia/takeda-can-continue-paying-off-debt -thanks-to-growth-from-core-drugs-ceo.

49. Garcia, Mauricio Holguin. 2021. "Takeda Pivoting to Growth Amid Renewed Focus on 'Core Assets.' " *Pharma Boardroom*, May 20, 2021. https:// pharmaboardroom.com/articles/takeda-pivoting-to-growth-amid-re-focusing -on-core-assets/.

CHAPTER 11

1. Edmans, Alex. 2011. "Does the Stock Market Fully Value Intangibles? Employee Satisfaction and Equity Prices." *Journal of Financial Economics* 101, no. 3 (September 2011): 621–640.
Edmans, Alex. 2012. "The Link Between Job Satisfaction and Firm Value, With Implications for Corporate Social Responsibility." *Academy of Management Perspectives* 26, no. 4 (November 2012): 1–19.

2. Bettinazzi, Emanuele L. M., and Maurizio Zollo. 2017. "Stakeholder Orientation and Acquisition Performance." *Strategic Management Journal* 38, no. 12 (December 2017): 2465–2485.

3. Ovide, Shira. 2010. "Ziff Davis Agrees to Buyout." *Wall Street Journal*, June 4, 2010. https://www.wsj.com/articles/SB10001424052748704764404575286 771576211704.

4. Shields, Mike. 2014. "How Ziff Davis Came Back from the Dead by Embracing Ad Tech." *Wall Street Journal*, May 15, 2014. https://www.wsj.com /articles/BL-269B-562?mod=article_inline.

5. Mullin, Benjamin. 2021. "Ziff Davis Is Returning to Public Markets with a Mandate to Make Deals." *Wall Street Journal*, August 17, 2021. https://www .wsj.com/articles/ziff-davis-is-returning-to-public-markets-with-a-mandate -to-make-deals-11629205200.

6. Feldman, Emilie R. 2014. "Legacy Divestitures: Motives and Implications." *Organization Science* 25, no. 3 (May–June 2014): 815–832.

7. Lee, Peggy M. 2001. "What's in a Name.com?: The Effects of '.com' Name Changes on Stock Prices and Trading Activity." *Strategic Management Journal* 22, no. 8 (August 2001): 793–804.

8. Cooper, Michael J., Ajay Khorana, Igor Osobov, Ajay Patel, and P. Raghavendra Rau. 2005. "Managerial Actions in Response to a Market Downturn: Valuation Effects of Name Changes in the Dot.com Decline." *Journal of Corporate Finance* 11, no. 1–2 (March 2005): 319–335.

9. Rodriguez, Salvador. 2014. "Confusion with Google Nest Acquisition Causes Penny Stock to Jump 1,900%." *Los Angeles Times*, January 17, 2014. https:// www.latimes.com/business/technology/la-fi-tn-google-nest-nestor-penny -stock-1900-20140117-story.html.

10. Ibid.

11. Neate, Rupert. 2020. "Zoom Booms as Demand for Video-Conferencing Tech Grows." *The Guardian*, March 31, 2020. https://www.theguardian.com /technology/2020/mar/31/zoom-booms-as-demand-for-video-conferencing -tech-grows-in-coronavirus-outbreak.

12. Prang, Alison. 2021. "Meta Shares Surge. No, Not Facebook's Meta." *Wall Street Journal*, October 29, 2021. https://www.wsj.com/articles/meta-shares -surge-no-not-facebooks-meta-11635516376.

13. Stoll, John. 2019. "In 'Mergers of Equals,' One Side Is Always a Bit More Equal." *Wall Street Journal*, June 14, 2019. https://www.wsj.com/articles/in -mergers-of-equals-one-side-is-always-a-bit-more-equal-11560528068.
Hoffman, Liz, and Rachel Louise Ensign. 2019. "A Truist Story About the Perils of Combining Company Names." *Wall Street Journal*, June 13, 2019. https://www.wsj.com/articles/a-truist-story-about-the-perils-of-combining-company-names-11560464391.

14. Jenkins, Holman W. 2001. "Enron Is History, Says History." *Wall Street Journal*, November 28, 2001. https://www.wsj.com/articles/SB10069063437 80246320.

15. Strom, Stephanie. 2012. "For Oreo, Cadbury and Ritz, a New Parent Company." *New York Times*, May 23, 2012. https://www.nytimes.com/2012/05/24 /business/mondelez-is-new-name-for-krafts-snack-foods-company.html.

16. Jargon, Julie. 2013. "Snack War: Peltz vs. Rosenfeld." *Wall Street Journal*, July 21, 2013. https://www.wsj.com/articles/SB1000142412788732426340457 8617962513937962.

17. Lieber, Ronald B. 1996. " 'What? Fortune Makes Golf Balls?' Studies In Corporate Nomenclature." *CNN Money*, December 9, 1996. http://money.cnn .com/magazines/fortune/fortune_archive/1996/12/09/219335/index.htm.

18. Smith, Elizabeth A., and Ruth E. Malone. 2003. "Altria Means Tobacco: Philip Morris's Identity Crisis." *American Journal of Public Health* 93, no. 4 (April 2003): 553–556.

19. Derived from data analyzed in Feldman, Emilie R. 2014. "Legacy Divestitures: Motives and Implications." *Organization Science* 25, no. 3 (May–June 2014): 815–832.

20. Ibid.

21. Ramachandran, Shalini. 2016. "Sir . . . Sir! You Need to Call the 'Other' Time Warner." *Wall Street Journal*, June 1, 2016. https://www.wsj.com /articles/time-warner-makes-game-of-thrones-confused-customers-think-its -the-cable-company-1464790213.

22. Ramachandran, Shalini. 2016. "Oops! The Senate Just Summoned the Wrong Time Warner." *Wall Street Journal*, October 27, 2016. https://www .wsj.com/articles/oops-the-senate-just-summoned-the-wrong-time-warner -1477598253.

23. AT&T Inc. 2016. "AT&T Statement on TWX-TWC Confusion." Form 425 Filing. https://www.sec.gov/Archives/edgar/data/732717/000119312516744963 /d266536d425.htm.

24. Lewis, Hilary. 2016. "John Oliver Takes on Print Journalism Woes with Fake Trailer Featuring Jason Sudeikis, Rose Byrne, Bobby Cannavale." *Hollywood Reporter*, August 8, 2016. https://www.hollywoodreporter.com/tv/tv -news/john-oliver-journalism-segment-stoplight-918019/.

25. Newton, Casey. 2016. "One of the world's most storied media companies has gloriously rebranded itself as Tronc." *The Verge*, June 2, 2016. https://www .theverge.com/2016/6/2/11846538/tribune-tronc-rebranding-lol-ayfkm.

26. Snavely, Brent. 2014. "Masco to Spin Off Division, Cut Corporate Staff by 40%." *Detroit Free Press*, September 30, 2014. https://www.freep.com/story /money/business/michigan/2014/09/30/masco-spin-division-cut-hq-staff /16474313/.

27. Estes, Adam Clark. 2011. "After Sale, New York Times Regional Employees Brace for Layoffs." *The Atlantic*, December 28, 2011. https://www.theatlantic.com/business/archive/2011/12/after-sale-new-york-times-regional-employees-brace-layoffs/333781/.
28. Walton, Rod. 2012. "ConocoPhillips Streamlines with Phillips 66 Refining Side Spinoff." *Tulsa World*, April 29, 2012. https://tulsaworld.com/business/conocophillips-streamlines-with-phillips-66-refining-side-spinoff/article_41650214-ba70-569e-bce9-06cbc75f5a56.html.
29. DiStefano, Joseph N. 2017. "Counting Down the Final Days of a Stand-Alone DuPont Co." *Philadelphia Inquirer*, August 23, 2017. https://www.inquirer.com/philly/blogs/inq-phillydeals/counting-down-the-final-days-of-a-stand-alone-dupont-co-20170823.html.
30. Gopinath, Chirukandath, and Thomas E. Becker. 2000. "Communication, Procedural Justice, and Employee Attitudes: Relationships under Conditions of divestiture." *Journal of Management* 26, no. 1 (February 2000): 63–83.
31. Luu, Anthony, and Paul Roche. 2020. "Deciding to Divest? Make Your Preparation Time Count." McKinsey & Company, November 3, 2020. https://www.mckinsey.com/business-functions/strategy-and-corporate-finance/our-insights/deciding-to-divest-make-your-preparation-time-count.
32. Holmes, Paul. 2003. "An Employee Relations Program to Communicate Divestiture." *Provoke Media*, February 26, 2003. https://www.provokemedia.com/latest/article/an-employee-relations-program-to-communicate-divestiture.
33. Henisz, Witold J., Sinziana Dorobantu, and Lite J. Nartey. 2014. "Spinning Gold: The Financial Returns to Stakeholder Engagement." *Strategic Management Journal* 35, no. 12 (December 2014): 1727–1748.
34. Walker, Dionne. 2007. "Altria Closing North Carolina Plant." *USA Today*, June 26, 2007. https://usatoday30.usatoday.com/money/economy/2007-06-26-4197533990_x.htm.
35. Ibid.
36. Swoboda, Rod. 2016. "Pioneer seed will still have roots in Iowa." *Wallaces Farmer*, March 14, 2016. https://www.farmprogress.com/blogs-pioneer-seed-still-roots-iowa-10736.
37. Noble, Breana. 2019. "Dow Spinoff Keeps Midland on Edge." *Detroit News*, March 28, 2019. https://www.detroitnews.com/story/business/2019/03/28/dow-spinoff-keeps-midland-on-edge/3149895002/.
38. Lyons, Kayley. 2019. "Community Connections: Employees Are Center of DuPont's Community Outreach Strategy." *Midland Daily News*, November 15, 2019. https://www.ourmidland.com/opinion/voices/article/Community-Connections-nbsp-Employees-are-center-14834181.php.
39. Rio Tinto. 2016. "Bougainville Copper Limited shareholding." June 30, 2016. https://www.riotinto.com/en/news/releases/Bougainville-Copper-Limited-shareholding.

40. Wilson, Catherine. 2017. "Rio Tinto Walks Away from Environmental Responsibility for Bougainville's Panguna Mine." *Mongabay*, April 6, 2017. https://news.mongabay.com/2017/04/rio-tinto-walks-away-from-environmental-responsibility-for-bougainvilles-panguna-mine/.

41. Flitton, Daniel. 2016. "Rio Tinto's Billion-Dollar Mess: 'Unprincipled, Shameful and Evil.'" *Sunday Morning Herald*, August 19, 2016. https://www.smh.com.au/world/billiondollar-mess-a-major-disaster-the-people-do-not-deserve-to-have-20160817-gquzli.html.

42. "Rio Tinto: Mining Giant Accused of Poisoning Rivers in Papua New Guinea." *BBC*, September 29, 2020. https://www.bbc.com/news/world-asia-54340227.

43. He, Laura, and Angus Watson. 2020. "Rio Tinto CEO Resigns After Destruction of 46,000-Year-Old Sacred Indigenous Site." *CNN Business*, September 11, 2020. https://www.cnn.com/2020/09/10/business/rio-tinto-ceo-intl-hnk/index.html.

44. Hume, Neil, and Jaime Smyth. 2020. "Rio Tinto Faces Tough Task to Rebuild Reputation." *Financial Times*, September 12, 2020. https://www.ft.com/content/761b0c40-1d7d-4d1f-81d3-3c2dfb920557.

45. Ibid.

CONCLUSION

1. Gioia, Ted. 2022. "Is Old Music Killing New Music?" *The Atlantic*, January 23, 2022. https://www.theatlantic.com/ideas/archive/2022/01/old-music-killing-new-music/621339/.

2. Ibid.

3. Berkshire Hathaway Inc. 2015. "2014 Annual Letter to Shareholders." February 27, 2015. https://www.berkshirehathaway.com/letters/2014ltr.pdf.

4. Berkshire Hathaway Inc. 2021. "2020 Annual Letter to Shareholders." February 27, 2021. https://www.berkshirehathaway.com/letters/2020ltr.pdf.

APPENDICES

1. Mazza Jr., James J., and Zahed A. Haseeb. 2020. "Rights Offerings in Chapter 11 Bankruptcies." *Review of Banking & Financial Services* 36, no. 7 (July 2020): 77–86. https://www.skadden.com/insights/publications/2020/08/rights-offerings-in-chapter-11-bankruptcies.

2. Reckert, Clare M. 1964. "Expansion Is Set by Socony Mobil; Oil Concern Acquires Stock of Big Gas Company for Nearly $78 Million." *New York Times*, July 30, 1964. https://www.nytimes.com/1964/07/30/archives/expansion-is-set-by-socony-mobil-oil-concern-acquires-stock-of-big.html.

3. "Briefs." *New York Times*, May 23, 1983. https://www.nytimes.com/1983/05/23/business/briefs-184936.html.

4. Derived from data gathered from Refinitiv (formerly Thomson One) and SDC Platinum. Accessed: January 24, 2022, and February 4, 2022.

INDEX

Page numbers followed by *e* refer to exhibits. Page numbers followed by n*, n†, or n‡ refer to footnotes.

ABOUT THE AUTHOR

Emilie R. Feldman is the Michael L. Tarnopol Professor and Professor of Management at the Wharton School of the University of Pennsylvania. Her research focuses on corporate strategy and governance, with particular interests in the role that divestitures, spinoffs, and mergers and acquisitions play in corporate reconfiguration, the internal functioning of multi-business firms, and the impact that large shareholders have on strategic decision-making and outcomes. She has served as an external consultant, expert witness, and collaborator to some of the world's largest law, accounting, and consulting firms, and to major corporations. She currently serves as a Senior Editor of *Organization Science*, and she previously served as an Associate Editor of the *Strategic Management Journal*. Her work has been featured extensively in popular press outlets such as the *Wall Street Journal*, the *New York Times*, the *Washington Post*, the *New Yorker*, and *Fortune*. She graduated *magna cum laude* from Harvard College, where she studied Economics and French Literature, and she received her master's and doctoral degrees in Strategy from the Harvard Business School. She also holds a Diplôme Oenotropae from the National Wine School.